Advance Praise

In this study of the deep discipleship inspired by a generation of world-famous gurus, Somak Biswas splits open the seams of sentimentalism that underwrote transatlantic Indophilia in the context of colonial modernity. Swami Vivekananda, Rabindranath Tagore and Mohandas K. Gandhi were household names. They were also the objects of longing and love for men and women who gave their lives over to them in pursuit of earthly transcendence and revolutionary politics. Biswas explores both the social geographies and the cultural practices of these radical devotees, producing a lively account of utopian communities stitched together by spiritual desire and preserved in a rich and vivid archive of letters that testify to the power of affective politics in the making of global history.

—**Antoinette Burton,** University of Illinois

An elegant account of the mutual but also rival desires that constituted the now classic relationship between Indian sages and their Western followers starting early in the last century. The combination of counter-cultural transgression and conservatism that Biswas describes in such relations makes for a highly original argument.

—**Faisal Devji,** University of Oxford

Weaving together modern guru–disciple relationships and the journeys of Western figures in pursuit of Indian gurus, this significant work explores a strikingly unusual theme. It inverts the dominant tenor of interactions between the coloniser and the colonised by looking at Western men and women who were entranced by Indian religious and political figures in times of intensifying anticolonialism. It probes the manifold complexities that are involved in such inversion, which defied the logic of 'normal' colonial encounters. By counter-posing histories of several gurus and their disciples, the book, moreover, describes the relationships on different registers. Each relationship is situated against a broad historical backdrop of contemporary politics and faith, of gender and emotions, in Britain and America as well as in India.

—**Tanika Sarkar,** Jawaharlal Nehru University

Passages through India puts flesh on the bones of the familiar trope of the Indian guru and the Western disciple. It is a useful reminder of the important work of 'white solidarity' in reshaping the global image of India for an anti-colonial project. At the same time, it is clear-eyed about the exclusionary effects of relying on Hindu high culture and a politics of respectability for this image makeover.

—**Mrinalini Sinha,** University of Michigan

Passages through India

Passages through India offers a study of the phenomenon of Western Indophilia: romanticised engagements around Hindu ideas of India. It argues that affective practices cultivated between major Indian guru-figures (Gandhi, Tagore and Vivekananda) and their white disciples serviced a larger politics of respectability, tied to the exigencies of Indian cultural and nationalist politics. Indophile deployments in transnational projects like the abolition of indentured labour and global Hinduism, while anti-colonial, were not quite emancipatory. Such deployments – in Africa, America, Fiji and India – frequently reproduced deep hierarchies around race, class, caste and gender. Unifying distinct strands of western discipleship within a shared tradition of Indophilia, *Passages through India* offers a new methodological framework that situates self and subjectivity as central to processes of global mobility and migration.

Somak Biswas is Junior Research Fellow at the Institute of Historical Research, London. He works on the intersections of South Asian, British, imperial and global history. He is also a member of the Global History and Culture Centre, University of Warwick.

Passages through India

*Indian Gurus, Western Disciples and the
Politics of Indophilia, 1890–1940*

Somak Biswas

CAMBRIDGE
UNIVERSITY PRESS

Shaftesbury Road, Cambridge CB2 8EA, United Kingdom

One Liberty Plaza, 20th Floor, New York, NY 10006, USA

477 Williamstown Road, Port Melbourne, VIC 3207, Australia

314–321, 3rd Floor, Plot No.3, Splendor Forum, Jasola District Centre, New Delhi – 110025, India

103 Penang Road, #05–06/07, Visioncrest Commercial, Singapore 238467

Cambridge University Press is part of Cambridge University Press & Assessment, a department of the University of Cambridge.

We share the University's mission to contribute to society through the pursuit of education, learning and research at the highest international levels of excellence.

www.cambridge.org
Information on this title: www.cambridge.org/9781009337984

First published 2023

Printed in India by Avantika Printers Pvt. Ltd.

A catalogue record for this publication is available from the British Library

ISBN 978-1-009-33798-4 Hardback

To Dalit seers, peers and queers

Contents

Figures

Acknowledgements

It is difficult not to read our own despair in the subjects we study. Fortunately, an array of dazzling people has constantly supplied me with constant wisdom and warning. It is a pleasure to thank them all. The History Department at Warwick University has been my refuge, its people a source of great comfort and conviviality. Even after I finished my PhD in 2020, I linger in love of the place and its people. The Global History and Culture Centre provided an exceptionally exciting place. I am grateful to the *Past and Present* for a research fellowship that allowed me time to finish this book. The Institute of Historical Research, London, helped me settle into a flexible postdoctoral life just when COVID struck.

Sarah Hodges's sharp tutelage has moulded this work in important ways. Aditya Sarkar's generous engagement helped me hone key arguments made in this book. Anne Gerritsen has been a wonderful mentor, offering counsel and courage as and when needed. James Poskett, Meleisa Ono-George, Guido Van Meersbergen and Rebecca Earle provided help and advice whenever I reached out. Outside Warwick, Ruth Harris has been the most wonderfully supportive mentor.

Poorva Rajaram's delayed but definitive entry in my life has been a high point; her friendship has nourished me in every possible way. Cheri Kuncheria, Vidya Subramanian and their two adorable felines have been the most excellent hosts. Saba Hussain and Anjali Thomas made life in Coventry full of laughter, sharing advice, agony and great gossip. I became friends with Andrew Burchell over seven years ago; I am most glad he remains so. Poorva, Cheri, Adhitya Dhanapal, James and Andrew's comments on several draft chapters have been most useful. Andrew, Martin Schauss, Matteo and Pierre (Botcherby) translated relevant sections of

Romain Rolland's 'Indian Diaries' from the French original. For all their labours, rendered freely, I have only gratitude.

I would like to thank the following for their warm friendship and inspiring work, in no particular order: Anna Sailer, Kalyani Prajapati, Adhitya Dhanapal, Sam Strien, Tarangini Sriraman, Jason Cyrus, Awanish Kumar, Anisha George, Arun Kumar, Komal Mohite, Paloma Perez-Galvan, Shounak Ghosh, Paromita Sinha, Ishita Chakraborty, Maroona Murmu, Shrikant Botre, Joeeta Pal, Sohini Chattopadhyay, Bobby Tam, Mouli Banerjee, Lavrentis Galanoupoulos, Koonal Duggal, Vincent Kelly, Maria do Mar Pereira and Aya Nassar. Friendships forged outside of the history circuit have been refreshing. Thanks to Ria Bari, Prachi Singh, Harpreet Kaur, Abhinav Mishra, Preeti Thakur, Sumeet Tsering, Arindan Mandal, Abhishek Verma, Kanhaiya Lal, Harshita Asthana, Shailesh Yadav and Shashikant Manishwar for many wonderful evenings spent in impromptu *antakshari*s and midnight bike trips for *masala chai* in Murthal.

Friendships with Sue Lemos, Madi Simcock-Brown and Nazifa Zaman have been most rewarding, both personally and politically. J. Daniel Luther, Shantanu Singh and the *Queer Asia* collective taught me queer kinship. Thanks are due to Sara Bamdad, Daniel Papadopoulos, Martin Schauss, Mantra Mukim, Anna Rivers, Anna Carolina Rocha, Virinder Kalra, Laura Schwartz, Claire Bielby, Hilary Marland, Asma Abdi, Clare Langhammer, Kalyan and Kalyani Bhattacharya, Uttara and Subhas Chakraborty for a great many things. Sohini Ghosh, Anwesha Rana and Qudsiya Ahmed have been exceptional editors and an author's dream. It is a pleasure to thank the two anonymous reviewers for their generous comments. Thanks to Priya Das the production process has been a smooth experience.

My parents Ankita and Subodh Biswas have been bewildered with my never-ending research quest, and mostly glad to see something tangible in the form of a book. Aunts, uncles and family chipped in to do their pastoral bit; their worries often taking surreal forms of surveillance. Rupa and Alakesh Biswas provided a caring home in Delhi to fall back every time I needed. Trips to my aunt Geeta Bairagi's home were wildly anticipated affairs. Chhanda and Chandra Biswas opened their home to me in Philadelphia during a long archival trip. My brother Sayak and sister-in-law Namrata helped me navigate episodes of our very own mint-edition family drama, besides much else. The cousins' collective has been furiously loyal to a fault; much love and thanks to Arpita, Arnab, Aarushi, Amitesh, Rony, Roshni, Shubho and Vastika for stepping up as and when. My niece Mishita's arrival has been a wildly happy affair. I wish my grandmothers Nirmala and Kalpana Biswas were alive to see this book. They represented two sharp ends of an early generation of Dalit womanhood. Nirmala was rural and unlettered, immersed in her world of *haribhakti* and conjugal duties. Kalpana was educated, urbane and aspiring to respectable gentility. I miss them both terribly.

Librarians and archivists across three different continents provided invaluable material help that made this book possible. I would like to thank the following places (and people): the Nehru Memorial Museum and Library; National Archives of India; Shantiniketan (Shovan Ruj); Sabarmati (Kinnari Bhatt); Bodleian, Dartington Hall Trust, Edinburgh University Library and the British Library; Cambridge Historical Society, Boston; University of Pennsylvania Library and the Swarthmore College archives in Philadelphia. Archival dust is a real thing. It imbues meaning in the way we read sources. Visits to Sabarmati, Shantiniketan and Almora helped me understand these places and their enchantments.

Jawaharlal Nehru University has been the most significant influence in my adult life. Thanks to the teachers who taught us history, it was entering a world of sheer delight and intellect. The late M. S. S. Pandian was the first scholar who taught us pride in being Dalit; that is a lesson for life. Tanika Sarkar has been brilliant, offering the most astute advice on life and work. Radhika Singha is simultaneously awe-inspiring as a scholar and humane as a person. Meeting Janaki Nair in the London Coal Drops Yard provided the perfect backdrop to reminisce her classes on the history of capitalism. Meeting them all recently reminded me of the kind of historian I want to be. At a time when India is almost completely gripped by the frenzy of Hindu nationalism, a whole generation of JNU teachers and students offered hope.

Matteo has been my steady source of happiness and strength for several years now. He has suffered my delightful wit and banter every single day with the stoic indifference of a great martyr. He remains convinced of my general 'un-funniness' and stoutly pities those who have fallen to my charms. Our cats Ludo and Lucrezia have meowed their love into our lives. Matteo's family has been exceptionally kind: heartfelt thanks to (mamma) Maria, Gino (the papa), Michela, Giuseppe, Ebe, baby Annamaria, the dogs (Smile, Griffin, Leo), cats (Raja, Sgat) and Gino (the parrot).

Finishing this work under dark times has been a challenge. Both in India and Britain, contemporary debates on ethnic violence and national borders have inflected my study of western Indophilia and its long-term stakes in producing 'good' and 'bad' immigrants. As Britain finally makes me feel like a 'familiar stranger', it is perhaps apropos that a presentist despair creeps into my conclusion. But if the times are dark, the songs will be of dark times. Why should our history writing be any different?

PART I

Introduction

Indophilia and Its Wider Worlds, 1890–1940

Gurus are forever.

A lock of silvery-grey hair fell off a sheaf of papers I was working on (Figure I.1). An attached note detailed its origins: the dead poet Rabindranath Tagore's beard. On his death, this was sent as a keepsake to his English disciple Leonard Elmhirst in Devon.[1]

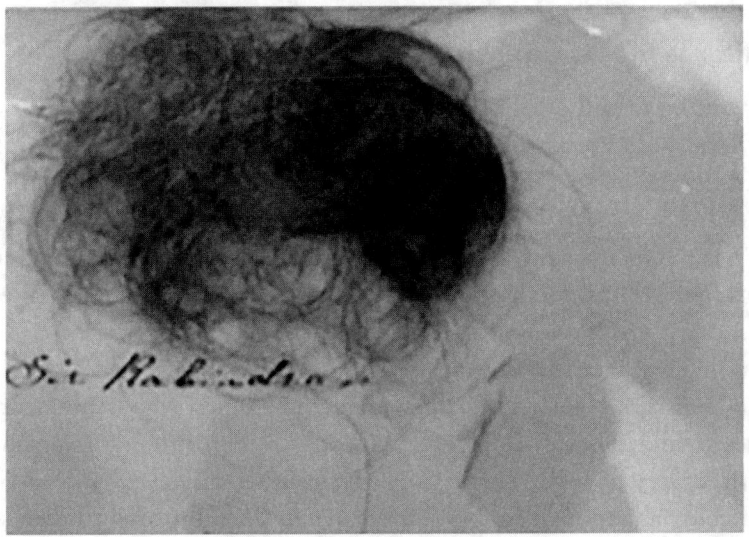

Figure I.1   Tagore's beard hair.
Source: Dartington Hall Trust.

The hair exemplifies what I refer to in this book as deep discipleship. How did a cast of sympathetic Western subjects come to immerse and identify themselves almost completely within the aspirational communities of their Indian gurus? This book follows their lineages. *Passages through India* analyses the phenomenon of Western Indophilia (romanticised engagements around idealised forms of Hindu India) in late colonial British India, its ideological and affective composition, and its political implications. Rooted in disquiet with forms of industrial modernity, it looks at the nature of intimacies cultivated between major Indian guru-figures (Gandhi, Vivekananda, Tagore) and some of their Western disciples through ashrams and letters. Western disciples' love and longing for their mentors were harnessed to service the divergent needs of an expansive Indian nationalism. Bringing together themes such as intimacy, discipleship, religion and migration, the book argues that Indophile deployments around transnational projects like abolishing indentured labour and global Hinduism, while anti-colonial, were not necessarily emancipatory. Such deployments in India, the United States, Fiji and South Africa frequently reproduced the very hierarchies of race, class, caste and gender that they sought to transgress. Unifying distinct strands of discipleship within a shared tradition of Indophilia, this volume sheds light on influential Indo-Western encounters and their profound consequences, both in India and abroad.

Framing White Indophilia

This work builds on a set of relationships between key Indian figures and their Western disciples to explore the phenomenon of Western Indophilia. The romanticised engagements of sympathetic white Westerners for idealised forms of India, usually rooted in upper-caste Hindu imaginaries, is illustrated through the influential and intersecting networks around three major figures of modern India: the Hindu monk and missionary Swami Vivekananda, the poet and educationist Rabindranath Tagore and the nationalist leader Mohandas K. Gandhi. Together their careers broadly bookend the decades 1890–1940. Indophile disciples comprised largely men and women who made definitive passages to and through India. They belong to that important category of Western actors who refuse to fit neatly within either official colonial discourse or anti-colonial nationalism. Not Orientalist in the influential Saidian sense, they fit more closely within the description of 'affirmative Orientalists', who were apologists of Indian culture.[2] Their passages to India were initially made in non-official, if not strictly anti-colonial, capacities. However, their trajectories diverged significantly from the dominant narrative of early imperial careering represented by British officialdom, merchants and military men.[3]

As Western actors who ultimately refused to own up to the racial privilege afforded by the nexus of imperial mobility and migration, their personhoods fragment our understanding of European agency, demonstrating the dissonances that exposed the serious limitations of the colonial project in action.[4] The empire, or imperial geographies, however, remained an important field to substantiate their work. In this, they were similar to other European men and women who sought and often found in the empire a space for vibrant opportunities – missionaries, feminists, Theosophists – in ways that may not have been possible within Britain itself.[5] Living and being in imperial locations exposed them first hand to empire's violence; such experiences were essential in eroding their belief in its munificence. The desire for alternative languages of affection and alliance with particular Indians was no less produced out of great despair at their own nation's (and the West more generally) betrayal of its enlightened civilising mission. However, this was not the only reason for the making of such discipleships. Disillusionment with Britain's manifest destiny was framed by deep disenchantment with forms of industrial and colonial modernity; Indophilia was an expression of that wider disquiet.[6] These were actors who desired to escape the 'techno-modernist' excesses of Western society. It led them to seek alternative models of living and being in 'non-modern' societies such as India and around forms such as the ashram.[7] This work, therefore, through a study of these figures and their networks, seeks to intervene in debates linked to questions of selfhood, modernity and religion, and more interestingly, on mobility and migration.

These networks helped consolidate some of the most sympathetic global opinions on India and Indians. An extensive literature already exists on each of these figures, given their importance in the national and international pantheon. Vivekananda, Gandhi and Tagore each have a proliferating body of scholarship that have examined those figures and their disciples/collaborators in numerous cultural, political and intellectual histories.[8] Few have, however, analysed the affective as an important site of analysis. I argue that a focus on this elusive intimacy is important; it determines the fraught-ness of their investments. These cannot be folded only within 'friendships of largeness and freedom', measured by the inevitable touchstone of Indian nationalism, where Western disciples seem star-struck by their Indian gurus.[9] By analysing how aspects such as space, emotions and embodiment were fundamental in producing and sustaining those relationships, I examine the experience of Indophile discipleship and its wider uses.[10]

Given that Indophile archives are shot through with what might be conceived as uncertain attempts to create intimacy, what did these transnational networks produce? I argue that these relationships, invoked and sanctified in the name of spiritual, cultural and political freedom, were also mobilised by an Indian nationalist elite anxious to settle respectable ideas of India that inhered in the representations of Vivekananda, Gandhi and Tagore. Inasmuch as these intimacies were guided by a profound sense of love, longing and idealism, their actions often had sharp exclusionary effects. This work interrogates the shifting meanings of radicalism as they travel in time and place.

C. F. Andrews and William Pearson, Gandhi and Tagore's English disciples, are celebrated figures in the history of abolishing indenture. Scholars have noted how the abolitionist movement was fundamentally tied to a more bourgeois desire for Indian respectability against an immoralised labour community.[11] A study of Indophile interiority reveals how notions of respectability were crucially inflected by their extended experience in prominent modern ashrams, experimental spaces that projected forms of upper-caste Hindu living as ideal. Nationalist or hagiographic practices of memorialisation frequently occlude the larger politics of their doing. Margaret Noble, the Irish disciple of Vivekananda, gets portrayed as a 'Celtic lioness',[12] Andrews as the 'rebel-saint'.[13] That all these figures have commemorative stamps, roads, statues or projects in their names sponsored by postcolonial Indian governments attest to this celebratory mode. Allusions to homoeroticism or (sexual) sublimation are carefully read away or left untouched, leaving behind a smoothened narrative of 'pure' discipleship.

This work foregrounds emotional experiences of discipleship as essential to analysing Indophile cultural politics. The chapters consequently move from the affective to the discursive, showing how personal enchantments inter-braided their political investments, the attachment to significant Indians providing a critical impetus for their subsequent self-transformations. This book follows the tension in sublime friendship: always partial, often instrumental, and regularly producing forms of Indophilia that arguably undermined Indophile claims of universal moral and material uplift.

The exclusionary effects of Indophile politics were not always obvious within India itself; a transnational scale helps chart their broader implications. The Hinduism deployed in the United States by Vivekananda and his Western disciples was different from that popularised within India; yet Western discipleships were instrumental in its moulding as a transnational discourse, manifest in its cultural nationalist and universalist registers.

Western disciples, through an essential whiteness, evidenced the arrival of a putative world that affirmed Indianist projects. Tagore's 'habit' of English secretaries – Andrews, Elmhirst, Pearson – (noted in a sarcastic aside by the spurned translator Edward J. Thompson) during his many travels after 1913 was arguably a visible demonstration of that world, exemplified aptly by educated Oxbridge Englishmen. This 'world' entered forms of Indian public discourse, evoking and validating Indian cultural and civilisational superiority to Indians themselves. The various chapters in this book map the scale of this Indophilia and its expansive cultural geographies, even as India remained a focal point of their investments. Diaries of the French pacifist and littérateur Romain Rolland provide a sense of the scale of this Indophilia and its cumulative convergences. His accounts list the many overlaps and broader effects of these actors and networks outside India, even as they remained divergent within India itself.[14]

Intersections: The Late Nineteenth Century

By the late nineteenth century, Britain's naval superiority, financial reach and near-absolute hegemony in trade, commerce and territorial expansion confirmed the formidable magnitude of an Anglocentric world order.[15] The gradual economic subordination of India as a colonial dominion within global capital networks catalysed the emergence of an colonial intelligentsia in various provinces of British India. Many sought in indigenist categories of thought an inspiration for culturalist politics that explained away India's material subordination by refiguring India as an ancient repository of religious, spiritual and ethical values. This essential, spiritually whole India, part of a larger 'Orient', was in sharp contradiction to a grossly materialist and unethical West.[16] For Westerners disenchanted with the onslaught of industrial modernity and what they felt was a decline in moral living, the positioning of India as a site of age-old spiritual wisdom carried viable appeal. In adopting various public Indian figures as their master, mentor or friend, they made substantive investments in numerous projects undertaken by these figures.

Westerners disenchanted with forms of industrial modernity saw this turn as a profound 'crisis of faith' moment in Western civilisation. Indophilia came to represent the nostalgic pursuit for an idealised world whose spatial and temporal frames intimated a world outside of modernity, but accessible to those inside it. This modernity rested on 'rupture',[17] but this rupture also produced the desire for a utopian 'lost world', a point the chapter on ashrams takes up in fuller detail.

The vibrant cosmos of *fin-de-siècle* Europe and America, and the many movements that populated its subcultures, became a fertile ground to produce and perform this Indophilia. Movements such as feminism, vegetarianism, social utopianism or non-conformism cherished alternative traditions with 'Eastern' origins. Direct and indirect encounters with these movements supplied almost all of Vivekananda, Gandhi and Tagore's Western followers.

Several scholars have already pointed to the fluid, fertile ground this nexus provided for anti-colonial politics.[18] Intersections between European anti-imperial traditions and the radical discourses of vegetarianism, animal rights, feminism, theosophy, homosexuality and socialism are hard to miss. These intersections enabled contrarian engagements in Europe and America with forms of utopian community that challenged the sway of liberal imperialism, scientific racism and laissez-faire economism.[19] Indian religious and cultural formulations provided critical ways to explore, if not escape, closures wrought by capitalist modernity. These formulations generally did not displace popular Orientalist typologies of a spiritual, mystical India. Yet, such cultural appropriations were not necessarily one way, as Vivekananda, Tagore and Gandhi demonstrate. They mobilised important Western resources and networks in stabilising their own projects.

Western individuals and institutions attracted to these personalities and their causes saw a fulfilment of their own personal and spiritual quests. Women followers such as Besant or Noble, coming from the British suffragist tradition, found in certain emanations of Hinduism and Buddhism a closer spiritual opening compared to the patriarchal ethos of high Anglicanism.[20] Notwithstanding these dissatisfactions, some form of belief in imperial munificence remained intact in these curious seekers and sympathisers but guided by a liberal aspiration of India as an essential, if not always equal, partner within the British Empire. In such circles, Indian preachers, politicians and artists were eagerly avowed and listened to. The desire for a closer connection with charismatic Indian figures and through them, a closer access to their idea of India produced determinate forms of Indophilia.

Indophiles who declared their love and longing for India could not – and generally did not – escape the bind nationalist politics placed on them. They saw their political endeavours for India as integral to the larger 'service of love' for their respective guru-figures. Anti-colonial identification with India and Indians came at a cost. These disciples variously courted arrest, got beaten up by white settler mobs, wrote incendiary literature, and aided civil disobedience and revolutionary terrorist movements wherever they could for the expansive cause of Indian nationalism.

Accessing Intimacy: Affects, Objects, Spaces

Cultural-material artefacts were integral to the lives of disciples.[21] Spatialising emotional practices, as Chapters 2 and 4 on the experience of discipleship will show, suggest how intimacies were contingent on disciples' desire to enter certain spaces. Ashrams and spiritual geographies provided Western disciples with the special frame to experience place-making. The desire to relate to specific places produced a range of practices through which they entered their mentors' worlds.[22] The concept of 'emotional community' provides an apt way to describe aspirational spaces like ashrams that provided sites for intensive self-reflection and transformation.[23]

The experience of discipleship was premised on emotional regimes that depended on the regular enactment of literary, physical and material practices. These practices were embedded within hierarchies of race, caste, class and gender that rendered specific acts of inversion, subversion or immersion meaningful. What value did the 'dust' of Indian gurus' feet hold for Western disciples? [24] Dust had deep material significance.[25]

New materialist interventions have reflected on how 'worlds' are produced – and made sense of – through a range of human practices in relating to that world.[26] This 'world' – the aspirational spaces and places that Indophiles sought to be a part of – produced the form and fantasy of Indophilia; the habitus of that 'world' insistently naturalising a set of cultural values as normative.

Reading intimacy is always a fraught proposition for 'unused to pushing the affective up against the political', we tend to dismiss emotive negotiations as elusive.[27] The anxieties of contact and contagion around interracial relationships provided much impetus for sexual control and policing of racial, cultural and moral borders.[28] It also produced the curious ellipses, silences and ordering logics of the colonial archive through which certain kinds of sexuality (or sexual difference) registered their presence. The chapter on indenture draws on this insight to show the convergence of normative social hierarchies in the *Fiji Report* drawn up by C. F. Andrews and William W. Pearson (and supported by Gandhi and the Hindu nationalist leader Madan Mohan Malaviya), central to the abolition of indenture.[29] Based on their investigation of indentured sugar plantations, the report abounded in the language of sexual immorality and 'moral panic' around a fallen purity. Letters written around this time show them constantly evoking and mobilising a pure ashram life in their critique of sexual transgressions that blurred social lines in plantation colonies. This was further troubled by their own lineages as celibate Christian missionaries.

Important insights coming from the field of feminist, queer and postcolonial scholarship have been crucial in grappling with ambivalences that inhere in intimate deployments.[30] Private letters form an extremely important site to analyse interiority.[31] There are, however, limits to how such desires could be named. Love and longing for mentors could be expressed only through desexualised tropes. Idioms of spiritual love helped contain potent affections from spelling itself out clearly, leaving in its wake a rich trace of allusions and ambiguities. To recover such articulations is to also note their limits and failure, formative as they were of the larger politics in such representational hermeneutics. Failure shaped the unsteady politics of performance.[32]

Lofty languages of discipleship helped contain the 'problem of desire'. Madeleine Slade and Margaret Noble were relentlessly made to fit desexed, celibate roles of sisterhood or motherhood. In male disciples' articulations of affection, there is much homoerotics at work. Andrews' letters to Tagore exemplify the agony of affection: 'O my dear, dear friend, I can never tell you in words how I love you.'[33] A similar tension appears in Gandhi's relationship with followers-cum-associates such as Hermann Kallenbach and Polak, though Gandhi was more open to reciprocal intimations and practices of (homoerotic) male intimacy than Tagore. Sublime friendship became an invocation to express feelings that could otherwise not be named.

Homoeroticism could be framed in remarkably heteronormative terms.[34] Male Indophile letters to their mentors testify to this framing; Gandhi could confidently send 'love-letters' to both Andrews and Kallenbach without any overt displacements of gender. It is precisely this ability that made male–male desire speakable, preserved in a language that was deeply homoerotic but not sexual. Indeed, the tendency to collapse all desire as ultimately sexual tends to make both desire and intimacy rather impoverished categories. A history of intimacy is not only one of sexuality, but a larger set of practices that comprise the tactile, the embodied and the material. Personalised projections were integral to the imagining of this intimacy. In the way Gandhi's mahatma-hood was circumscribed and enforced by mythopoeic imaginations of the Indian peasantry, disciples' excess of projections made and remade their gurus.[35] At the centre of such projections lay the body of the guru, around which practices of embodiment were rendered meaningful.

Following influential theoretical interventions, narratives of embodiment have received close scholarly attention.[36] Letters from the guru and their bodily artefacts re-enacted this experience. MacLeod's attempt to feel Vivekananda after his death by inhabiting the rooms he lived in reflected this desire to imagine and invest in an embodied co-presence. In a similar way, Mira and Andrews sought to feel the larger presence of their gurus through their letters; to touch their handwriting was to feel the guru's presence. Bull's desire for Sarada Devi's photograph and rosary blessed by her, and Saradananda's cramming of his small room with Bull, Noble and MacLeod's possessions instantiate the many forms through which things, spaces and places embody selves. Practices of embodiment were valuable in the ways they made disciples feel connected to their mentors' worlds. There was distance, sometimes insuperable, but it was often seen as creating wonder and mystique, an enchanted world around their Indophilia.

Worlding Indophilia

There has been a benign tendency in certain influential strands of recent scholarship to view India's elite entanglements in largely affirmative terms. In her study of *fin-de-siècle* anti-colonial thought, the literary scholar Leela Gandhi has termed the ability of individuals such as Andrews, Pearson or Nivedita to form 'cross-cultural friendships' as constitutive of 'affective communities'.

Framing such friendships as the 'lost trope of anti-colonial thought', such mobilisations for a variety of anti-colonial projects have been portrayed as constitutive of an 'affective cosmopolitanism' that emerged in late nineteenth-century Europe.[37] In a similar vein, some historians have argued for a 'peak period of anticolonial struggle in South Asia from ca 1890 to the mid twentieth century' that saw the emergence of an 'aspirational cosmopolitanism' across lines of difference.[38] As Kris Manjapra asserts: 'If nationalism was the main political project of resistance in the anticolonial era, cosmopolitanism was the main ethical project.'[39]

This work takes issue with all such claims and terminologies. Affective or aspirational cosmopolitanism remain uninterrogated categories that seem to suggest a coming-of-age universalism in Indian anti-colonial entanglements, a universalism that is generally presumed to be emancipatory in its tendencies. That there was greater connection and awareness of anti-colonial movements around the world is widely acknowledged; less emphasised is the strategic and hegemonic nature of this cosmopolitanism.[40] The spread of pan-Aryanism, for instance, shows how racial (mis)identification was strategically used by high-caste Indians to reify their claims to equal citizenship in the United States.[41] Nor was this just a westward move. The 'Greater India' hypothesis, developed and deployed in the early twentieth century to assert India's civilising influence in Southeast Asia, subsumed the region's Hindu–Buddhist influences as an extension of India's own history. Tagore played a key role in popularising the 'Greater India' hypothesis, seeing Java and Bali as 'forgotten outposts of Indian civilisation', sitting rather uneasily within a Muslim Indonesia.[42] Pan-Asian claims easily accommodated different kinds of internal hierarchy.

All three big Indian figures – Vivekananda, Tagore and Gandhi – shared in the pride of Aryan civilisational greatness. On a visit to Iran in 1932, Tagore waxed eloquently about the common 'Aryan inheritance' that unified the Indo-Iranian civilisation:

> Coming to think of it, my relations with Persia are even more intimate, for am I not an Indo-Aryan! Persians have throughout their history taken pride in their Aryan descent, and that feeling is gaining strength under the present regime [Reza Shah Pahlavi]. So they are looking on me as a blood relation…. In thus feeling me to be their own, they have made no mistake, for I too feel quite close to them.[43]

It is easy to read this as a moment of anti-colonial solidarity formed in the wake of the Qajars' fall in Iran. But as Chapter 3 on ashrams will show, Tagore's identification was part of a larger inheritance in Aryan civilisational pride and superiority. Belief in an imputed Aryanism created its own logic of difference and exclusions, some of which have been shown in greater detail for Vivekananda and Gandhi in two subsequent chapters (Chapters 4 and 6). Gandhi initially defined Africa (except for Arab Africans) as outside of the pale of empire and India, a view that he modified later in his life.[44] Almost all Western disciples, but particularly Andrews and Nivedita, forcefully argued for this belief in Aryan superiority, borne by contemporary 'scientific' claims about the distinctiveness of this 'racial stock'. If Aryanism was considered a strategic ally of anti-colonial articulations, its limits were soon exposed as the imputed claims of equality remained largely unheard in British imperial (and even American) circles.

Indophile politics was deeply complicit in the reproduction of such identifications and their internal hierarchies. The proliferation of mainstream nationalist discourse within India from the late nineteenth century produced severe anxieties around the representation of India in the empire and beyond. India's position within the British Empire as the biggest supplier of cheap labour – both indentured and non-indentured – was increasingly seen at odds with the respectable aspirations of its nationalist elite. Indophile intimacies were sensitive to realising such aspirations, if not always self-consciously. Andrews, Polak and Pearson's efforts to abolish indenture were driven by this representative anxiety to produce a respectable India and Indians fit for assimilation anywhere, but particularly in settler colonial territories. Vivekananda's American disciples were similarly engaged in the accrual of learned audiences in the West, in their attempts to shore up the glory and greatness of Hindu culture and civilisation. Together, these deployments produced India as the site and signifier of high culture and civilisation, manifested in the exemplary personhoods of Tagore, Gandhi and Vivekananda.

The transnational-global turn in South Asian historiography has persuasively argued against the insular tendencies of methodological nationalism.[45] The period between 1890 and 1940 is a useful referent to capture the increasingly diverse movements of India in global flows of trade, migration and exchange. Institutional protocols aimed at regulating migration, particularly labour flows from India and China, have been key to the discourse of integration and segregation that came to characterise international mobility.[46] The historical nationalisation of migration produced un/foreseen eruptions of 'fervent nationalist claims', a point that sets the context for Indophile deployments in the chapter on anti-indenture campaigns.[47] This has been particularly true for issues of labour migration, where labour became embroiled in a triangulated contest between the British colonial state, an anxious Indian nationalist elite and the demands of global labour supply.

Several scholars have argued against the usage of 'transnational' as it conceptually reifies the very borders it attempts to transcend, preferring instead 'international' to encapsulate the steady stream of engagements between South Asian actors and networks in the interwar period that took nationalism as its framing principle.[48] I have retained transnational as a valid analytical category precisely for this reason. For a country that imagined itself as a nation, though not yet so, 'transnational' became an aspirational move to consolidate that very 'nation' through an act of transcending. Adopting a transnational scale allows us to grapple with the ambivalence of Western entanglements. It reveals that in trying to settle respectable ideas of India as they did, Indophiles reinforced troubling hegemonies in the names of their mentors and anticolonial causes.

The rapid proliferation of transnational political networks such as abolitionism, socialism, pacifism, revolutionary terrorism or religious networks such as Theosophy, Pan-Asianism, Pan-Buddhism and Pan-Islamism, fostered remarkable overlaps.[49] Emergent forms of anti-colonial and cultural nationalism found close solidarity in these networks.[50] Vivekananda's success in the United States (US) contributed to a growing stream of students and nationalist politicians migrating to New York and California from the first decades of the twentieth century. With the ascendancy of the US in global politics, America became a site to counterpose British claims to superiority among the English-educated nationalist elite, particularly on grounds of science and technology.[51] Its liberal Press laws proved conducive to the circulation and distribution of revolutionary journals such as the *Indian Sociologist*, run by the India House patron Shyamjii Krishnavarma. There were important strategic alliances made with Irish nationalists, developments that greatly worried the British imperial government. Pan-Asian connections rose with the victory of Japan over Russia in 1905. As relations between the Pan-Asian thinker Kakuzo Okakura and Sister Nivedita demonstrate in the backdrop of the Swadeshi movement in Bengal, there was much hope in a resurgent Asia led by Japan at the helm.[52] Nivedita wanted to revive Indian spirituality in Japan through

Okakura: 'I can not think of a better personality through wh[ich] to revive the old tradition of the Indian Sadhu in Japan.'[53] While in Tokyo, Pearson published *For India* (1917), a searing indictment of British rule in India, while arguing 'Home Rule is inevitable'. [54] The book was proscribed, and Pearson promptly detained by the British imperial government. In a chapter titled 'Is India Ready?' he listed an array of literary, political and industrial Indian luminaries as evidence of its readiness: Tagore, Jagadish Bose, Gokhale, Natesan, Ratan Tata. In a confidential report to the Director of Criminal Intelligence, James Campbell Ker noted how Vedanta Societies in the US were disseminating Indian nationalist ideas: '… the teachings of the Vedanta Society tend towards Nationalism in politics. Swami Vivekananda himself generally avoided the political side of the case, but by many Hindu nationalists he is regarded as the guru … of the movement.'[55]

Tomoko Masuzawa's important intervention in the global history of religion – particularly around Asian religious forms coming to the West – argues that the category of 'World Religions' was invented to preserve the superior claims of European universalism in a pluralist framework.[56] While reading such imports as constitutive moments in the history of Western religious liberalism, we need to study the kinds of misrecognition this fostered within Asian sites and actors themselves, as well as their Western interlocutors. The final chapter on the making of 'Vedanta as a World Religion' attempts to illustrate the politics of such a move. Embraced by sections of progressive and heterodox liberal circles in the West, this embourgeoisement is eagerly vaunted by cultural nationalist discourse in India that aspired to global respectability. The ideal type to settle such a belief is the largely upper-caste cultured Indian, not the lower caste or class labour-immigrant whose inferior social and cultural status threatened to destabilise that project.[57] Creeds such as Baha'i and Hindu Universalism might have destabilised the categories of East and West,[58] but did not displace them; they were reconstituted and mobilised to make claims for Indian religious or civilisational superiority. A global or transnational scale lets us see how white discipleship embodied and intensified (counter) hegemonic narratives emerging out of Indian nationalist discourse.

Brief Outline of Chapters

The five chapters (excluding the introduction) that span this book try to unify these concerns with some coherence. Chapters 1, 2 and 4 take up the theme of Indophile interiority through letters, ashrams and spaces of spiritual domesticity. I analyse how intimacies are produced and sustained between Indian gurus and their Western disciples through practices of letter-writing and prolific networking. Chapter 2 shows how ashrams provided the physical space to territorialise disciples' intimacy.

Foundational in conceptualising alternative formulations of modernity, the ashramic habitus, for Tagore and Gandhi's disciples, emerged as the centre of their spiritual and social striving. This is where the guru's physical presence could be deeply felt, where self-making practices could be rendered meaningful. Chapter 3 continues with the theme of being, showing how cultural values of the ashram – seen as the ideal aspirational form of Indian community life – profoundly inflected Indophile interlocution of anti-indenture campaigns. Andrews and Pearson repeatedly invoked their affections for Tagore, Gandhi and Gokhale, and the ideal of ashram life while making a case for the immorality of indenture. Their consistent critiques of indenture as a 'festering evil' jutted them into mainstream prominence, vindicating their representative claims in Indian nationalist discourse.

Chapters 4 and 5 focus closely on the affective and discursive practices of Vivekananda and his Western disciples. Chapter 4 – 'Practices of Discipleship' – returns to the theme of Indophile interiority, this time between Vivekananda and a select group of British and American women whose discipleships were crucial in consolidating his global legacy. I look at a series of affective landscapes – spiritual retreats, pilgrimages and household spaces – that produced their enchantment around a particular vision of India inflected by Orientalist typologies. In the final chapter on 'Vedanta as a World Religion', I see how the fantasy of India as a glorious civilisation produced an anxious soliciting of 'learned audiences' in the US.

Chapters 1, 2 and 4 show how intimacy was created and sustained through a series of material, affective and spatialised practices, while Chapters 3 and 5 show their mobilisation for cultural and nationalist projects that curated respectable ideas of India for the world. The Epilogue sums up the main arguments of the book, commenting on the broader entanglements of 'white solidarity' and Indophilia in the colonial and postcolonial world.

Spanning five decades between 1890 and 1940, the narrative is, however, not chronologically aligned. Even though a late nineteenth-century figure, the section on Vivekananda and his Western networks is placed later. The making of Vivekananda's Western discipleships happened around 'ashram-like' spaces, the discussion of which cannot be broached without analysing what the modern ashram is. As such, the chapters on Tagore and Gandhi's ashram projects and discipleships precede Vivekananda's. That Vivekananda is also a central figure in contemporary Hindu nationalism makes him a particularly apposite figure to end with, suggesting how well he has travelled over a century. Tagore and Gandhi's public legacies in India have suffered serious erosion in contemporary times. The Vedanta story anticipates in many ways the deepening entanglement of Hindu cultural forms in global processes of mobility and migration. This work is an attempt to tell some of that story.

Notes

1   Papers of Leonard K. Elmhirst, Dartington Hall Trust Collection, Devon Heritage Centre, Exeter. Within Indian lineages of guru-hood, bodily relics have long been central in sustaining a language of discipleship. A similar counterpart animates European traditions of Christian sainthood, where relics have been continuously institutionalised to inspire religious devotion. For Dartington, see Michael Young, *The Elmhirsts of Dartington: The Creation of an Utopian Community* (New York: Routledge, 1982). Inspired by Tagore's educational and agricultural ideas at Shantiniketan and Sriniketan, Elmhirst had founded the Dartington Hall Trust in England in the 1920s, a major educational experiment that advocated unconventional ideas of utopian communitarianism. The Dartington Hall School was a major experiment in alternative pedagogy in Britain. The historian Anna Neima aptly refers to it as 'Practical Utopia'. See Anna Neima, *Practical Utopia: The Many Lives of Dartington Hall* (Cambridge: Cambridge University Press, 2022).

2   Richard G. Fox, 'East of Said', in *Edward Said: A Critical Reader*, ed. Michael Sprinker (Oxford: Blackwell Publishing, 1992), 152.

3   David Lambert and Alan Lester, eds., *Colonial Lives across the British Empire: Imperial Careering in the Long Nineteenth Century* (Cambridge: Cambridge University Press, 2006).

4   Fred Cooper and Ann Stoler, *Tensions of Empire: Colonial Cultures in a Bourgeois World* (Berkeley: University of California Press, 1997), 21.

5   Vron Ware, *Beyond the Pale: White Women, Racism, and History* (London: Verso Books, 1992), 120. Ware shows how white women found new fields of work through empire and the expansion opportunities afforded by it of female independence and employment (Ware, *Beyond the Pale*, 126).

6   See, for instance, Charles F. Andrews, *The Relation of Christianity to the Conflict between Capital and Labour* (London: Methuen, 1896), for his take on capitalist modernity and Christian Socialism. Andrews regarded trade unions as not only timely outlets of labour grievance but also effective instruments of social and political control (Andrews, *The Relation of Christianity*, 62). Ashis Nandy has noted how the Enlightenment project had subordinated the feminine aspects of Western culture, whose qualities were projected on to the Orient. See Ashis Nandy, *The Intimate Enemy: Loss and Recovery of Self Under Colonialism* (New Delhi: Oxford University Press, 1983).

7   Nandy, *The Intimate Enemy*, 36.

8   I have engaged with some of this scholarship in various chapters more substantially instead of here. Faisal Devji's work on Gandhi stands out for its fresh take on Gandhi as a radical thinker. Faisal Devji, *The Impossible Indian: Gandhi and the Temptation of Violence* (London: Hurst and Co., 2012).

9   Uma Dasgupta, *Friendships of 'Largeness and Freedom': Andrews, Tagore, and Gandhi: An Epistolary Account, 1912–1940* (Oxford: Oxford University Press, 2018); Susan Visvanathan, 'S. K. Rudra, C. F. Andrews and M. K. Gandhi: Friendship, Dialogue and Interiority in the Question of Indian Nationalism', *Economic and Political Weekly* 37, no. 34 (2002).

10   Ruth Harris, 'Rolland, Gandhi and Madeleine Slade: Spiritual Politics, France and the Wider World', *French History* 27, no. 4 (2013): 580. Several historians have grappled with integrating the small scale of the biographical with the big scale of global history, such as Francesca Trivellato, 'Is There a Future for Italian Microhistory in the Age of Global History?', *California Italian Studies* 2, no. 1 (2011); Brice Cossart, '"Global Lives": Writing Global History with a Biographical Approach', *Entremons, UPF Journal of World History*, no. 5 (2013). Maxine Berg has outlined the challenges posed by global microhistory in Maxine Berg, 'Introduction', in *Writing the History of the Global Challenges for the 21st Century*, ed. Maxine Berg (Oxford: British Academy, 2013), 11–12. The history of emotions in South Asia have taken important strides with Margrit Pernau's work. See Margrit Pernau, 'Feeling Communities: Introduction', *Indian Economic and Social History Review* 54, no. 1 (2017). A more recent intervention argues for a history of feeling vis-à-vis the coming of modernity in urban South Asia: Elizabeth Chatterjee, Megan Robb and Sneha Krishnan, 'Feeling Modern: The History of Emotions in Urban South Asia', *Journal of the Royal Asiatic Society* 27, no. 4 (2017): 541. Pernau et al.'s important volume *Civilising Emotions* indexes the emergence of a high imperial order in the nineteenth century and how it reordered the control

and management of a set of emotions around the categories of civility and civilisation in different parts of Asia and Europe: Margrit Pernau et al., eds., *Civilizing Emotions: Concepts in Nineteenth Century Asia and Europe* (Oxford: Oxford University Press, 2015).

11 The recent work of Ashutosh Kumar, *Coolies of the Empire: Indentured Indians in the Sugar Colonies, 1830–1920* (Cambridge: Cambridge University Press, 2017), gives an excellent overview of this.

12 Lizelle Reymond, *The Dedicated: A Biography of Nivedita* (New York: The John Day Company, 1953); Barbara Foxe, *Long Journey Home: A Biography of Margaret Noble (Nivedita)* (London: Rider, 1975).

13 Benarsidas Chaturvedi and Marjorie Sykes, *C. F. Andrews: A Narrative* (London: George, Allen and Unwin, 1949); Nicol Macnicol, *C. F. Andrews: Friend of India* (London: J. Clarke, 1944); Daniel O'Connor, *A Clear Star: C. F. Andrews and India 1904–1914* (Delhi: Orient Blackswan, 2015).

14 Romain Rolland, *Inde: Journal, 1915–1943* (Paris: Albin Michel, 1960). A systematic scholarly study of his journals, written in French, is yet to be undertaken. Separate studies, though largely within a nationalist or hagiographical framework, exists on Rolland and Gandhi; Rolland and Vivekananda; Rolland and Tagore.

15 Kris Manjapra, *Age of Entanglements: German and Indian Intellectuals across Empire* (Harvard: Harvard University Press, 2014).

16 For a nuanced understanding of how this binary played out, see Edward Said's classic book *Orientalism: Western Conceptions of the Orient* (New York: Pantheon Books, 1978).

17 Saurabh Dube, 'Introduction', in *Enchantments of Modernity*, ed. Saurabh Dube (London: Routledge, 2009), 1.

18 In her recent book, the literary scholar Priyamvada Gopal has argued that a history of the British Empire is also a history of its own dissidence. Priyamvada Gopal, *Insurgent Empire: Anticolonial Resistance and British Dissent* (London: Verso, 2019).

19 Leela Gandhi, *Affective Communities: Anticolonial Thought and the Politics of Friendship* (New Delhi: Duke University Press, 2006).

20 Several historians of British feminism have studied the importance of alternative religiosities and suffragists. See Joy Dixon, *Divine Feminine: Theosophy and Feminism in England* (London: Johns Hopkins University Press, 2001); for a more secular feminist engagement, see Laura Schwartz, *Infidel Feminism: Secularism, Religion and Women's Emancipation in England, 1830–1914* (Manchester: Manchester University Press, 2013).

21   Material culture history has prompted a 'renewed interest in understanding experience, the senses and emotions in history', in relation to objects: Anne Gerritsen and Giorgio Riello, eds., *Writing Material Culture History* (London: Bloomsbury, 2014), 7.

22   The two influential contributions of Edward Soja, *Postmodern Geographies: The Reassertion of Space in Critical Social Theory* (London: Verso, 1989); and David Harvey, *The Condition of Postmodernity: An Enquiry into the Origins of Cultural Change* (Oxford: Blackwell, 1990), have informed my understanding of space and practices of spatiality.

23   Barbara H. Rosenwein, *Emotional Communities in the Early Middle Ages* (Cornell: Cornell University Press, 2006).

24   There are, of course, deep Christian overtones of Christ washing his disciples' feet and modern parallels of that in different Christian dispensations; but this is not the same as its everyday performance between disciples touching the guru's feet often multiple times within the same day.

25   Carolyn Steedman, *Dust* (Manchester: Manchester University Press, 2002), 160. Also, for dust as an archival metaphor, see the brilliant exploration by Marijn Nieuwenhuis and Aya Nassar, 'Dust: Perfect Circularity', *Cultural Geographies* 25, no. 3 (2017), who explore the role of dust as 'archival metaphor' that blurs the line between order and disorder.

26   Ben Anderson and Paul Harrison, eds., *Taking-Place: Non-representational Theories and Geography* (Farnham: Ashgate, 2010).

27   Ann Stoler, *Carnal Knowledge and Imperial Power Race and the Intimate in Colonial Rule* (Berkeley: University of California Press, 2002), 12. Her work on colonial Indonesian plantations has shown how sexual arrangements and affective attachments have been key to the production of colonial categories for its control and management. See also Ann Stoler, 'Intimidations of Empire', in *Haunted by Empire: Geographies of Intimacy in North American History*, ed. Ann Stoler (Durham: Duke University Press, 2006).

28   Stoler's corpus has indexed the place of 'tense and tender ties' in governing the education of racialised desire. Stoler, *Carnal Knowledge*, 77.

29   Charles F. Andrews and W. W. Pearson, *Report on Indentured Labour in Fiji: An Independent Enquiry* (Calcutta: Star Printing Works, 1916).

30   As Anjali Arondekar argues, refiguring the archive as a subject allows us to read its silences and elisions meaningfully. An archival lack is not necessarily absence. Anjali Arondekar, *For the Record: On Sexuality and the Colonial Archive in India* (Durham: Duke University Press, 2009), 11. Her work

on sodomy trials in colonial India suggests that if homosexuality remained absently present, largely anecdotal or in passing, it is precisely because of the language employed to record it (Arondekar, *For the Record*, 76).

31 A critical mass of theoretical and empirical insights on epistolarity have emerged out of the Oliver Schreiner Letters Project, http://www.oliveschreinerletters. ed.ac.uk/GiantRaceArticlePDF.pdf (accessed on 13 March 2023). Also see Liz Stanley, 'The Epistolarium: On Theorizing Letters and Correspondences', *Auto/Biography* 12, no. 3 (2004): 201–235; Rebecca Earle, ed., *Epistolary Selves, Letters and Letter Writers, 1600–1945* (Aldershot: Ashgate, 1999).

32 Jack Halberstam, *The Queer Art of Failure* (Duke: Duke University Press, 2011).

33 Andrews to Tagore, 2 October 1913, File No. 4–11, Original Letters from C. F. Andrews to Rabindranath Tagore, CFA Papers, File 1–26, 28 (ii), CD No: RBVB-018, Rabindra Bhavan, Visvabharati.

34 The literary scholar Santanu Das has noted in the context of World War I 'trench letters' how the homoerotic 'kiss' between British men or the Victorian cult of 'romantic friendship' made possible the articulation of male desire without any serious threat to their masculinity. See Santanu Das, *Touch and Intimacy in the First World War* (Cambridge: Cambridge University Press, 2006), 109–110. Elsewhere, in a discussion on the representation of homosexuality in Indian novels, Ruth Vanita has observed how even disapproving portrayals of such themes aroused a degree of sympathy and limited identification in the early decades of the twentieth century. Ruth Vanita, 'Introduction', in *Chocolate and Other Writings on Male Homoeroticism*, ed. Pandey Bechan Sharma [Ugra], trans. Ruth Vanita (London: Duke University Press, 2009).

35 Shahid Amin, 'Gandhi as Mahatma', in *Selected Subaltern Studies*, ed. Ranajit Guha and Gayatri Spivak (Delhi: Oxford University Press, 1989), 292.

36 Based on a broad reading of the following works of these authors: the body is the centre of a range of influential works by Foucault, particularly *The History of Sexuality*, vol. 1 (New York: Pantheon Books, 1978); and *Discipline and Punish* (London: Allen Lane, 1977); Judith Butler, *Senses of the Subject* (Fordham: Fordham University Press, 2015); and Brian Massumi, *Parables of the Virtual* (Durham; London: Duke University Press, 2002).

37 Gandhi, *Affective Communities*, 17. Gandhi draws from Jacques Derrida's influential work *The Politics of Friendship* (1994), that conceptualises the possibilities of radical friendship, based on his readings of Western canonical texts. A similar line of argument is advanced by the literary studies scholar

Elleke Boehmer. She conceptualises collaborations between figures such as Sister Nivedita and the extremist leader Aurobindo Ghose as exercises in 'cross-border interdiscursivity', fostered between marginalised subjects across the empire. See Elleke Boehmer, *Empire, the National, and the Postcolonial: Resistance in Interaction, 1890–1920* (Oxford: Oxford University Press, 2005), 8. Other scholars, such as Chris Bayly, have sought to portray these intersections as part of a 'Global Idealist Moment'.

38   Kris Manjapra, 'Introduction', in *Cosmopolitan Thought Zones: South Asia and the Global Circulation of Ideas*, ed. Sugata Bose and Kris Manjapra (London: Palgrave Macmillan, 2010), 1.

39   Ibid., 2. Nico Slate's work *Coloured Cosmopolitanism* acknowledges the strategic nature of these collaborations, generally between elite Indian actors and their American (both white liberal and African-American) counterparts. Nico Slate, *Coloured Cosmopolitanism: The Shared Struggle for Freedom in the United States and India* (Cambridge, MA: Harvard University Press, 2012). In general, however, the work on global idealist convergences skate over the exclusionary projects that such figures helped authorise in their own home-countries in colonial South Asia.

40   Ali Raza, Franziska Roy and Benjamin Zachariah have strongly emphasised that a cosmopolitan openness is 'wishful thinking'; the hope for an imputed globalism have always been fragmented and imaginary. Ali Raza, Franziska Roy and Benjamin Zachariah, eds., *The Internationalist Moment: South Asia, Worlds, and World Views 1917–39* (New Delhi: SAGE Publications, 2015), xx.

41   Tony Ballantyne, 'Knowledge, Empire and Globalisation', in *The New Imperial Histories Reader*, ed. Stephen Howe (New York: Routledge, 2010), 231. Sheldon Pollock has noted how German Orientalism fed the myth of the Indo-European superiority and contributed to the Aryan purity narrative in Germany. Sheldon Pollock, 'Deep Orientalism? Notes on Sanskrit and Power Beyond the Raj', in *Orientalism and the Postcolonial Predicament: Perspectives on South Asia (South Asia Seminar)*, ed. Carol A. Breckenridge and Peter van der Veer (Philadelphia: University of Pennsylvania Press, 1993).

42   Marieke Bloembergen has dwelt insightfully on the trajectories of the 'Greater India' discourse in her article 'The Politics of "Greater India", a Moral Geography: Moveable Antiquities and Charmed Knowledge Networks between Indonesia, India, and the West', *Comparative Studies in Society and History*, 63, no. 1 (2021): 193–194.

43   Rabindranath Tagore, cited in Afshin Marashi, 'Imagining Hāfez: Rabindranath Tagore in Iran, 1932', *Journal of Persianate Studies* 3, no. 1 (2010): 58.

44 Proponents of African nationalism such as John Dube (African National Congress) also pitted the 'heathen' Indians against Christian Africans viewing them as outsiders usurping native control over resources. Isabel Gaskel Hofmeyr, *Gandhi's Printing Press* (Harvard: Harvard University Press, 2013), 20.

45 This is an increasingly influential argument made by many historians and scholars. Harald Fischer-Tiné, 'Indian Nationalism and the "World Forces": Transnational and Diasporic Dimensions of the Indian Freedom Movement on the Eve of the First World War', *Journal of Global History* 2, no. 3 (2007), 325–344; Hofmeyr, *Gandhi's Printing Press*; Raza, Roy and Zachariah, *The Internationalist Moment*; Radhika Mongia, *Indian Migration and Empire: A Colonial Genealogy of the Modern State* (Durham: Duke University Press, 2018); and others.

46 Adam McKeown, 'Integration and Segregation in Global Migration', *Connecting Seas and Connected Ocean Rims: Indian, Atlantic, and Pacific Oceans and China Seas Migrations from the 1830s to the 1930s,* ed. Donna R. Gabbacia and Dirk Hoerder (Leiden: Brill, 2011), 63. Also Radhika Singha, 'The Great War and a "Proper" Passport for the Colony: Border-Crossing in British India, c.1882–1922', *Indian Economic and Social History Review* 50, no. 3 (2013): 289–315, in the context of Indian immigration.

47 Mongia, *Indian Migration and Empire*, 6.

48 Raza, Roy and Zachariah, *The Internationalist Moment*, xv–xxv.

49 Fischer-Tiné, 'Indian Nationalism and the "World Forces"', 329–332.

50 Mrinalini Sinha shows the effective ways through which these transnational networks were brought to bear on the Mother India controversy in 1927, and the subsequent restructuring of a global empire as effect. Mrinalini Sinha, *Specters of Mother India: The Global Restructuring of an Empire* (Durham: Duke University Press, 2006).

51 Ross Bassett, *The Technological Indian* (Cambridge, MA: Harvard University Press, 2016), 15.

52 Fischer-Tiné, 'Indian Nationalism and the "World Forces"', 333–336.

53 Nivedita to Josephine MacLeod, 11 October 1902, *Letters of Sister Nivedita-II*, Calcutta, 512. Henceforth, *LSN*.

54 W. W. Pearson, *For India* (Tokyo: Asiatic Society of Japan, 1917), 43.

55 James Campbell Ker, *Political Trouble in India, 1907–1911* (Calcutta: Editions India, 1917), 215–217.

56 Tomoko Masuzawa, *The Invention of World Religions, or How European Universalism Was Preserved in the Language of Pluralism* (Chicago: University of Chicago Press, 2005), 13.

57   Except for Har Dayal, who seems to have been the only prominent nationalist leader who managed to bridge the gap between student politics and the Indian agricultural labourer in the US. See Fischer-Tiné, 'Indian Nationalism and the "World Forces"', 335.

58   Ruth Harris, 'Vivekananda, Sarah Farmer, and Global Spiritual Transformations in the Fin de Siècle', *Journal of Global History* 14, no. 2 (2019): 180.

CHAPTER 1

Languages of Longing

Indian Gurus, Western Disciples and the Politics of Letter-Writing

An Archive of Feelings

This chapter will look at the formative role of letters as a medium in constituting discipleship. It examines the guru-figures Swami Vivekananda, Rabindranath Tagore and Mahatma Gandhi and their relations with a cast of close Western disciples. In the context of high British imperialism, letters moulded sympathetic Western men and women into intimate disciples serving a range of Indian causes.

The cast of Western disciples gathered around these guru-figures came from a variety of lineages. C. F. Andrews and William Pearson were Christian missionaries (Anglican and Baptist respectively); Margaret Noble, Sara Bull and Josephine MacLeod were involved in various heterodox initiatives (some linked to Hindu eclecticism); Madeleine Slade was the daughter of a British Admiral. Sister Nivedita (Margaret Noble), C. F. Andrews and Mira Behn (Madeleine Slade), came to occupy major roles in Indian cultural and political nationalism. Western followers' profound spiritual disquiet was rooted in the pervasive mechanisation of life produced by industrial modernity; gurus and ashrams constituted part of a larger 'seeking'. All of them were attracted to some form of immanent spirituality that inhered in the figures of Vivekananda, Gandhi and Tagore.

The Modern Letter in Colonial India

The coming of the modern letter in India is intrinsically tied to the expansion of communication networks used to order empire. Building on an earlier system of *dak*, the rapid proliferation of postal networks scaled time and distance, emerging as key to imperial governance.[1] The introduction of the Indian penny post in 1854, following its British counterpart in 1840, saw an explosion of postal communication over the next century. Aimed at aiding the unrestricted flow of information, a series of postal reform measures made post cheaper and hugely popular in India. From 43 million in 1860–1861 it increased to nearly 250 million in 1900–1901, a figure that included not only letters but also the cheap quarter anna postcards.[2] The Indian Postal Service was one of the fastest to Indianise, with over half of the 214 senior appointments (ranks between Superintendent to Post Master General) being held by Indians.[3] It marked the intensification of the postal system and its penetration deep into the countryside, integrating the empire as never before, with negligible violence. The rapid proliferation of postal networks spawned new literary publics and practices across a range of languages and populations.[4]

Letter-writing manuals existed since the eighteenth century in Britain, used as prescriptive guides for 'model letters'. In Victorian Britain, they offered instruction in the art of letter-writing, which was considered necessary education for building characters of young men and women in their public conduct.[5] With the popularisation of the penny post in Britain after 1840, letters became part of new cultural and political economies of knowledge circulation. Transatlantic networks of abolitionist activism, for instance, allowed for conversation to take place between geographically disparate people.[6] Prescriptive or actual, private letters were understood to reveal the 'authentic character of an individual even if their public conduct could not'.[7] The private letter was a site to produce and perform a true individual moral self away from public glare. It was to this epistolary tradition that Western disciples like Andrews, Pearson, Noble, Slade belonged.

Indian correspondents, on the other hand, came from a different if not unrelated tradition. The coming of print culture had brought forth important breaks and continuities from earlier traditions of orality in the subcontinent. The rationalising of postal communication, while introducing new forms of letter-writing, transformed pre-colonial forms as well. Of particular importance was the emergence of the personal letter and the ways it changed conventions and meanings around letter-writing practices for the English-educated Indian elite. It helped chart a process of self-individualisation in an emergent private sphere, while also partaking in a larger colonial modernity.

There has been a long tradition of epistolary manuals and compilations since at least the Mughal times.[8] Much of these letters focused on diplomacy, and there was no broad private–public distinction in epistolary categories. Medieval-era love letters came closest to any form of personal letter, but they were generally written in effusive courtly language that showed off nobility and refinement.[9] As Francesca Orsini notes, the coming of colonial literary modernity gave birth to a new critical individual subjectivity that took itself very seriously.[10] Older epistolary forms were not effaced, but the advent of a modern selfhood greatly affected the kind of authors and audiences emerging around the form.

The gradual development of a loose but distinctive public–private sphere made personal letters an imaginative space where selves were creatively deployed and cultivated. As discourses of the colonial elite sought to catch up with their metropolitan counterparts, the glamour, distance and status associated with English as a language of power, in relation to vernacular languages, made letters written in English something of a marker of culture and high learning.[11] Conversely, the ability of certain educated Indians to correspond and converse in English (alongside their own native languages) generally invested them with the potential to be part of an Anglicised colonial symmetry.[12] This is not to deny the significant growth that vernacular letter-writing practices had within elite and non-elite Indian audiences. Nonetheless, knowledge of English endowed their authors with the possibility to engage with Western actors and networks beyond India. Rammohan Roy's prolific contacts with important British and American figures bear an early testimony to this possibility of 'reaching out' to a wider world through colonial networks.

This influential class of English-educated (and bilingual) colonial elite pioneered ideas of citizenship and civil rights within the colonial public sphere.[13] Western Indophiles formed a precipitating point in this interlocution, vocally arguing for the extension of metropolitan rights and privileges to imperial subjects. To this end, they collaborated in various colonial elite-led projects. Their active presence in Indianist enterprises became a morally legitimising force.

Their epistolary corpus offers insights into the intimacies forged between iconic Indian figures hailing from a critical class of Western educated elite and their Western disciples. They form a minor if influential trend in a time of high imperial consolidation, of Western men and women who willingly accepted the discipleship of Indian figures and stood against the imperial politics of their own nation and/or racial privilege. Tagore and Vivekananda of course made concessions in distinguishing Western culture from Western imperialism, but this distinction was generally under strain.

Epistolary Communities

The community of letters formed out of this cast of Indian and Western characters was expansive. Anxious for physical and emotional proximity to their mentors, letters compensated both. Enthralled by their mentors' personalities, disciples wanted a larger stake in their lives and work. The letters passing through this small but influential community could be broadly categorised into primary and secondary epistolary networks. Primary epistolary networks constituted the corpus of letters exchanged directly between Western disciples and their Indian gurus. In these, disciples poured out their hearts to mentors and sought instruction. As emotional practice, letters between mentors and their disciples recorded the gradual shifts and shifting sensibilities made possible by letter-writing. Despite initial enchantments, these relationships were not forever beholden to the greatness of the guru. They came under frequent strain and primary epistolary networks provide a rich narrative of this densely constituted interiority.

Undergirding these major epistolary networks lay various ancillary connections that refer to lateral correspondence exchanged (*a*) within followers and their close confidantes; and (*b*) between various Indian mentors and their wider circles. These include Noble's correspondence with other Western disciples of Vivekananda such as Sara Bull and Josephine MacLeod, or the accounts of Gandhi's associates Mahadev Bhai and Pyarelal that shed light on primary networks. Letters exchanged between Gandhi and Tagore, Andrews and Pearson, or members of their wider circles such as the French litterateur Romain Rolland, Tagore's British associate Leonard Elmhirst, the Moderate Congress politician Gopal Krishna Gokhale, the Arya Samaj leader Munshi Ram[14] and the Wesleyan missionary Edward J. Thompson belonged to this category. Secondary epistolary networks consist of these parallel epistolary connections. They illuminate the relationships forged between gurus and disciples.

Romain Rolland's diaries provided the most consistent record of these intersecting networks.[15] A unique European pacifist literary figure with a deep interest in Indian culture and philosophy, he had personally met Vivekananda, Gandhi and Tagore, as well as all their Western disciples. He had even 'gifted' Slade to Gandhi. Each of them confided in Rolland their doubts, hopes and fears. Rolland's diaries unified these different sets of disciples within a shared tradition of Indophilia. Rolland's diary entries, culled from his personal exchanges, offer valuable comparative insights into the broader convergences at work.[16]

Secondary epistolary networks between disciples or other confidants constantly referred to the state of their relations with mentors. Noble, for instance, wrote of her initial days of training in Hinduism to her fellow-disciple and friend Josephine MacLeod:

> The hot season has begun again. I teach now from 7 till 11 in the morning.... At 11 I bathe – eat – rest – and then write, like a veritable Hindu. In future, I mean to dress in this fashion for those hours....
>
> I am visiting Swami's little cousin in her zenana and teaching her English. Swami says that if I bring her into this work and make her my spiritual and intellectual heir I shall be conferring the greatest benefit that he could ask on him. Just fancy![17]

Vivekananda's influence loomed large in these adoptions, in her dress, food and living habits and her teaching English to zenana women.

A similar, if more intense inter-braiding, can be seen in Andrews's letters to Tagore. Written to William Rothenstein, a British artist and literary associate of Tagore, Andrews bared his heart:

> It is hard even yet to get over the pain of separation from the Poet [Tagore] ... I have never known love such as this, that has been given me from him.[18]

Secondary epistolary relations provided that useful space where this excess of meaning was performed.

Letters to the Guru

C. F. Andrews joined the Cambridge Brotherhood Mission in Delhi (St Stephen's College) in 1904 as an Anglican missionary. Known for his reformist and unorthodox views, Andrews courted frequent controversy within missionary and Anglo-Indian circles in India and England, particularly the Society for the Propagation of the Gospel in England. Influential in the selection of S. K. Rudra as the first Indian Christian to head St Stephen's College, Andrews strongly advocated for an Indianisation of Christ and Christianity.

Between 1905 and 1910, years that saw the proliferation of the Swadeshi movement in Bengal, along with the rise of extremist politics and revolutionary terrorism, Andrews emerged as a distinctive liberal Christian voice. He was condemned by the Anglo-Indian community but highly regarded by Moderate Indian nationalists for his denunciation of violence.

Pearson was a Baptist missionary teaching at the London Missionary College in Calcutta. Dissatisfied with its 'narrow' theological atmosphere, he sought to quit the mission in 1911, and wished to continue in India as an independent worker. Andrews's eclecticism (his position against conversion, belief in a fulfilment theology) had already spread by then in Indian missionary circles. Pearson was attracted to Andrews' reformist if polarising streak, and introduced him to Tagore in London.[19] Both men had a shared experience of Cambridge education and missionary service in India.

Pearson and Andrews first met Tagore at a London reading session, in 1912. Tagore had by then left behind his former association with the Swadeshi movement. Increasingly disillusioned with the exclusivist strains of Hindu cultural nationalism that came to dominate the movement, he moved towards pantheism and a language of universal humanism. In 1912, his *Gitanjali* poems – translated into English from their Bengali originals – had created a stir in London literary circles.[20] Its mysticism and lofty sentimentalism stirred poets like W. B. Yeats, and eventually paved the path for a Nobel Prize in 1913.

Andrews and Pearson were greatly moved by Tagore's poetry and personality. Within weeks of their first meeting, Andrews wrote to Tagore:

> My thoughts are with you so constantly and I seem at times to pass whole days with you altogether, remembering you in my prayers and thinking of you … also longing to be with you…. I want you to tell me anything you would wish me to do to help you.[21]

Tagore became part of this projection: in their daily prayer and longing, thought and habit. Pearson was ready to give up his missionary vocation and join Tagore's utopian ashram-school at Shantiniketan:

> You told me in London that you wanted to capture me for Shantiniketan and now I am able to write and tell you that I am a willing captive and that it is only a question of time now for the captive to enter the place where the bonds of affection have been woven.[22]

Through letters, both Andrews and Pearson could imagine an intimacy with Tagore, already the vaunted *gurudev* (the Guru as God) (Figure 1.1). Tagore, in turn, warmly reciprocated both Pearson and Andrews's overtures in lofty terms. Pearson's letter 'stirred [Tagore's] heart to its depths'. Affirming Andrew's affection, Tagore wrote: '… your love has made my life richer and I count it as one of the gains of my life that will abide. Have faith in my love when I am silent.'[23] Andrews and Pearson visited Tagore's ashram in his absence to help with daily activities, while writing letters that affirmed their loyalty.

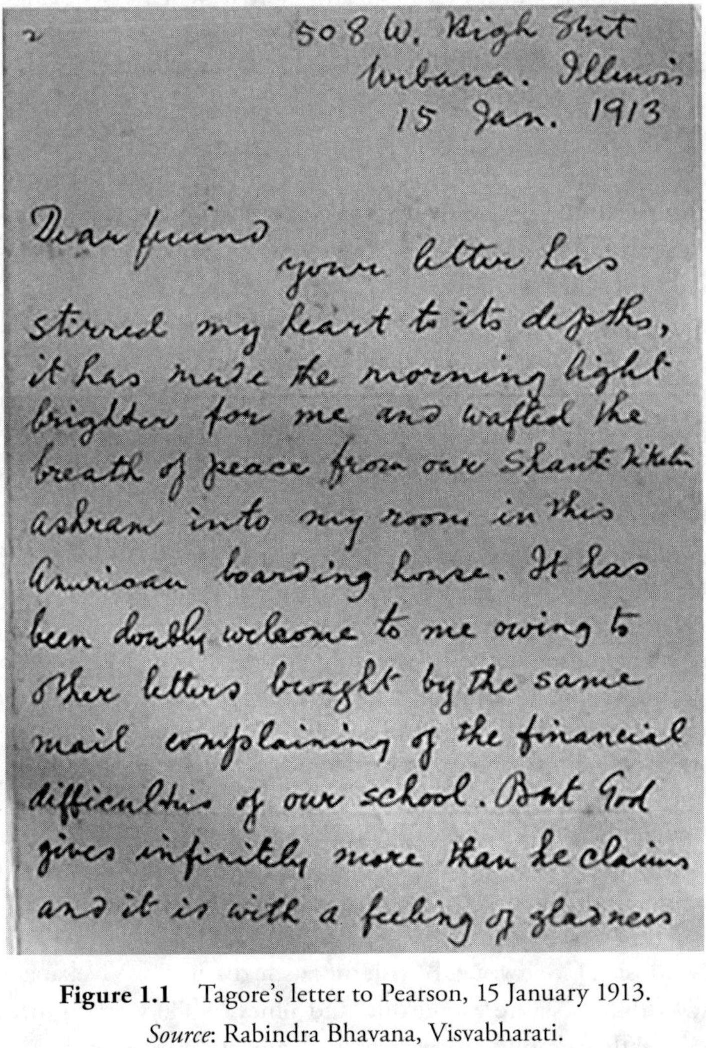

508 W. High Street
Urbana. Illinois
15 Jan. 1913

Dear friend your letter has stirred my heart to its depths, it has made the morning light brighter for me and wafted the breath of peace from our Shanti Niketan ashram into my room in this American boarding house. It has been doubly welcome to me owing to other letters brought by the same mail complaining of the financial difficulties of our school. But God gives infinitely more than he claims and it is with a feeling of gladness

Figure 1.1 Tagore's letter to Pearson, 15 January 1913.
Source: Rabindra Bhavana, Visvabharati.

Like Andrews and Pearson, Noble and Slade too wished to be part of their mentors' lives and work. Letters became the medium to express their desires. Never having met Gandhi in person, Slade came to know of him through Romain Rolland in 1924.[24] She wanted to join his ashram at Sabarmati immediately. Gandhi had then professed caution and a preparatory interval of one year. After a year, Slade reiterated her request:

> Most Dear Master,
>
> ... The first impulse has never faded, but on the contrary my desire to serve you has grown ever more and more fervent.... My being is filled with a great joy ... of giving all I have to you and your people and the anguish of being able to give so little. I pine for the day when I shall come to India.
>
> Dear Master, may I come?[25]

She gave up 'the drinking of all wines, beers or spirits', 'meat of any kind' while learning to spin and read Hindi.[26] In a similar vein, Noble's guru Vivekananda too advised against her coming to India. Noble was already active in the London Vedanta Society that Vivekananda established with the help of British disciples. Vivekananda acknowledged that she had 'the making ... of a world mover' but felt she 'could do more work for us in England than by coming here.'[27] A cautious Vivekananda confided in Sara Ole Bull, a wealthy American patron-disciple, who also knew Noble:

> I do not think any European or American will be of any service here just now, and it will be hard for any Westerner to bear the climate. Mrs. Annie Besant with her exceptional powers works only among the Theosophists and thus she submits to all the indignities of isolation which a Mlechha is made to undergo here. Even Goodwin smarts now and then and has to be called to order. He is doing good work as he is a man and can mix with people. Women have no place in men's society here, and she can do good only among her own sex in India. The English friends that came over to India have not been of any help as yet and do not know whether they will be of any in the future, with all these, if anybody wants to try she is welcome.[28]

In 1898, Josiah Goodwin, a British monastic disciple of Vivekananda, had passed away due to severe exhaustion and illness while working in India.[29] Goodwin's death exemplified Vivekananda's anxieties. It was only after other disciples interceded on Noble's behalf that he conceded.[30] Both Gandhi and Vivekananda warned Slade and Noble of the general lack of European comforts and everyday deterrents that ranged from casteism, racism and poverty to language and climate barriers. However, aspiring disciples regarded these ordeals as testaments to the purity of their resolve.

Self-abnegation and suffering formed a common arc for disciples to prove their worthiness. Exalted references such as Master, Bapu and Gurudev served to underscore a relationship of worshipful subservience. Nivedita yearned to serve Vivekananda:

> ... today I want to do things only because they are my Father's [Vivekananda's] will.... One longs to serve for serving's sake, for ever and ever, dear Master – not for our miserable little life.[31]

Declarations of subservience placed them at par with Indian disciples, who were already familiar with the cultural idiom of *gurubhakti* (devotion to the guru). Yet, even as it rendered them in equal relation to their fellow Indian disciples, their extraordinariness was well understood. Their letters, suffused with (spiritual) invocations of complete surrender, continued to perform physical and symbolic inversions of hierarchy.

Love in Letters

Reciprocity was fundamental to the act of letter writing.[32] Its promise led disciples to continue writing, in the hope that their gurus would read and reply. Vivekananda comforted Noble: 'Every word you write I value' and 'every letter is welcome a hundred times ... whenever ... and whatever you like[d], knowing that nothing will be misinterpreted, nothing unappreciated'.[33] For Noble, writing to her guru was an eagerly anticipated act. She would playfully assert its joy:

> All day I have been promising myself the joy of writing to you. Haven't I been a bad daughter? To my poor old father, too![34]

Seemingly light, the assertion of a filial relationship between Vivekananda and Nivedita was also part of a continual attempt to frame that relationship in sacred terms.[35] Fellow women disciples such as MacLeod felt she had the 'lover's adoration' for Vivekananda.[36] Relations between male gurus and their women disciples were largely framed within father–daughter relationships, containing potential slippages.

Feelings of love and affection were framed through different kinds of operative limits. Gandhi was the least inhibited in declaring and naming this love for both male and female disciples. Gandhi cherished writing 'love-letters' to his disciples, that included his South African Jewish colleagues Henry Polak and Hermann Kallenbach, and later Andrews and Slade. Gandhi referred to Kallenbach's letters as 'charming love notes' and both had, at least on one recorded occasion, pledged deep love for each other, while regarding Gandhi's wife Kasturba as his 'mother'.[37] Gandhi did not shy away from acknowledging the homoerotics in his relationship with Kallenbach.[38] In a letter from London, Gandhi reminisced:

> Your portrait (the only one) stands on my mantelpiece in the bedroom. The mantelpiece is opposite to the bed.... The pen I use ... in each letter it traces makes me think of you. If, therefore, I wanted to dismiss you from my thoughts, I could not do it.... The point ... is to show to you and me how completely you have taken possession of my body. This is slavery with a vengeance.[39]

Material artefacts – portrait, bed, pen – came together to stage a 'possession' of Gandhi's body. The highly charged language of absence evoked romantic longing. Love-letters helped imagine co-presence. That Gandhi destroyed many of Kallenbach's early letters to preserve their confidentiality limits us from speculating too much on the nature of this 'possession'. In this, he seemed to have acted on Kallenbach's insistence on their not being read by anyone else.[40] Gandhi censured his powerful love but did not forbid or dissuade him: 'Everyone considers that your love for me is excessive.'[41] Homoeroticism figured not infrequently under the benign sign of mentor–disciple relationship.

Kallenbach's 'excessive' love soon manifested in resentment towards C. F. Andrews, who became close to Gandhi within a few weeks of his arrival in South Africa in 1914. Andrews's emergence as a trusted aide stoked Kallenbach's jealousy. Gandhi assured him repeatedly: 'Though I love and almost adore Andrews so, I would not exchange you for him.'[42] Apparently, the reassurance was not enough, for within two months we find sterner replies to Kallenbach: 'You seem to have been hasty in judging Andrews. I fancy that I know him better.'[43] Gandhi chided Kallenbach for being 'petty'.[44] Interestingly, it was

to Andrews that Gandhi turned for help in getting Kallenbach to India in
1915, after his return from South Africa and the outbreak of World War I
(Kallenbach was German, and later became a Zionist).[45] From Shantiniketan,
where Gandhi's Phoenix School boys were temporarily lodged, he remembered
Kallenbach while working on sanitary reform:

> Extraordinary changes have been made in the Santiniketan school,
> Andrews and Pearson rose to the occasion and Pearson and I, whilst
> we were working away at sanitation reform, thought of you – how
> you would have thrown yourself into the work.[46]

It is difficult to say if such letters soothed Kallenbach's jealousy. But he
did identify correctly Andrews as a major contender for Gandhi's affections.
Andrews, not always registering these upsets, continued to nestle himself deep
within Gandhi's discipleships, both Indian and Western. In a letter to Mahadev
Desai, Andrews invoked both Polak and Kallenbach: 'I am so glad Bapu was
able to see Henry Polak. Give my dearest love to Bapu and tell him I am in
correspondence with Hermann Kallenbach and am trying to get him to take
an interest in African handloom work.'[47]

On their first encounter in 1914, Andrews had stooped to touch Gandhi's
feet in a racially polarised South Africa.[48] He was shunned by the White press
and population. But this act gained him immediate affections from both
Gandhi and the Indian community. Though his stay was brief, he played an
important role in brokering the Gandhi–Smuts[49] Agreement. Andrews's regard
for Gandhi found clear expression in his letters to Tagore, his other (already)
great love:

> The English in Natal are far worse than the English in Calcutta. What
> is exercising them at present is the fact that I [as an Englishman] took
> the dust of Mr. Gandhi's feet – the feet of an Asiatic – on landing. I
> am afraid I shall never be forgiven.[50]

Andrews hoped to Gandhi that his transgressive acts in Natal would make
him worthy of Tagore's love:

> I long – Oh! How deeply I cannot tell you to take this love itself and lay
> it at the feet of Gurudev. I am longing and hoping that by and through
> this experience I shall not be made less unworthy of his love.[51]

The need to love became an existential need for Andrews. Dust connected many things: spiritual subservience, racial transgression and male intimacy, all inspiring a love for India. He constantly compared his feelings for Gandhi and Tagore and initially found the former falling short: 'I could not love him immediately, instinctively, as I loved you when I saw you in England.'[52] Unlike Tagore and Shantiniketan, he felt he had to 'cut channels, for love to run freely ... and to get past the barriers of mere kindness and friendliness which falls short of true love'.[53] Compared to the rustic, unfettered freedom of Shantiniketan, Phoenix and Tolstoy Farm were highly regulated spaces, made with the object of carrying out political struggles. In his letters, he would confide his love for Gandhi to Tagore, that for Tagore to Gandhi, and for both Gandhi and Tagore to Gokhale, creating a thick affective trail linking everyone. Aboard a ship bound for India from Capetown, he yearned for 'Mohan':

> I have been thinking so much about you on this voyage – more even, I think, than on my voyage from the Cape. It is the coming closer to India that brings me even closer to you ... how sane and true you were, Mohan [Gandhi], when we were in Pretoria and I was questioning myself of going to the [passive resistance] march with you if it were to begin once more....[54]

Reciprocating this embrace, Gandhi's 'love-letter' playfully noted:

> If you cannot have a nurse like me, who should make love to you but at the same time enforce strict obedience to doctor's orders, you need a wife who should see that you had your food properly served, you never went out without an abdominal bandage.... But marriage is probably too late. And not being able to nurse you I can only fret.[55]

The attention to material details of care – food, bandages – or the invocation of specific roles such as nurse and wife, virtually re-constituted co-presence. The reference to 'love-making' and wifely care by a strictly celibate Gandhi evoked a language of conjugal intimacy. Like a doting wife, he vividly portrayed Andrews as the suffering husband, evoking a vision of conjugal care.

Andrews's desire to love and be loved by prominent men such as Munshi Ram, S. K. Rudra, Tagore and Gandhi helped him realise his 'feminine' self. As he confided to his Stephens colleague and friend S. K. Rudra, another of his great loves, he was 'too much of a woman by nature ... and [he] cannot help' not expressing his love and concern.[56] Perhaps anticipating its potently risqué aspects, Andrews qualified this 'feminine' self as essentially maternal:

> ... it is because of this unchanging motherly influence that the 'mother' in me has grown so strong. My life seems only able to blossom into flower when I can pour out my affection upon others as my mother did upon me.[57]

To love India was construed as essentially an effect of this strong maternal urge.

Andrews felt powerfully attracted to different kinds of masculinity embodied by all these 'great' Indian men. Glad to add Gandhi to his initial acquisition of the trio of Tagore, Munshi Ram and Rudra, Andrews wrote gushingly to Desai:

> ... what Bapu used laughingly to call the 'Trinity' (whom I worshipped in South African days) – Gurudev, Mahatma Munshi Ram, and Mr Rudra – It is a supreme joy to me to find that, in not one single instinct of the 3, have I been betrayed; and if my Trinity of worship has become a Quaternity – I need not tell you which name has been added to the list![58]

To be able to come in their close confidence and affection was a dual affirmation of his 'womanliness' and their manliness. It evinced his 'feminine' ability to 'love' and 'long' for their presence while also sublimating it under an abstracted Indophilia.

Love letters provided the perfect site to hold homoeroticism. Potent attractions of disciples for their mentors could be contained, their sexualities sublimated into non-threatening idioms of affection. Epistolary spaces manifested and indeed celebrated these intimate transgressions less readily achievable in more formal spaces. It 'queered' languages of intimacy within standard idioms of discipleship, a point rarely recognised within mainstream scholarship.[59]

When the discipleship was heterosexual, as with Gandhi and Mira, love letters helped cultivate suitable distance. Like Nivedita, Mira too had the 'lover's adoration' for Gandhi, as Rolland astutely noted.[60] To cultivate physical distance, Mira was continuously sent to different ashrams to learn Hindustani, and more importantly, stem her over-attachment to Gandhi. Letters also became a mode of instruction in Gandhian syncretism: 'I have all your love letters. The one about the repugnance against Mussalmans is disturbing. It is the fear of conversion that has caused this repugnance.'[61]

Though letter-writing is based on reciprocity, the desire to please Gandhi led Mira to forfeit that expectation. Yet, Gandhi insisted:

> Though you absolve me from having to write to you I cannot deny myself the joy of writing to you every Monday. Writing love letters is a recreation, not a task one would seek an excuse to shirk.[62]

At times, Mira did not even seek an acknowledgement of her 'love-letters', satisfied in the quiet knowledge that they would be read by him. She wrote voluminously, sometimes, as Gandhi complained, not 'shorter than ten pages'.[63] For Mira, to be replied to was a privilege in itself, even if this was a two-liner. Gandhi's replies, often short and curt, were hardly effusive. He always followed up on her training in the ashram and practicalities:

> You should give me your day's doings, and describe the prayers, the studies and the meals. Tell me what you are eating. How are your bowels acting? What is the quantity of milk you are taking? … Are there mosquitoes there? Do you take your walks regularly? Do you write any Hindi?[64]

Gandhi's ashram letters generally served a didactic function. They reflected his constant pursuit of ideal dietary regimes and a minimalist lifestyle.

Disciples sought an amplified sense of their gurus' selves in letters and generally found them. Through letters, they felt the guru's touch. Distance imparted meaning to the letter's embodiment, compensating for actual physical absence. Andrews wrote to Tagore:

> It was such an intense pleasure to see your dear handwriting again. I had been looking for it mail after mail hoping against hope … and my heart overflowed when it came at last with its opening word of 'friend'. I wish I could tell you what that means to me, but it must be told in other ways than letters![65]

The 'mail' – embedded in a longer history of imperial networks and postal modernity – ordered epistolary meanings of intimacy in space and time. The wait for the letter created the momentum for fulfilment. Postal modernity came to manifest new languages of emotion around the private letter, shaping its correspondents' intentions and expectations. Both handwriting and signature came together to reconstitute this cultural-material embodiment of the self. Even as Andrews fretted, 'I could never tell you in words how I love you', letters came closest to instantiating this love.[66]

Anxieties of Longing

Disciples' love for gurus could not remain opaque to the anti-colonial ethos of their projects. While Tagore did not participate in mainstream political endeavours as Gandhi, he nevertheless remained a critic of empire. Epistolary texts bore testimony to confessions of complicity and failure. An anguished Andrews confessed to Tagore about his failings:

> I have failed many times. The greatest failure was last year when to my surprise the missionary societies, one and all, asked me to write a book for their younger people to study. I accepted the task ... I was ashamed of the book..., especially when I met you and stayed with you. But the sense of shame has increased since I came back to India and visited the ashram ... but I will *never* [emphasis added] write a book on those lines again! I want to realise a truer self ... and I am going to make a great claim upon your friendship and ask you to help me to do so.[67]

Andrews's book *The Renaissance in India: its Missionary Aspect* (1912) credited the advent of missionary Christianity in India for its new social, cultural and political awakening. In letter after letter to Tagore, he expressed torment for this deed and sought penitence (Figure 1.2). Tagore's letters seemed to give him new life: '... since your letter came my mind has been wonderfully relieved. The assurance of your love and the call to your side have changed the aspect of affairs, and I am happy.'[68]

Andrews could not wait to be 'freed from all ... claims, as soon as possible, of Government and Mission and Anglo India with its social calls and conventions'. Meeting Tagore had only made the 'longing stronger' along with a 'liberalising of [his] own Christian thoughts'.[69] Pearson underwent a similar experience. He was impatient to offer his services for Tagore's ashram 'with the humility and reverence of a worshipper', trying to give up the 'poverty and failures of [his] own life and ... fix a steadfast gaze on the ideal for which the as[h]ram stands'.[70] Pearson wanted to quietly work on his Bengali and leave his Baptist missionary obligations before immersing himself in Shantiniketan. Pearson's love for Tagore elicited in Andrews a similar feeling:

It has been very beautiful on this voyage to watch Willie's love
for you, and it has given me a deep joy which I cannot express in
words....To speak of you, as we do together, has been his great and
widest comfort.[71]

He wished to follow in Pearson's footsteps: learn Bengali and Sanskrit, travel
and live widely in India and with Indians, engage with Indian philosophy.
Like Pearson, he wanted to try, from a 'completely independent standpoint
(not as a paid agent)', to express Christian thought in the 'East': 'I have been
proud and conceited in the past and underrated Hinduism; I would be so
no longer'.[72] Love for Tagore spilled into new investments, linking them in a
relationship of transitivity:

> ... there has come ... through my love for you, a new confidence ...
> I have entered into the heritage of India herself and been made one
> with her spiritual experiences and felt its depth and power.... But
> the fountain of my own heart was still partly sealed and only since I
> have learnt to love you has it burst its bonds and overflowed.... It has
> taught me to love ... all the dear friends I have made at the ashram.[73]

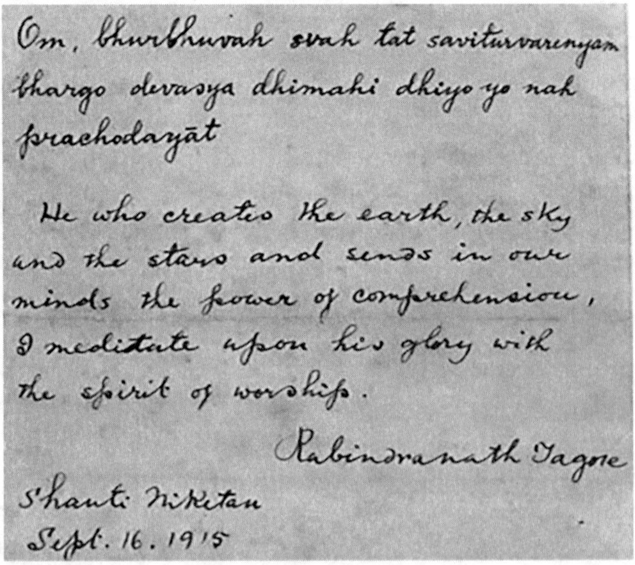

Figure 1.2   Tagore sends a Vedic prayer of peace to Andrews. Tagore occasionally
sent lofty Sanskrit verses to Andrews, a famous *Shantimantra*, or Vedic prayer of
peace in this case.

Source: Rabindra Bhavan, Visvabharati.

Andrews's 'love talk' was, however, interpreted as a sign of going native by missionary colleagues and Anglo-Indian society.[74] He wrote to Gandhi:

> That attack on me in the English newspapers for my 'Hindu' proclivities goes on. The missionaries are probably saying ... that I am going to become a 'Hindu' and if I go to Bolpur and resign the Delhi Mission this will be universally believed....[75]

Coming closer to Tagore intensified his desire to leave his missionary ties:

> I could not be true to my love for you, if I did not seek to share them with you and I trust your love enough to be sure that you will welcome the burden ... it was my very meeting with you, which made has made me realize more clearly my own position and become dissatisfied with it. I could not share your life, without feeling the confinement of the narrow walls of my own.... If I remain a missionary, in a somewhat narrow Missionary Society, I am in a sort of bondage.[76]

Tagore and Shantiniketan continued to figure in almost every letter from and between Andrews and Pearson, reminding them of the promise ashram life held. Visions of being and working with Tagore heightened their yearning.

Work became worship and gurus became near-divine characters. Mira, bouncing between ashrams all over India, remained 'immersed in [her] Bapu'. Her letters to Gandhi show the painful negotiation of a new cultural self, and fear of failure:

> Bapu dearest, another long and precious letter from you has just arrived!
>
> I could not, even if I tried, be anything else but what I am before you, and that is why, however I am ashamed of my weakness, I have to lay bear [sic] before my Bapu – Yes – you are indeed father and *mother* and what is more than all, you are Bapu, *my Bapu* – in whom I live, and in whom I have that utter confidence that only boundless love can inspire – and it is Bapu alone who can make me what I should be. The strength and love of my Bapu are ever with me now.... Nothing that bears the slightest shade of *untruth* can stand before you....[77]

Gandhi's replies to Mira are almost clinical in their brevity and directness. He referred to his disciplining of Mira's passionate desire as a necessary 'operation':

> I sent you away too quickly after a serious operation. But the sending you away was part of the operation.... Jamnalalji says I should have kept you with me. Well, you are going to belie their fears and be and keep quite well and cheerful.[78]

Almost like a mandate, Gandhi's instructions to Mira brought more sorrow than solace. The attempt to excise personal attachment almost broke Mira. 'Love-letters' bore testimony to this continued cycle of distress and relief that characterised their relations.

Becoming Idealised Objects

The bodies of white women and their investments became gendered sites of nationalist spectacle. Both Noble and Slade adopted vows of Hindu celibate asceticism, or *brahmacharya*, becoming Nivedita and Mira respectively. Vivekananda anticipated for Noble her role of India:

> What was wanted was not a man, but a woman; a real lioness, to work for Indians. India cannot yet produce great women, she must borrow them from other nations. Your education, sincerity, purity, immense love, determination and above all, the Celtic blood make you just the woman wanted.[79]

In letter after letter, Vivekananda continued to spell out what the Indian nation needed Noble to embody: purity, education and a Celtic racial valour mobilised to deliver manhood. He continued to warn her of people who stood in the way of such a project:

> ... as long as you go on mixing with that [Tagore] family, I must go on sounding my gong. Remember that that family has poured a flood of erotic venom over Bengal ... my mission is simply to bring MANHOOD to this people [*sic*].[80]

Nivedita, in due course, became a central figure in the politics of deficit masculinity that dominated discourses of colonial Bengal and India in the early twentieth century. Creating a desexualised but forceful language of discipleship was central to Vivekananda.

Gandhi, attuned to a different vision of Hinduism and masculinity than Vivekananda, exercised another set of expectations on Mira. She chose to adopt celibacy and took her vows in Gandhi's presence in 1927. Her letters were frequently circulated by Gandhi as objects of education for ashram inmates:

> … you should perhaps know that I send most of your letters to the Ashram for being read to the members. They are so beautiful. Those that contain criticism of the attitude of the Kanya Gurukul I did not send. I destroyed them.… I do not want you to restrain yourself because other eyes may see the letter …[81]

The practice of circulating letters gave them a performative role. This simultaneous gesture of approval, through circulation of her appreciative letters, and control, by destroying more critical letters, formed part of a larger disciplining exercise.

Mira's coming closer to a syncretic and 'essential' Hinduism reflected her desire to identify with an aspirational collective:

> Everyday of my life I become more and more deeply in love with the Hindu nature – I don't know how to express it Bapu – I just feel as if it were the highest development of humanity which we have in this world, with its inborn gentleness, forgiveness and tolerance – its simpleness and natural feeling for God.… I get the feeling that to pass into the Hindu nature is the natural, perhaps the road to salvation … as long as one remains to any extent outside it, one feels oneself to be to that extent a barbarian.… I now realise that barbarism in myself and sooner or later I will overcome it.… If I can not all together overcome it in this life, then I ask nothing better than to be born a Hindu in the next birth – and this the Blessed Way will at last become open to me.[82]

The strong desire to be Hindu produced the experience of being so. Mira was far less vocal than Nivedita in Hindu nationalist discourse, but both became extraordinary examples, affirming an Indianness they were not born into. Indian cultural and nationalist politics generally remained sensitive to the strategic use of these figures. Racial difference made Western discipleships extraordinary, and in that sense, useful. The bind this claim created on white women disciples led to further disciplining of their bodies and desires.

Conclusion: Archipelago of Affect

The anthropologist Monique Scheer has argued that emotions are not merely cognitively rooted but also consistently material, embodied and embedded in practice.[83] Letter-writing is a distinctive mode of such emotional practice. The act of writing made physical acts around them more real. Conversely, physical acts informed by epistolary dialectics reinforced their convictions.

Since historians can only access the expression of an emotional experience, not the experience itself, languages of expression assume primacy in understanding emotions as practice. Every act of writing became an act of memory. Letters made possible a dense archipelago of affect. Mentors resisted, not infrequently, the proprietary appropriations of their disciples. Vivekananda and Gandhi continued to sermonise on the dangers of 'personal love'. The 'problem of the personal' lingered in relations with women disciples. Letters became a means of inserting distance. Vivekananda clarified to Nivedita that despite 'persons giving [him] almost the whole of their love', he 'must not give any one the whole of [his] in return, for that day the work would be ruined ... a leader must be impersonal'.[84] Similarly, Mira's desire for physical proximity and willingness to please Gandhi irked him:

> Why hanker after my company! Why touch or kiss the feet that must one day be dead cold? There is nothing in the body ... experience and effort will unravel it before you, never my association in the manner you wish.... Why so helplessly rely on me? Why do everything to please me? Why not independently of me and even in spite of me? ... Break the idol to pieces if you can and will.[85]

Gandhi pushed back against Mira's constant 'clinging'. Invocations of impersonality and the idea of a greater (implicitly spiritual) cause served to stem the dangers of excessive personal adoration. Gandhi was always fearful of sexual transgression, and his own lifelong experiments with celibacy bore witness to this anxiety. Gandhi pontificated that Mira 'must not cling to [him] as in this body. The spirit without the body is ever with [her]'.[86] Vivekananda struggled with the incessant rumour-mongering about his chastity, usually spread by detractors.[87] Creating a sacralised language of discipleship was essential, given the prominence of celibacy or *brahmacharya* to Gandhi and Vivekananda's projects. The conjoining of *gurubhakti* and *deshbhakti* has long been an integral part of the nationalist project in India, since at least the late nineteenth century, and with important consequences for many forms of *bhakti*.[88]

With male disciples, disenchantments played out differently. There was no imminent fear of sexual transgression that loomed large. Tagore and Gandhi agreed to share Andrews between themselves. As Gandhi wrote to Tagore:

> Much as I should like to keep Mr. Andrews with me a little longer, I feel sure that he must leave for Calcutta tonight.… And you must have him while you need him.… I would ask you … to lend me … Andrews now and then. His guidance at times is most precious to me.[89]

Secondary epistolary exchanges such as these reveal what Indian mentors thought about their Indophile mentees and each other. It brought to fore doubts, differences and dismissals. Tagore, for instance, did not hesitate to criticise Gandhi's practices to Andrews, anticipating much of their later differences:

> Only a moral tyrant like Gandhi can think that he has the dreadful power to make his ideas prevail through the means of slavery. It is absurd to think that you must create slaves to make your ideas free. I would much rather see my ideas perish than to leave them in charge of slaves to be nourished. There are men who make idols of their ideas and sacrifice humanity before their altars.[90]

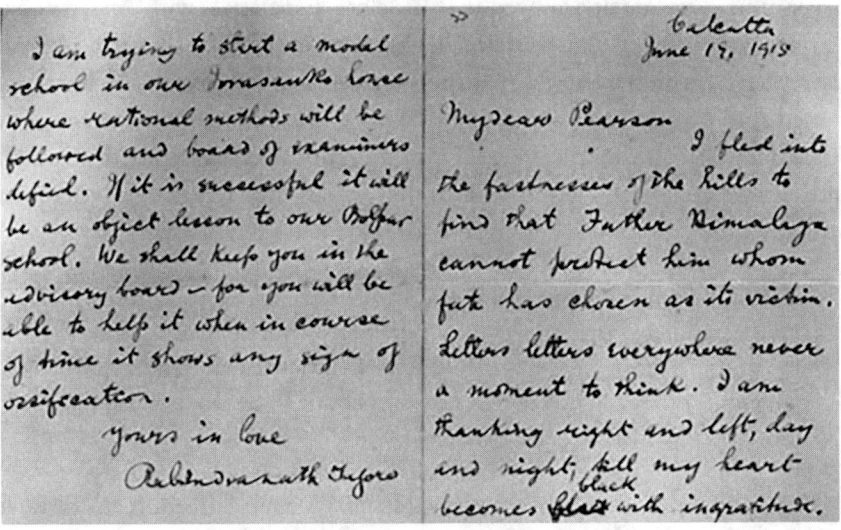

Figure 1.3   Tagore playing 'truant', 1914.
Source: Rabindra Bhavana, Visvabharati.

Tagore continued to air his differences with Gandhi, but Andrews remained a shared emissary. Even as disciples sought to stake their claims on Tagore, he resisted their zealous overtures in his ashram and literary endeavours. Playing truant (Figure 1.3) whenever his disciples' desires for physical proximity became exasperating, he continued to dispense transcendent wisdom from suitable epistolary distance. Andrews recognised the strain his tendency to act as custodian put on his relation with Tagore.

> I was too eager to be continually present with the Poet ... whom I deeply loved, and it became an oppression to him because he saw with his fine instinct that it was weakening my individual character. Therefore, in the gentlest manner possible he warned me from this.[91]

The 'oppression' such declarations of love conferred on Tagore was not minor. Edward J. Thompson, a Wesleyan missionary, poet and admirer of Tagore, was scathing of Andrews as 'beneath contempt as regards judgement and intellect generally', and for fanning Tagore's vanity.[92] He did not hesitate to convey this to Tagore's British associates, including the poet Robert Bridges and the artist William Rothenstein. Thompson's offers to translate Tagore were often thwarted by the poet himself, who had 'every hope that Andrews will be willing to help me in this work'.[93] Yet, this closeness occasionally brought its own allegations. Always uncertain of the literary merit of his English translations, Tagore felt annoyed that his close association with Andrews had led people to suspect that he owed his literary success in a 'large measure to Andrews': '... which is so false that [he] can afford to laugh at it'.[94] Thompson blamed Andrews for 'annex[ing] Tagore as a private possession', a feeling shared by another British disciple, the agricultural educationist Leonard Elmhirst. Andrews wrote anxious letters to Elmhirst, when they went on international tours to China and South America, asking for news on Tagore:

> I should be so very grateful if you could send me news.... You will understand my anxiety, yet it is not merely my anxiety.... I know how very greatly Gurudev values letters, which I may send to him, giving him news about the ashram and about India itself. He almost hungers for this.[95]

Tagore frequently appealed to the lofty language of freedom to distance himself. Letters became vectors to intimate such distance. Yet, disciples too occasionally rebelled at the continuous demands made on their person. Pearson, often travelling with Tagore on his international voyages and having to act as secretary, chafed at this imposition. Tagore was startled at this revelation:

> You must have freedom, not only for your sake but for mine. That I had been forcing you to a life from which you had been struggling to be free is a discovery which is the most difficult of all the burdens that I am bearing at present.... You know I love you, and therefore any service you offer to me which is irksome to you is doing injustice to me.[96]

Declarations of love went both ways to act as reasons for control and freedom. Intimacies became reciprocal when mentors returned this gesture. The confiding of their hopes and fears made them accessible figures.

The tendency to overcompensate was writ large in much epistolary articulation. Letters laid bare Western disciples' continuous grappling with a new set of idioms and individuals all of which were distinctively Indian. Mediated by a politics of race, nation, class and gender, the letter became a point of convergence between individuals located in various positions of power. They became agentic in intermeshing big discourses in their everyday contexts and relations.

The letter lay at the heart of an affective geography that gave form and language to disciples' Indophilia. Letters abound in a language of loss, the will to intimacy constantly riven by disciples' doubts of self-worth. In time, these intimacies inspired wider investments both in India and abroad.

Notes

1   Devyani Gupta, 'Stamping Empire: Postal Standardization in Nineteenth Century India', in *Global Scientific Practice in an Age of Revolutions, 1750–1850*, ed. Patrick Manning and Daniel Rood (Pittsburgh: University of Pittsburgh Press, 2016), 219–220.

2   Mark R. Frost, 'Pandora's Post Box: Empire and Information in India, 1854–1914', *English Historical Review* 131, no. 552 (2016): 1043–1073.

3   Ibid., 1055.

4   Ibid., 1058.

5   James Poskett, *Materials of the Mind: Phrenology, Race, and the Global History of Science, 1815–1920* (Chicago: University of Chicago Press, 2019), 118.

6   Eve Tavor Bannet, *Empire of Letters: Letter Manuals and Transatlantic Correspondence, 1688–1820* (Cambridge: Cambridge University Press, 2005).

7   Poskett, *Materials of the Mind*, 118.

8   Francesca Orsini, ed., *Love in South Asia: A Cultural History* (Cambridge: Cambridge University Press, 2006), 234–235.

9   Ibid., 220.

10   Ibid., 235.

11   See, for instance, Gauri Viswanathan's analysis of the relationship between the institutionalisation of English and the exercise of colonial power. Gauri Viswanathan, *Masks of Conquest: Literary Study and British Rule in India* (New York: Columbia University Press, 2015), 3.

12   See Sabyasachi Bhattacharya, *Talking Back: The Idea of Civilization in the Indian Nationalist Discourse* (Delhi: Oxford University Press, 2012), on a representation of this discourse emerging out of a colonial elite. Homi Bhabha writes on this more tellingly, on how hybridity arises out of colonisation and creates forms of cultural collusion and conflict. Homi Bhabha, *The Location of Culture*, Routledge Classics Series (New York: Routledge, 1994), 159.

13   I use 'bilingual' in the sense of English and one vernacular language; there were, of course, vibrant traditions of non-English bilingualism in the subcontinent, but the colonial importance of English remained a constant factor.

14   Munshi Ram Vij, later Swami Shraddhanand, was a major leader of the Arya Samaj movement, active in the early twentieth century. He founded the Gurukul Kangri school in Haridwar in 1902 to train young boys in austere conservatism; C. F. Andrews visited Munshi Ram and his school when serving at the Cambridge Mission in Delhi. Munshi Ram later rose to prominence as a Hindu nationalist leader, at the forefront of the *shuddhi* (re-conversion) and *sangathan* (organisation) movements. He was assassinated in 1926.

15   Rolland, *Inde*.

16   Ibid. Parts of this text have been translated variously by Martin Schauss, Andrew Burchell, Matteo Mazzamurro, Paloma Perez Galvan, Pierre Botcherby and Natalie Hanley-Smith.

17   This was also a time of the plague epidemic in Calcutta, and Nivedita joined in the relief work, along with Vivekananda's followers, especially Swami Sadananda. Nivedita to Josephine Mcleod, [5 April 1899?], *LSN*-I, 99.

18   Andrews to William Rothenstein, [?] September 1916, Hugh Tinker, *The Ordeal of Love: C. F. Andrews and India* (Oxford: Oxford University Press, 1998), 129.

19   Tinker, *Ordeal of Love*, 45–46.

20   Rabindranath Tagore became the first Asian recipient of the Nobel Prize in Literature in 1913, when India was still a British colony.

21   Andrews to Tagore, 18 March 1913, Original Letters from C. F. Andrews to Rabindranath Tagore, Visvabharati, Shantinikentan, Rabindra Bhavan Archives. Henceforth, MSS/CFA/RBVB/F/4-11.

22   Pearson to Tagore, 17 December 1912, Folder 287(ii), Letters from William W. Pearson to Rabindranath Tagore, Rabindra Bhavan, Visvabharati. Henceforth, MSS/WP/RBVB/F/287(ii).

23   Tagore to Andrews, 13 May 1915, File No. 1, Original Letters from Rabindranath Tagore to C. F. Andrews, CFA PAPERS, File: 1-26, 28 (ii), CD No: RBVB-018. Henceforth, MSS/RT/RBVB/F/1-26, 28 (ii).

24   Vide the publication of Rolland's book: Romain Rolland, *Mahatma Gandhi: The Man Who Became One with the Universal Being*, trans. Caroline D. Growth (London: The Swarthmore Press, 1924).

25   Madeleine to Gandhi, 29 May 1925, Tridip Suhrud and Thomas Weber, eds., *Beloved Bapu: The Gandhi–Mirabehn Correspondence* (New Delhi: Orient Blackswan, 2014), 11–12. All letters between Gandhi and Mira/Madeleine Slade are taken from this volume unless otherwise stated.

26   Ibid.

27   Vivekananda to Nivedita, 23 July 1897, *Letters of Swami Vivekananda* (*LSV*), Advaita Ashrama, Almora, 1944.

28   Vivekananda to Ole Bull, 19 August 1897, *LSV.*

29   Josiah J. Goodwin (1878–1898), sometime journalist, stenographer and British disciple of Vivekananda. He is credited with transcribing most of Vivekananda's impromptu lectures. Goodwin is an underexplored figure in the Ramakrishna–Vivekananda tradition. Enlisted as a stenographer by Vivekananda's wealthy patrons in America, he went on to become one of his staunchest followers. In India, though, he could not fit in with Vivekananda's Indian disciples. For the only proper reference to his life, see Pravrajika Vrajaprana, *My Faithful Goodwin* (Calcutta: Advaita Ashrama, 1994).

30   Vivekananda to Nivedita, 29 July 1897, *LSV.*

31   Noble to Vivekananda, 13 January 1900, *LSN*-I, 297.

32   Sarah Poustie, 'Re-Theorising Letters and "Letterness"', Olive Schreiner Letters Project, Working Papers on Letters, Letterness and Epistolary Networks, no. 1 (2010): 12.

33   Vivekananda to Nivedita, 20 June 1897, *LSV.*

34   Noble to Vivekananda, 15 December 1899, *LSN*-I, 265.

35   See Leslie A. Fielder's comparable insight on inter-racial relationships: As long as there is no mingling of blood, love does not become a threatening enough force to reckon with in interracial relationships – '... soul may couple with soul in God's undefiled forest.' Leslie A. Fielder, *Come Back to the Raft Ag'in, Huck Honey, An End to Innocence: Essays on Culture and Politics* (New York: Beacon Press, 1972), 148.

36   Rolland writes of this in his Journal, Rolland, *Inde,* cited in Pravrajika Prabuddhaprana, *Tantine: The Life of Josephine MacLeod, Friend of Swami Vivekananda* (Calcutta: Sri Sarada Math, 1990), 217.

37   Gandhi to Kallenbach, 30 August 1909, *Complete Works of Mahatma Gandhi (CWMG)*, vol. 96, 25.

38   For instance, the agreement signed by both Gandhi and Kallenbach for 'more love, and yet more love ... such ... as the world had never seen', on the eve of Kallenbach's visit to his family in Europe on 29 July 1911 is particularly insightful (*CWMG*, vol. 96). Gandhi had destroyed Kallenbach's letters to him as he felt it would preserve the confidentiality of their relationship. We only have Gandhi's letters to Kallenbach, preserved by his family members and later taken in possession by the Government of India.

39   Gandhi to Kallenbach, 24 September 1909, *CWMG*, vol. 96, 28–29.

40   Gandhi to Kallenbach, 30 July 1909: 'I know that you do not want them to be read by anybody else.' *CWMG*, vol. 96, 21.

41   Gandhi to Kallenbach, 10 September 1909, *CWMG*, vol. 96, 26.

42   Gandhi to Kallenbach, 27 February 1914, *CWMG*, vol. 96, 166.

43   Gandhi to Kallenbach, Letters dated 7 April 1914, *CWMG*, vol. 96, 179.

44   Gandhi to Kallenbach, 12 April 1914, *CWMG*, vol. 96, 181.

45   Kallenbach's German nationality was a problem in his entering British India on the eve of the First World War. Gandhi consulted Andrews before writing to Viceroy Hardinge to see what steps could be taken. Gandhi to Kallenbach, 17 February 1915, *CWMG*, vol. 96, 202.

46   Gandhi to Kallenbach, 13 March 1915, *CWMG*, vol. 96, 205.

47   CFA to Mahadev Desai, 21 June [1920s?], Sabarmati Ashram Archives.

48   C. F. Andrews and Pearson were both sent as envoys to help Gandhi in South Africa by the Moderate nationalist leader Gopal Krishna Gokhale. More on this aspect in the ashram chapter.

49   General Jan Smuts, a major architect of racial apartheid in South Africa, and a key Cabinet Minister in the Union of South Africa established in 1910. A great believer in the idea of a Commonwealth as well as a policy of racial segregation, he helped write the Constitution of South Africa.

50 Andrews to Tagore, 6 January 1914, MSS/CFA/RBVB/F/4-11.

51 Andrews to Gandhi, 5 April 1914, MSS/CFA/RBVB/F/1-26, 28 (ii).

52 Andrews to Tagore, 14 January 1914, MSS/CFA/RBVB/F/4-11.

53 Ibid.

54 Andrews to Gandhi, 13 April [1914?], MSS/CFA/RBVB/F/1-26, 28 (ii).

55 Gandhi to Andrews, 6 August 1918, *CWMG*, vol. 17, http://www.gandhiashramsevagram.org/gandhi-literature/mahatma-gandhi-collected-works-volume-17.pdf (accessed on 29 September 2018).

56 Andrews to Rudra, 4 May 1915, C. F. Andrews' File, F. F. Monk's File, St Stephen's College.

57 Andrews to Tagore, 27 January 1914, Fraser–Tagore Collection, Press Clippings 91–200, University of Edinburgh.

58 CFA to Mahadev Desai, [undated, 1919], Sabarmati Ashram Archives.

59 As, for instance, Uma Dasgupta's framing of the relationship between Tagore, Gandhi and Andrews as lofty 'friendships of largeness and freedom', formed in the shadow of colonial rule and India's freedom struggle. Dasgupta, *Friendships of 'Largeness and Freedom'*.

60 Rolland, *Inde*, cited in Prabuddhaprana, *Tantine*, 217.

61 Gandhi to Mira, 27 December 1926.

62 Gandhi to Mira, 4 April 1927.

63 Gandhi to Rukminidevi and Benarsilal Bajaj, 8 January 1933, *CWMG*, vol. 52, 1932–1933, 400.

64 Gandhi to Mira, 11 December 1926.

65 Andrews to Tagore, 8 May 1913, MSS/CFA/RBVB/F/4-11. All letters from Andrews to Tagore are from this series unless otherwise stated.

66 Andrews to Tagore, 2 October 1913.

67 Andrews to Tagore, 8 March 1913.

68 Andrews to Tagore, 15 May 1913.

69 Andrews to Tagore, 8 May 1913.

70 Pearson to Tagore, 6 May 1913.

71 Andrews to Tagore, 5 October 1915.

72 Andrews to Tagore, 28 July 1913.

73 Andrews to Tagore, 13 December 1913.

74 While Hindu in a broad sense, Tagore himself belonged to the reformist Brahmo Samaj, generally seen as distinct from conventional Hindu orthodoxy. Detractors often castigated the Brahmo Samaj as Christianised. The Brahmo Samaj, started by Rammohun Roy in 1828, underwent much splintering over the next century. Tagore's father Debendranath advocated a return to Hindu

orthodoxy, which led to further divisions in the already dissipating movement. Tagore did identify as Hindu in a broader civilisational sense.

75   Andrews to Gandhi, 13 April [1914?].

76   Andrews to Tagore, 28 July 1913.

77   Mira to Gandhi, 15 May 1927.

78   Gandhi to Mira, 2 October 1927.

79   Vivekananda to Nivedita, 29 July 1897, *LSV.*

80   Nivedita to Josephine Mcleod, 12 March 1899, *LSN*-I, 82. Tagore's biographer Prasanta Pal has observed that it was Vivekananda's ignorance of Tagore's corpus that made him dismiss Rabindranth's literary work as erotic. See Prasanta Pal, *Rabijibani*, vol. 4 (Calcutta: Ananda Publishers, 2012), 230. At stake here, however, is Vivekananda's quest for manliness and what he perceived as lacking in Bengal due to the 'effeminate' poetry and attires practiced by members of the Tagore family, especially Rabindranath.

81   Gandhi to Mira, 24 January 1927.

82   Mira to Gandhi, 29 January 1929, Muzaffarpur.

83   Monique Scheer, 'Are Emotions a Kind of Practice (And Is That What Makes Them Have a History)? A Bourdieuian Approach to Understanding Emotion', *History and Theory* 51, no. 2 (2012): 194.

84   Vivekananda to Nivedita, 1 October 1897.

85   Gandhi to Mira, 24 June 1929, 233.

86   Gandhi to Mira, 22 March 1927.

87   See letter from his Brother Disciples to Vivekananda, March 1894, *LSV,* about rumours spread by the Brahmo preacher Protap C. Mazoomdar of him 'committing every sin under the sun in America – especially "unchastity" of the most degraded type!!!' Marie Louise Burke, *Swami Vivekananda in the West: New Discoveries*, vol. 2 (Calcutta: Advaita Ashrama, 1984), 90.

88   Jacob Copeman offers a comparative insight on the powerful role of the guru in influencing disciples' sacrifices around donating blood for the Indian armed forces in post-colonial India, and how this has been embraced by some sects influenced by reformist Hinduism. See Jacob Copeman, 'Violence, Non-Violence, and Blood Donation in India', *Journal of the Royal Anthropological Institute* 14, no. 2 (June 2008): 278–296.

89   Gandhi to Tagore, 30 April [1918], *CWMG*, vol. 14.

90   Tagore to Andrews, 7 July 1915.

91   Andrews to Rothenstein, 3 August 1916, Tinker, *Ordeal of Love*, 129.

92   Edward P. Thompson, *Alien Homage* (Delhi: Oxford University Press, 1993), 33. Thompson received an uneven response from Tagore throughout his engagement with the poet. He was also a literary aspirant desirous of translating Tagore's works from their Bengali originals.

93   Tagore to Thompson, 15 February 1914, Edward J. Thompson – General Correspondence – Tagore, E. J. Thompson Papers, MS. Eng c 5318, Fols 1–40.

94   Tagore to Rothenstein, 4 April 1915, Mary Lago, ed., *Imperfect Encounter: Letters of William Rothenstein and Rabindranath Tagore, 1911–1941* (Cambridge, MA: Harvard University Press, 1972).

95   Andrews to Leonard Elmhirst, 18 March 1924.

96   Tagore to Pearson, 23 December 1920.

Part II

CHAPTER 2

Home in the World

Indophiles and the Ashram

The modern ashram in India came to encapsulate a new kind of utopian community where alternative modes of living were imagined and put to practice. This chapter examines why Western disciples sought wilful participation in these aspirational worlds to territorialise their Indophilia. Ashrams acted as emotional communities with a set of practices and performances that mobilised the affections of Indophile followers around given spaces.

Prologue

Ashrams constituted a major preoccupation for both gurus and disciples. Tagore, Gandhi and Vivekananda instituted major ashram experiments from within, but not exclusively, a Hindu tradition. Only the former two lived long enough to see them grow into definite institutions. Shantiniketan and Sabarmati emerged as the loci of intense striving for their disciples. From 1913 onwards till their deaths, Pearson, Andrews and Mira actively inhabited and invested in their mentors' ashrams. Ashrams figured constantly in their letters, reinforcing ashramic and epistolary practice as sites of intimate self-making. Ashram engagements determined disciples' Indophilia.

The historian Barbara Rosenwein defines emotional communities as 'groups in which people adhere to the same norms of emotional expression and value – or devalue – the same or related emotions'.[1] Disciples' complex emotional responses in trying to relate to their gurus' ashrams produced a range of practices. Ashrams became spaces to rethink their own cultural and political subjectivities while making them available for anticolonial projects outside of the ashram, as shown in the subsequent chapter on indenture.

Andrews, Pearson and Mira's coming to these ashrams represented a coming closer to their mentors' worlds. All of them were drawn and captivated by the utopian communities built and fostered by their mentors. However, the senses of this captivation worked differently. Pearson and Andrews wanted to be 'captive' to the promise of freedom that Shantiniketan enjoined, with its unstructured method of life and education; Mira, on the other hand, sought to enter a tightly wound institution of strict discipline and control, and make herself a pliant subject for the ashram and Gandhi to mould. The difference in the emphases of Gandhi and Tagore's ashrams was reflected in their disciples' experiences. While Gandhi put Mira through rigorous discipline to become an ideal disciple for the ashram, 'to shed all angularities' as he put it,[2] Tagore neither demanded nor imposed any sacrifice that was not already offered. Both saw Andrews, Pearson and Slade as 'gifts of the West' who would act as bridges to the 'East'.[3] Yet, in their own ways, Indophile gestures revolved around a performance of excess: of respectful obeisance, zealous proprietorship, and general adoption of ashram habits. As their mentors' abodes, ashrams territorialised disciples' desires for intimacy.

I focus largely on Tagore and Gandhi's ashrams (Figure 2.1), given their disciples' frequent passage and traffic through them. Sabarmati and Shantiniketan were two extremely prominent and inclusive (inter)national experiments, its founders and interlocutors constantly engaged in dialogues integral to Indian nationalist discourse. Other important Hindu ashramic spaces included the monastic Ramakrishna Mission founded by Vivekananda and the puritanical Gurukul Kangri ashram established by Munshi Ram (later Swami Shraddhanand of the *shuddhi*/reconversion movement fame). Both figure in Indophile movements. Their treatment, however, remains cursory. Outside of these upper-caste Hindu undertakings lay several low-caste ashram initiatives markedly different in their constitution and membership. All these institutions were part of a wider Hindu ashramic modernity arising out of colonial encounter; however, I shall only consider Tagore and Gandhi's ashrams in this chapter.

The Modern Ashram

The ashram emerged as a 'curious category' in Indian nationalist imagination.[4] By the early twentieth century, the modern ashram had become a significant mode to think about the nation, as well as imagine and invest a new life for it. Despite a similarity of mode, all the aforementioned ashrams differed in their methods, impulses and thrusts. What made the ashram such a unique mode for colonial subjects to experiment and cultivate ethical selves for the nation?

As an institution, the ashram has been in existence since at least the Vedic times in ancient India. It is derived from the Sanskrit root *shram* – to toil – and is characterised by intense spiritual striving. Very broadly, an ashram has been described as a forest hermitage, with a 'spontaneous community of disciples gathered around a spiritual leader' or guru who guides them in the practice of *sadhana* or spiritual learning.[5] The guru or Acharya (usually male) occupies a central role in ashram life. He is deeply venerated by disciples, his charismatic

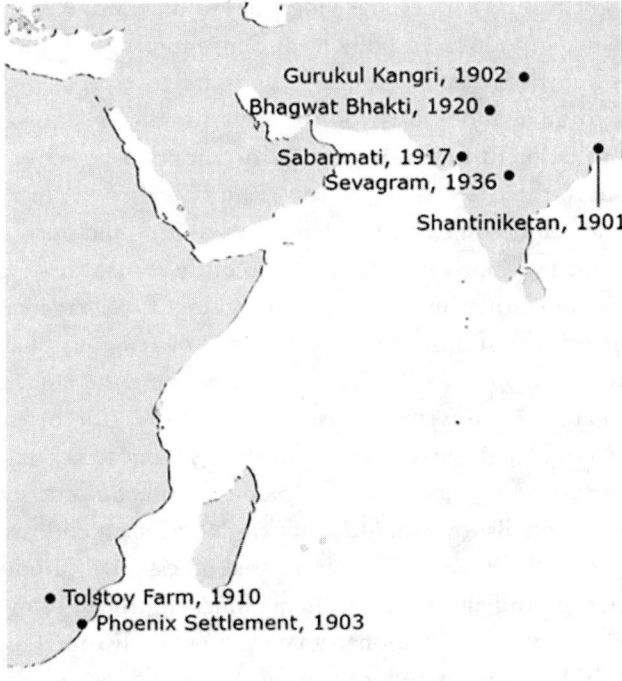

Figure 2.1   Ashrams and utopian settlements inhabited by Gandhi and Tagore's Western disciples.
Source: Matteo Mazzamurro.

authority a source of wisdom and instruction for ashramites.[6] *Deeksha* gurus offered formal initiation to disciples within their *sampradaya*, or sect, while *shiksha* gurus dispensed instruction to those who sought it. The ashram is also related to the *varnashrama dharma*, or the four stages of life for upper-caste Hindu men: student, householder, renouncer and ascetic. Throughout ancient and medieval Indian history, the ashram remained a common phenomenon for those who sought spiritual life and learning.

The ashram was recovered from this precolonial past as a romanticised theme in colonial Indian discourse through Orientalists such as Max Müller and Paul Deussen.[7] From this Orientalist romanticising, as Ajay Skaria argues, the nationalist category of ashram emerged as a representative site of ancient Hindu spirituality that had degenerated ever since.[8] The nationalist ashram was a call to resuscitate such spaces and, through them, the Indian nation.

As the British colonial state increasingly consolidated imperial rule, the rhetoric of spiritual power became a logic of Hindu cultural sovereignty. The ashram became a mode to embody its ancient prototype – as repositories of spirituality, knowledge and wisdom – necessary to escape the disciplinary regimes of colonial modernity. Spiritual or moral power, even as it was considered superior to forms of political or temporal power, was necessary for any claim to the latter. A loss of spirituality justified the loss of temporal power, and the tables could be turned only by restoring and nurturing that lost vitality described variously in nationalist discourse as manliness, morality and freedom. The modern ashram became a new site of convergence for various forms of bhakti (devotion): the older, spiritual or religious bhakti was now distinctively tinged with *deshbhakti*, or love for the motherland. Older forms of territorial attachment were increasingly co-opted within or effaced by the new but powerful language of nationalism.[9] This is not to say that spirituality was only purposed to service an incipient nation; but the ever-looming discourse of nationalism wrought its imprint on all such endeavours. Tagore privileged the 'social' repeatedly to emphasise an essential Hindu syncretism that characterised Indian life.[10] Yet, the national continued to overdetermine the social, if ambivalently. Nationalism continued to disrupt Tagore's ashram community in Shantiniketan; his vigorous denunciations did not necessarily insulate its members. Andrews and Pearson were often the instigators.

In a wide-ranging commentary on 'modernity and its enchantments', the historian Saurabh Dube observes that the 'idea of modernity rests on rupture'[11] – a rupture that is premised on a series of oppositions 'embedded within formidable projects of power and knowledge', enlightenment, empire and nation.[12] In other words, if modernity is constitutive and constituted by what it perceives as anti/non-modern, the ambiguities that surround such propositions are, in effect, responses to aspects of modernity itself. An enchantment with modernity is coupled with disenchantments, producing formations that are coeval as 'subjects of modernity' negotiate for themselves traditions with specific truth claims. Propositions for alternative or anti-modernity were often rooted in disenchantments that modernity assumed in its imperial guise.

The modern ashram embodied this disenchantment and shaped the colonised desire for an idealised lost world, a world that also held value for those disenchanted with the closures of industrial modernity. Ashrams manifested the yearning for a romanticised past, through a form and category that was decidedly indigenist but readily lent itself to modern adaptations. It was a mode to insert the moral, religious and spiritual into the liberal 'secular' discourse of nation and nationalism. As a mode, it could inhabit modernity not only discursively, 'but through [the] regulation of everyday habits and practices, and cultivation of technologies of self'.[13]

As an indigenist mode, ashrams could fold both the sacred and the secular within their habitus, disrupting the movements of secular space and time. These disruptions were necessarily partial; the desire for alternative forms of community could never fully escape the deep transformations wrought by colonial modernity. This tension, for instance, was manifest in the way modern clock time was central to almost all early twentieth-century ashrams that saw themselves as creating new subjects and subjectivities for an emergent Indian nation, howsoever differently.

Sabarmati, Shantiniketan and Other Ashrams

The geographer Edward Soja has observed that modernity transformed the three most basic dimensions of human existence: space, time and being.[14] The modern ashram did all of these. The ashram space, even as it responded to or against certain historical determinations of modernity, produced its own formulations of alternative space and time. It could accommodate a wide range of intentions and imaginations, from the most pragmatic to the rigidly idealistic.

The ashram as a collective social space emerged out of its members' aspirations. At the same time, as a space, it powerfully drew and shaped the self-making of aspiring members.

Disquiet with the effects of industrial and colonial modernity was shared by both Andrews and Pearson in the course of their missionary work; Mira's was also tinged with experiences of the First World War.[15] Ashrams sought to reimagine a collective life against the proliferating individualisation produced by industrial modernity.[16] Both Tagore and Gandhi were critical of the mechanisation of human life produced by modern science and its technicism. Both stressed simplicity of lifestyles (that differed in degrees, if not in kind), *brahmacharya* (celibacy) for ashram members and vegetarianism as the prescribed dietary practice.[17] This appealed to prospective Western disciples as a call to remake their own selves. The Gandhi scholar Thomas Weber refers to these experiments as 'intentional communities', where alternative lifestyles were pursued with a marked ethical content.[18] In the wake of the First World War, some of these ashrams joined a global cluster of utopian experiments in Europe, the US, Japan and India. Seeing wartime violence and dehumanisation as a symptom of the failure of industrial and capitalist modernity, they proposed and practised ideal visions of life and society through utopian communes (Figure 2.2).[19]

Early Gandhian ashrams relied on critical support from several Western followers for their sustenance, all of whom were drawn to alternative religiosities and ways of living that professed self-abnegation.[20] Inspired by turn-of-the-century London trends such as radical vegetarianism, Gandhi saw his early ashram efforts as creating a 'community of men of religion', away from industrial cities.[21] The Russian novelist Leo Tolstoy's critique of industrial modernity and the social alienation bred by such modernity influenced Gandhi deeply, as also the late nineteenth-century British social critic John Ruskin's similar take on social inequality. Both Tolstoy and Ruskin saw in modern civilisation's avowal of materialist excess a 'devastating retreat from morality'.[22] They inspired Gandhi's early experiments in commune living as a way to flatten hierarchies created by capital, religion and caste. It spoke to larger trends since the early nineteenth century that saw several British thinkers such as Robert Owen experimenting with socialist communes in response to the growing inequalities caused by industrialisation.[23]

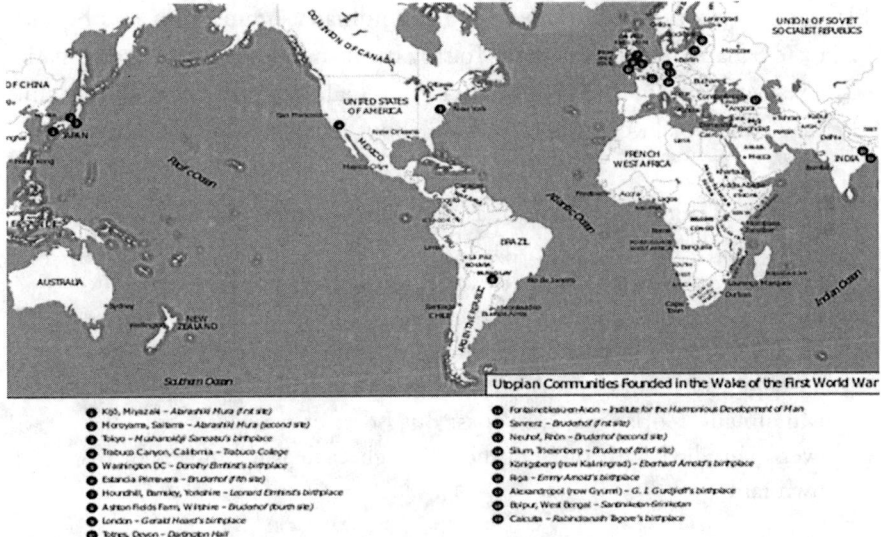

Figure 2.2   An index of utopian communities in the early twentieth century.
Source: Anna Neima, *The Utopians: Six Attempts to Build the Perfect Society* (London: Picador, 2021).

In South Africa, Gandhi founded the Phoenix settlement (1904) and Tolstoy Farm (1908), along with his close followers and colleagues Henry Polak and Hermann Kallenbach.[24] Both Polak and Kallenbach were part of a group of radical young Jewish intellectuals in Johannesburg drawn to Hindu and Buddhist thought through their engagements with theosophy.[25] With Polak and Kallenbach's assistance, Gandhi

> … determined to take Indian Opinion [a mouthpiece for Gandhi's mobilising activities in South Africa] into a forest where I should live with the workers as members of my family. I purchased 100 acres of land and founded Phoenix Settlement, which neither we nor anyone else called an ashram. It had a religious basis, but the visible object was purity of body and mind as well as economic equality. I did not then consider brahmacharya (chastity) to be essential.…[26]

The 'forest' – a metaphor for seeking alternative modernity – became an ideal space to experiment in a rural setting. Neither Phoenix nor Tolstoy were labelled as ashrams yet. However, these anti-modern experiments were often based on a 'classically modern set of technologies' such as the printing press.[27]

This ambiguity continued to inhere in all Gandhian ashrams from Tolstoy and Phoenix to Sabarmati and Sevagram. Tolstoy Farm and Phoenix Settlement made possible experiments in shared domesticity and male intimacy between Gandhi, Kallenbach and Polak. Gandhi recounted about himself and Kallenbach:

> Both of us were living a sort of ashram life ... we led a comparatively very simple life in the sparsely populated country, and were religiously minded. Kallenbach purchased a farm of 1,100 acres and the Satyagrahi families settled there. Religious problems confronted us now at every step and the whole institution was managed from a religious standpoint. Among the settlers there were Hindus, Musalmans, Christians and Parsis. But I do not remember that they ever quarrelled with one another, though each was staunch in his own faith.[28]

A significant section of these settlers came from indentured labour backgrounds, and the early commune became a major testing space for syncretic practices. Gandhi felt the presence of multiple sects, religions and castes made children immune to the 'infection of religious intolerance'.[29] He undertook numerous dietary and living experiments in these communal settlements, including vegetarian diets and nature cures such as mud and water therapies, refusing to concede to Western medicine.

Figure 2.3 Sabarmati Ashram, Ahmedabad, founded by Gandhi in 1917.
Source: Sabarmati Ashram Preservation and Memorial Trust.

These practices continued with his Satyagraha Ashram, or Sabarmati, established in 1917 near Ahmedabad in India (Figure 2.3). The Sabarmati Ashram was an attempt to create an ideal non-hierarchical society, emphatically effacing boundaries of class, caste and religion. Gandhi saw in such a society a possible utopia and rescue from the dehumanisation and fragmentation of life enforced by an aggressive techno-modernity.[30] In Gandhian ashrams, individual selves had to be diminished to cultivate a uniform ashram ethic that was highly regulated, a practice Slade found exacting even as she desired it. Ashramites were to consider themselves vessels for collective moral action, rather than engage in pursuits of curiosity or creative impulses.[31] Their bodies and bodily desires were rigidly policed and shamed for any subsequent lapse.[32] Gandhi built the Sabarmati Ashram to train satyagrahis for future anti-colonial movements and nation-building activities like promoting *khadi* and removing untouchability. Restating on multiple occasions his critique of modernity and the ashram as bearer of anti-modern experiments, Sabarmati was nonetheless sustained by generous donations from Bombay and Gujarati industrial capitalists.

Gandhi's asceticism was also a powerful political capital, bestowing purity to his intentions. Tagore was neither ascetic nor monastic, though he himself never remarried after his wife's early death. Both Tagore and Gandhi had platonic relationships with women in their mature age,[33] in addition to troubled relationships with young women in the ashram.[34] Gandhi indulged in a widely publicised series of celibacy tests that involved 'sleeping' (non-sexual in principle) with young women, for which he courted considerable controversy.[35]

Shantiniketan, on the other hand, grew out of Tagore's growing dissatisfaction with the inadequacy of colonial pedagogy. He felt that modern schools were in reality 'a factory, and the teachers [were] part of it'.[36] The focus on a radically different kind of learning mattered to Andrews and Pearson, both of whom had experience in missionary education. They found it refreshingly different from the rigidly hierarchical and condescending world of Christian missionary education.[37] Andrews and Pearson wanted to be part of this space.

The ashram sought to emulate ancient *tapovan*s, or forest hermitages, as sources of knowledge and wisdom, located in the wilderness of nature. Well read in Sanskrit classical poetry, the idyllic *tapovan* life portrayed by the poet Kalidasa moved Tagore: it was a place that radiated peace and transcendent love, where people abjured their violence, even animals like lions.[38]

Figure 2.4   Shantiniketan, founded on the ideal of a community in the forest.
Source: © 2022 Gandhi-Informations-Zentrum e.V.

Shantiniketan sought to be a modern *tapovan* (Figure 2.4), where human life was not fragmented from its place in nature:

> At the centre of the tapovan is the guru. He is not a machine, he is a being. Not in any passive way, but actively.... To quicken the minds of his disciples in the forceful flow of tapasya [penance] is part of his sadhana/spiritual practice.[39]

Tagore believed that the modern school was a machine that produced clerks instead of thinkers. In its stead, the Shantiniketan ashram would be a place where the guru/Acharya would strive along with his pupils, embracing their creative impulses, a 'school of nature', uncaged by the time-discipline of colonial schooling.[40] Tagore was very much the *shiksha* guru.

The ashram, begun as Brahmacharyashrama in 1901, was influenced by Vedic Brahminism and upheld the hierarchies of the *varna* system (Brahmin and non-Brahmin students dined separately till at least 1915).[41] Till 1907, the ashram remained conservatively Brahminical in practice, Tagore's own shifts coinciding with the Hindu revivalist turn around the Partition of Bengal in 1905. The ashram was opened only later in the 1910s to be more inclusive.[42] Tagore's ashram was based on an idealised Vedic form of community, rooted in the vision of an unsullied Hindu cultural past and civilisational greatness.[43] In 1921, the ashram was renamed Visvabharati (the world in India) to indicate the universal humanitarian turn in Tagore, shedding its former conservatism. Even while Tagore emerged as a bitter critic of nationalism, the Shantiniketan ashram was widely considered a 'nationalist' institution, not in the sense

Tagore was critiquing the concept, but as a space that was distinctively Indian, if predominantly Hindu upper caste of a reformist type, and rooted in pan-Indian traditions, celebrating music, art and culture.[44] Major political leaders, from Gandhi and Jawaharlal Nehru to the more radical Subhash Bose and the Hindu nationalist leader Shyamaprasad Mookerjee would often visit the ashram. As the Hindi literary figure Shivani, who studied there, noted: 'Be it Gandhiji or Pandit Nehru, the ashram bell would always ring on its own time.'[45]

Tagore was quite in step with 'world cultural' trends and a pioneer of pan-Asianism. Shantiniketan was very much a representation of the best of high culture, art and learning that Tagore thought civilisation could muster. He was captive to the notion of civilisation as a universal category that would expand continuously to include hitherto uncivilised geographies.[46] His ashram, he believed, was a particular way of reaching or celebrating that universal in civilisation.[47] Tagore also established the sister institution Sriniketan in 1922, to promote rural reconstruction experiments in adjacent villages. Smaller in scale, Sriniketan embraced a wide range of initiatives around co-operative farming, scientific cultivation, and rural arts and crafts. Throughout Tagore's lifetime and later, both institutions drew very different sets of people and projects.[48]

Both Sabarmati and Shantiniketan ashrams were variable responses to aspects of capitalist modernity Tagore and Gandhi were deeply dissatisfied with. For Gandhi, it was the dehumanisation caused by techno-modernity, while for Tagore it was the mechanised pedagogies of modern schooling. As Slade would succinctly put it: Sabarmati and Shantiniketan were not irreconcilable but complementary institutions, one focusing on the 'ascetic', the other on the 'artistic'.[49]

Tagore and Gandhi's ashrams offered a critique of Western modernity not only discursively but also through everyday habits and practices. Vegetarianism and *brahmacharya* were practised rigorously, aspects that greatly appealed to their Western disciples. The denial of meat and material desire came to represent control over appetite and urges. Rathindranath, Tagore's son and one of the earliest students of his ashram, averred that their life was

> not only simple but austere. The ideal of Brahmacharya was the keynote of everything. The yellow uniform, which covered up the poverty of clothes … the vegetarian meals comparable to jail diet in their dull monotony – these were the standards laid down. Nobody wore shoes or even sandals and such luxuries as toothpaste or hair oil were taboo.[50]

This aspiration to austerity fit in with Andrews and Pearson's quests. Though Tagore was never one to advocate extreme austerities, Pearson and Andrews found in ashram life an opportunity to merge their lives in the service of a larger community, an urge that resonated with their own deeply held convictions of self-abnegation and Christ-like sacrifice. Young men and women students in Shantiniketan, however, revelled in the air of freedom, romance and cultural activity.[51] Pearson was captivated at the 'Sanskrit prayer chanted by the boys of Bolpur [the town closest to Shantiniketan]':

> I wish it were possible to preserve the freshness of one's first impressions, for then the very sound of the prayer would be a constant and never fading inspiration. I cannot describe the thrill which I felt as I listened to that ascending chant filling the fresh morning air with its solemn notes of youthful aspiration.[52]

Andrews yearned from afar to be back in Shantiniketan every 'Wednesday and Thursday morning to join with them in their service of prayer'.[53] Prayer played a central role in assembling the community.

In Sabarmati, Gandhi's injunctions on sex and dietetics were much more severe. Slade had found, on her arrival to Sabarmati, its rigorous moral discipline quite demanding:

> Moral standards were poised at a height where the slightest wavering by an inmate from the strictest truth, honesty and rectitude was noted down and made the subject of public discussion between Bapu and the rest of Ashramites. Physical standards regarding diet, labour and hours of rising and going to rest were rigidly severe, and economic ideals required that everyone should use only hand-spun and hand-woven cloth, and other hand-made articles as far as possible, besides living a life of the utmost simplicity, even by Indian standards.[54]

Gandhi's prayer service involved singing devotional bhakti hymns, culled from a wide range of Hindu, Christian, Muslim and modern inheritances. They served a pedagogic function in the making of ideal satyagrahi subjects, instilling moral and spiritual purity.[55] Gandhian prayer meetings were also a more didactic affair. It was used as an opportunity to discuss breaches in ashram discipline. Even though Mira was unable to follow the prayer service initially as it was largely in Gujarati, she later became proficient in Sanskrit chants, leading the ashram's 'Morning Prayer'.[56]

Simulations of the forest inspired both Tagore and Gandhi's utopias. Sabarmati and Shantiniketan represented their founders' romanticised visions of a lost world that could recover India's spiritual and civilisational greatness. Western followers of Gandhi and Tagore found in such enchanted spaces a remarkable resonance of their own dissatisfactions with industrial modernity.

Reconfiguring space was crucial in the arrangement of ashram life. Shantiniketan reflected Tagore's acute sensitivity in matters of art and aesthetics, visible in the relentless experimentation that blended forms, styles and construction materials. Tagore's ashram aesthetics and architecture fused pan-Asian influences, differing sharply from the colonial styles that came to proliferate building in British India.[57] Gandhi's ashram buildings were largely unassuming and spartan (Figure 2.5), purposely built to serve as sites of social and behavioural reform.

Figure 2.5   Hriday Kunj: Gandhi's residence in the Sabarmati Ashram from 1918 to 1930. The architecture was minimalist.

Source: Photo by author.

Prioritising local needs and building materials, they sought to order a more egalitarian space that challenged caste taboos and sustained a dense collective life. In this, Gandhian designs, as the historians of architecture Peter Scriver and Amit Srivastava argue, anticipated elements of Soviet socialist architecture that consciously tried to move beyond the sentimental aestheticism associated with nineteenth-century nationalist planning.[58]

Andrews, Pearson and the World of Shantiniketan

Since at least 1910, Andrews insisted on missionary platforms that ashrams were the only true way to indigenise Christ in India.[59] At that time, he was exposed to only Munshi Ram's Gurukul Kangri in Hardwar in the northern Himalayas. Christian missionaries were aware of modern Hindu ashrams emerging at the beginning of the twentieth century but there was much opposition to it, as most held ashrams to be typically Hindu institutions. Christian ashrams, argued Andrews, greatly enabled the imagining of an Indian Christ. For disenchanted missionaries like him, a Christian spiritual quest could continue independently, outside of the narrow frame of formal mission work. By the end of his life, Andrews was able to conceive of a pan-ashram movement, spreading all over Asia and adapted to in the West:

> India may give this Ashram ideal, not merely to Ceylon, but to the Christian Church in the West …
>
> … What a wonderful thing it would be if the Indian Christian Church cd [sic] offer some greatly needed gift to the West: May not the Ashram Movement be one way to do so? … What a beautiful thing it would be, if now India cd [sic] give to the West one of its own treasures (Instead of missionaries being sent by the west) … You see the time is now ripe in the West.[60]

Shantiniketan fitted with his own spiritual quest to indigenise Christ and Christianity through Indian idioms and practices, which, if fruitful, could create a 'Christian Chaitanya or Christian Vivekananda'.[61] The ashram seemed to be an eminently suitable mode for such quests. Andrews's initial attempts at mobilising ashrams for the missionary propagation of Christianity later mutated into a personal quest for Christ through the ashrams of Tagore and Gandhi, neither of whom insisted on any kind of ritual conversion. Ashrams became a sacred locus for these disciples, through which their mentors' lives and works could be felt. To invest in their everyday habits was to merge oneself into this wider community of believers. This is not to say that the enchantments never wore off or these disciples were never critical of either gurus or ashrams. There were moments of rupture, disagreement and criticism but the validity of the mode itself was never contested. To enter the ashram was to stake a claim in the collective life of that emotional community. I explore these two ashrams and Indophile engagements around them individually and collectively, to understand what entering these aspirational worlds meant for them, and for the ashrams.

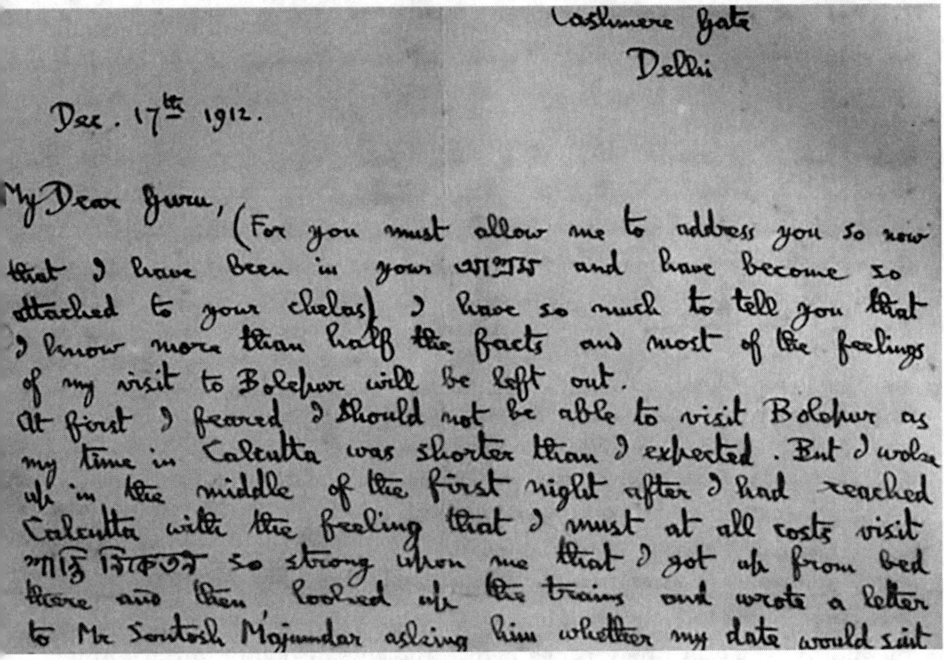
Cashmere Gate
Delhi

Dec. 17th 1912.

My Dear Guru, (For you must allow me to address you so now that I have been in your আশ্রম and have become so attached to your chelas) I have so much to tell you that I know more than half the facts and most of the feelings of my visit to Bolepur will be left out.
At first I feared I should not be able to visit Bolepur as my time in Calcutta was shorter than I expected. But I woke up in the middle of the first night after I had reached Calcutta with the feeling that I must at all costs visit শান্তিনিকেতন so strong upon me that I got up from bed there and then, looked up the trains and wrote a letter to Mr Santosh Majumdar asking him whether my date would suit

Figure 2.6 Pearson's letter to Tagore, asking he be allowed to call him 'Guru', 17 December 1912.

Source: Rabindra Bhavana, Visvabharati.

Note: The words 'ashram' and 'Shantiniketan' are spelt in Bengali, illustrating how language and space was imbricated in discipleship.

To re-cite a letter from Pearson to Tagore (referred to in the earlier chapter) more fully:

> You told me in London that you wanted to capture me for *Shantiniketan* and now I am able to write and tell you that I am a willing captive and that it is only a question of time now for the captive to enter the place where the bonds of affection have been woven. This I tell you in confidence for I want quietly to work at Bengali for the next year or two until I have completed my engagement in Delhi. After that I will gladly enter the service of the *ashram* if I am worthy of it.... Andrews is the only friend I have told here in India.[62]

Pearson repeatedly emphasised his sense of captivation (Figure 2.6). There was much doubt about his self-worth, but also a quiet promise to prove himself. He was willing to put in the hard work. Joining Shantiniketan would immediately raise heckles of 'going native' or Hindu in missionary and official circles, a fate that came to haunt Andrews brutally. Within a year, Pearson was signing off his letters with 'Bhaktipoorn Pranam' (worshipful obeisance) to 'Gurudev' Tagore.

Andrews expressed a similar wish to visit and join Shantiniketan, believing that 'it will be a pilgrimage and every step of the way will be sacred'.[63] His itinerant travels as an Anglican missionary to Munshi Ram's Gurukul Kangri in Hardwar exemplified this 'yearning':

> ... for the nearer presence of God – I found that fulfilled during those days at the Gurukula, and it came through you, my dearest friend. God has used you and your work as His spiritual temple and I was treading, all unworthy, in its courts ...[64]

Shantiniketan was a continuation of this quest. Pearson's first visit to the ashram was enough to captivate him for life. Its communal life, rustic setting and the morning 'Sanskrit prayers chanted by the boys of Bolpur' thrilled him.[65] He wrote back to Tagore, who was then abroad, about the touching farewell ceremony given to him:

> ... at 7.30 the whole school assembled outside the mandir to bid me Farewell with a service of parting benediction. The sloka which was uttered by Thakur dada [Dwijendranath Tagore, Rabindranath's

elder brother] was the one used when Sakuntala left the ashram and was a prayer that I might take the joy and peace of the ashram with me. I was quite overcome and utterly humbled by the affection ... and ... I couldn't help feeling as I stood there in the morning light with bowed head and full heart that this was really the ceremony of my dedication to the service of the ashram.... I have been captivated and captured.[66]

Letters became a chief way to evidence his feeling of oneness with the ashram. Andrews, a busier man owing to his high-profile commitments, visited the ashram a few months later in March 1913:

> ... the tiredness went away when I reached the ashram and saw the boys and was taken up to the very room where you had lived– with that wonderful balcony and all the dreaming[?] trees so close at hand and the distant view ... we went out and sat in the wood at evening and watched the sun set and the moon rise and Ajit sang to me from Gitanjali.... It was all so pure and still and sacred after dusty noisy Delhi and the wearisome train journey.... The excitement was too great and I spent most of the night in the balcony watching the moon in its glory and the dim silent stars and thinking of my mother in England and again of you and looking down upon the sleeping school.... Night is wonderful in Panjab but in Bengal it is far more wonderful still.... I was astonished by the bright intelligence of the children. It was an experience quite different from our dull Panjabi children. But the free unfettered life of the ashram was of course the main factor. [Your presence] each day became more real to me; but it was at night time, in the silence that it was most speaking.[67]

The ashram facilitated dense transferences: its idyllic unfettered life, Tagore's intangible spirit, music, the quiet nights, ashram students and members held for Andrews and Pearson visions of an enchanted world. The ashram and its ambience felt almost pristine and untouched, the excitement infectious. It was a world far removed from the bustle of modern city life and the moral exhaustion of missionary politicking. The presence of Santhal villages around the edges of Shantiniketan gave it a further air of primordiality. It served as a site of self-meditation, to reflect on their self-perceived moral lack. Pearson wanted to offer his service:

... for the asram [sic] with the humility and reverence of a worshipper who offers a few flowers at a shrine ... I try to give up thinking of the poverty and failures of my own life and try to fix a steadfast gaze on the ideal for which the asram [sic] stands.[68]

Andrews saw the 'call to Bolpur' [Shantiniketan] as an opportunity to resign from 'formal missionary society'.[69] His sense of shame increased after his visit to the ashram. Repentant for his complicity in the writing and dissemination of Christian missionary literature that patronised India and Hinduism, he wanted to realise

... a truer self ... to be with you, or to be in the ashram where your spirit will be to me itself the lesson that I need.... I am claiming you as my true Gurudev and I am truly one of your own pupils, however I may have failed to be worthy of the name.[70]

The claim on his 'true Gurudev' was not made lightly. He offered to help Tagore by 'taking charge' of the ashram in his absence (Figure 2.7), not in a position of superiority, but out of 'sympathy' and in subordination, as he clarified.[71] He prided himself on having worked 'for ten years under and with Mr. Rudra': 'the position of ... authority would be difficult for me'. He further stated that he had already been following a strict vegetarian diet under Munshi Ram's influence and found benefit in it, gesturing his preparedness.[72]

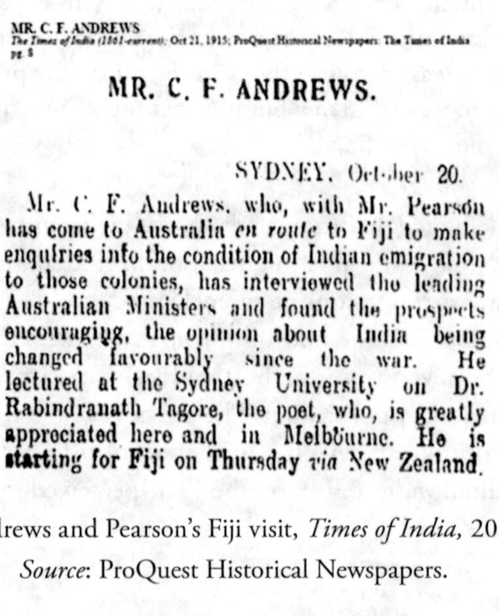

MR. C. F. ANDREWS
The Times of India (1861-current); Oct 21, 1915; ProQuest Historical Newspapers: The Times of India
pg. 8

MR. C. F. ANDREWS.

SYDNEY, October 20.

Mr. C. F. Andrews, who, with Mr. Pearson has come to Australia *en route* to Fiji to make enquiries into the condition of Indian emigration to those colonies, has interviewed the leading Australian Ministers and found the prospects encouraging, the opinion about India being changed favourably since the war. He lectured at the Sydney University on Dr. Rabindranath Tagore, the poet, who, is greatly appreciated here and in Melbourne. He is starting for Fiji on Thursday *via* New Zealand.

Figure 2.7   Andrews and Pearson's Fiji visit, *Times of India*, 20 October 1915.

Source: ProQuest Historical Newspapers.

Andrews's attachment to Shantiniketan and talk of resigning his mission alarmed the Cambridge Mission at Delhi. They thought he was converting to Hinduism. But for Andrews: 'If men in authority take my clergyman's orders away from me, I must all the more closely follow Christ himself'.[73] From afar, his heart kept drawing back to the ashram every day: 'I keep Wednesday and Thursday morning to join with them in their service of prayer. It has all become a part of my inner life'.[74] Andrews's impressions inspired Pearson further:

> I am happy too to hear from Shantiniketan of the great happiness of our friend Andrews. I hear from him constantly and he tells me how wonderfully and absolutely at home he is both with the Teachers and the boys.... I cannot tell you how happy I am at the prospect of beginning work there so soon for although I was there for only two days in December I feel deeply attached to the place and the boys and teachers, and the memory of my visit has been the most fragrant memory of the past six months.[75]

INDIANS IN SOUTH AFRICA.

Coming of New Legislation.

CAPETOWN, March 24

General Smuts announced in the Union House of Assembly that the Government would introduce legislation next session based on the report of the Indian Grievances Commission.

Mr. Pearson's Return.

Mr. W. W. Pearson who went with the Rev. Mr. Andrews to South Africa, arrived in Bombay yesterday by the steamer Umvolosi from Durban. On the way back Mr. Pearson stayed for about ten days in Portuguese East Africa, where he was able to enjoy the hospitality of Indians who are living in the Portuguese colonies. Mr. Pearson left last night for Delhi en route to Bolpur, where he is going to take up work as teacher in Rabindranath Tagore's Shanti Niketan School. Mr. Pearson spoke in glowing terms of the kind hospitality shown to him by Indians in South Africa as well as by Europeans.

Figure 2.8   Indians in South Africa, *Times of India*, 25 March 1914.
Source: ProQuest Historical Newspapers.

Shantiniketan became a sacred memory and metaphor for freedom. Desires manifested in dreams. Pearson continued to dream from a distant and dusty Delhi of the magical world of Shantiniketan:

> … twice during the past fortnight I have had vivid dreams of Bolpur. In the first dream I was present to welcome Gurudev and do you know I wept so bitterly as I thought how unworthy I was to be there. In the second dream, I was working at the ashram and talking to the boys.[76]

The ashram made them shed tears thinking of their unworthiness. Writing about these dreams made the space more real (Figure 2.8).

Shantiniketan occupied a tense position pedagogically, given its defiance to impose uniform methods of modern schooling.[77] Tagore's son Rathindranath wrote: 'People looked down upon the institution and ridiculed father's attempt to introduce new ideas in education'.[78] Indophile involvement in Tagore's ashram connected the ashram to larger political stakes, even at a time when he was increasingly critical of mainstream nationalist discourse. Andrews and Pearson's involvements in nationalist projects around anti-indenture or Gandhian causes made the ashram a relevant institution through the spaces they moved, not just nationally but transnationally. Wherever Andrews and Pearson toured and lectured – South Africa, Australia, Fiji, America or Europe – Tagore and Shantiniketan continually formed a crucial part of their interlocution for India and the prospect of an 'East–West' cultural union.

Mira and the Mahatma's Ashram

Born in 1892, Madeleine Slade was the daughter of British admiral Edmond Slade and had an aristocratic upbringing in England. She spent two years of her childhood in India, during her father's official posting, though this was limited to the world of British colonial officialdom.[79] A deep admirer of Beethoven's music, she helped organise classical music concerts at the end of the First World War that helped break the ban on German musicians in England. Shared love for Beethoven also led her to Romain Rolland, who introduced her to Gandhi. Horrified by the industrial scale of violence unleashed by the war, she was fascinated by Gandhi's doctrine of non-violence and powerfully drawn to his distinct blend of simplicity, spirituality and religion.[80] Moved, Slade wrote to Gandhi:

> Most Dear Master …
>
> May I come to your Ashram to study spinning and weaving, to learn to live your ideals and principles in daily life, and indeed to learn in what way I may hope to serve you in the future? In order to become a fit servant of your cause I feel the absolute necessity of that training and I will do my very best to be a not too unworthy pupil if you will accept me.
>
> In the meantime I continue my preparations as best I can. I spin and weave. With the aid of many kind Indian friends I perplex my head over long Hindustani exercises I read…. The more I enter into Indian thought, the more I feel as if I were reaching at last, a long lost home…. I have given up the drinking of all wines, beers or spirits, and I no longer eat meat of any kind.[81]

Her entering into Indian thought – mostly through French translations of the Bhagavad Gita and Rigveda – felt like reaching a 'long lost home'. Readying herself, Mira strove to follow Sabarmati's prescribed dietary regime. Having already bestowed on him the title of 'Master', she could not wait to give her all to Gandhi and '[his] people'. She pined for the day when she could come to India. Rolland, who introduced her to Gandhi, wrote that Slade

> has been touched by grace: she converted to Mahatma Gandhi's faith; she decided to give her life to serve it; she will leave to India, and enter in Sabarmati Ashram in Ahmedabad, where Gandhi has accepted her.[82]

She read all of Gandhi's works and learnt some Urdu, hoping they would be useful. This presumed relationship of herself as a humble servant and Gandhi as the merciful Master resonated with the idiom of complete self-surrender in the tradition of bhakti. She wished to become a 'fit servant' for his cause.

By the early 1920s, Gandhi was the pre-eminent figure in Indian politics. Riding high on his success of the satyagraha movement in South Africa in 1914, he consolidated his position in India through the Champaran, Kheda and non-cooperation movements. He also demonstrated his commitment to the principle of non-violent satyagraha through these movements and successfully ushered in the era of Congress-led mass agitations through boycotts and civil disobedience. Forever the conscientious imperial subject, Gandhi pledged not to resume direct political action till 1928, to mark the formal end of his original prison term. While corresponding with Slade, he was still serving prison for the Chauri Chaura incident.[83] Slade was made aware of Gandhi by Romain Rolland's book on him, published in 1924.[84] His political experiments were not the primary cause that drew Slade to the Mahatma. Gandhi's twenty-one-day fast for Hindu–Muslim unity in Delhi moved Slade to seek his spiritual discipleship.[85]

Seeking to combine the moral force of spirituality with politics, Gandhi had founded the Satyagraha Ashram on the banks of the Sabarmati, near Ahmedabad in 1915. Sabarmati Ashram was founded with the explicit object of producing satyagrahi subjects who would lead Gandhian movements. Departing from the conventional notion of the ashram as a spiritual-cum-religious commune, Gandhi was unique in his emphasis on the abolition of untouchability and the adoption of rigorous sanitary practices. Based on the idea of voluntary labour, ashramites were expected to spin their own yarn (*khadi*), cook their own food and clean their own refuse. Gandhi instituted eleven vows to be followed by his followers: non-violence, truth, non-theft, non-possession, bread-labour, celibacy, dietary control, fearlessness, respect for all religions, swadeshi and the abolition of untouchability.[86] Ashram members included people from the most ascetic to the worldliest. Householder followers, in their efforts to serve Gandhi in whatever way possible, often brought their families with them, who generally remained outside the pale of strictures applicable to themselves. The presence of non-Gandhian family members, often non-committal to the principles and austerities of the ashram, caused frequent furore that regularly violated one or the other foundational vows of the ashram.[87] There were intermittent instances of squabbles, homosexual incidents among boys and petty thefts that pervaded ashram life. It exerted much of Gandhi's patience to keep the place running. Sabarmati was a tightly wound space, unlike the more unstructured Shantiniketan ashram.

It was into this experimental semi-ascetic, semi-domestic space that Slade sought admission. She was insistent on leading an intensive ashram life under

Gandhi's tutelage. In the one year of probation advised by Gandhi, she already practised a simulated ashram life. She was learning to speak Hindustani, and spun and wove wool, whose sample she enclosed in the above letter. She also became a complete teetotaller and vegetarian, and slept on a hard bed. Her family members were concerned but did not protest as she gave up her small comforts gradually, including her passion for Beethoven and music. Rolland was excited that he was able to send Gandhi an able volunteer and proudly noted how her example had influenced her parents too: 'She says her example has carried along her parents; her mother is spinning, and her father, the admiral is weaving (cursing Gandhi all the time)'.[88]

Gandhi warned her that 'life at the Ashram is not all rosy, it is strenuous. Bodily labour is given by every inmate.'[89] Slade finally arrived at the Sabarmati Ashram in November 1925. As she entered:

> ... a slight brown figure rose up and came toward me. I was conscious of nothing but a sense of light. I fell on my knees. Hands gently raised me up, and a voice said: 'You shall be my daughter.' My consciousness of the physical world began to return, and I saw a face smiling at me with eyes full of love, blended with a gentle twinkle of amusement. Yes, this was Mahatma Gandhi, *and I had arrived*.[90]

Slade's first encounter was exactly what she had imagined it to be: a *darshan* or vision of her guru in his ashram abode. Gandhi preferred the more accessible term Bapu, the Gujarati word for father, than the lofty sounding 'guru', as 'no one in these days [is] competent to live up to the ideal', he opined.[91] However, the role of a paternal figure intensively mentoring his disciples in the enclosed space of an ashram remained similar. To Rolland she wrote enthusiastically that she 'had been prepared for a Prophet and [she] ... found an Angel'.[92] Soon, however, she found that the ashram was hardly the 'compact group' she had imagined it to be:

> I found a heterogeneous collection of one or two hundred people, men, women and children of all ages and all degrees of faith, from fanatical ascetics to sceptical family women.... Because Bapu himself was all-sided, he attracted people of the most varied types.[93]

As the novelty of the experience wore off, she found that instead of being a monastic retreat based on rigorous principles, the ashram 'was a miniature cross-section of the everyday world' and comprised of 'highly explosive material'.[94] Different members were drawn by different aspects of Gandhi to join the ashram, and there was often no unifying motive that bound them, exemplifying once again how the ashram as a space held different meanings for different members. Slade eventually came to side with the more ascetic group within the ashram, advocating greater austerity and adherence to ashram rules.

Slade soon busied herself with everyday ashram work, revelling in the presence of Gandhi and eager to follow his instructions. Among her first jobs in the ashram included cleaning communal latrines, reflecting Gandhi's emphasis on the primacy of sanitation work. His appreciation enthused her to work harder, ignoring the physical and mental strain these exertions had. Gandhi reported to Rolland: 'Miss. Slade is showing wonderful adaptability and has already put us at ease about herself'.[95]

Her first phase of training, as devised by Gandhi, involved learning Hindustani in the Devanagari script (a reflection of the Hindi–Urdu divide already at work), spinning cotton and carding, and sweeping ashram latrines daily.[96] We get a sense of the value of her discipleship – and also its relative difference from Indian discipleships – from Mahadev Desai's dairies. Desai, a close associate and ashram secretary, was chided by Gandhi for trying to learn French from Mira:

> Do you know that Miss Slade has come here, having burnt all her boats? Do you know that her sacrifice for our cause is greater than that of any one of us? Do you know that she is here to learn and study and serve and give all her time to the service of our people and thereby her own people, and that nothing that happens at her own home will swerve her from her appointed task here? Every minute of her time is therefore doubly precious and it is for us to give her as much as we can. She wants to know everything about us, she must master Hindustani.[97]

Desai publicised this anecdote in the ashram journal *Young India* as a moral lesson on the value of time for ashram readers. Desai did, however, continue to sneak in French lessons from Slade, whenever he could.[98] Nevertheless, it shows how Gandhi saw Mira, as 'doubly precious'. Gandhi saw her 'service to our people' as a service to 'her own people'.

Within two decades of her discipleship to Gandhi, she ventriloquised his political positions. She boldly represented Indian nationalist interests in influential British official circles (Figure 2.9). When Winston Churchill told her in an interview in 1934 that the 'Indian nation does not exist', Slade reassured him that 'being in India for a decade, she can vouch that there is a unifying culture throughout the land and from North to South and from East to West, wherever you go you find this yearning for freedom'.[99] And more bluntly, during the Quit India movement in 1942, to Gilbert Laithwaite, Principal Secretary of the Viceroy Lord Linlithgow, when the latter refused to see her:

> This time it will be impossible for you to hold him [Gandhi]. No jail will contain him, no crushing will silence him. The more you crush, the more his power will spread. You are faced with two alternatives; one to declare India's independence, and the other to kill Gandhiji, and once you kill him, you kill for ever all hope of friendship between India and England....[100]

She did not spare Linlithgow, making her loyalties clear, while invoking her lineage: 'I am the daughter of the late Admiral Sir Edmond Slade, who came to Gandhiji seventeen years ago, and has ever since been closely associated with him in all his activities.'[101]

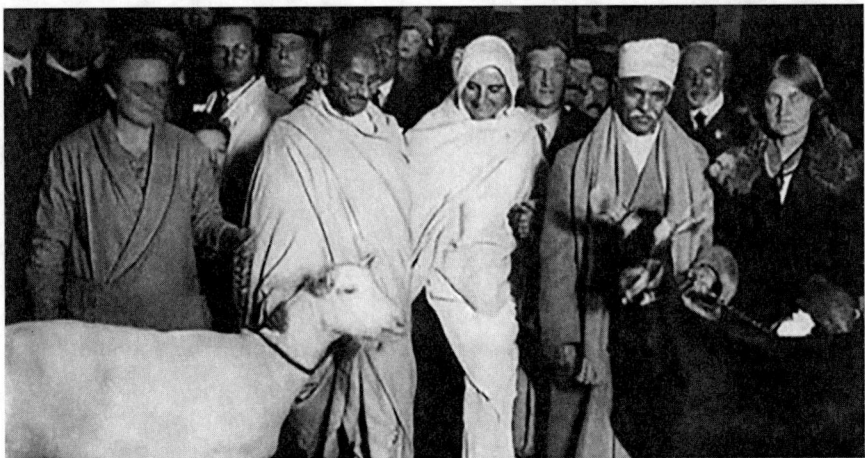

Figure 2.9   Gandhi inspecting goats at the Royal Agricultural Hall, London, 1931. Mira Behn and Madan Mohan Malaviya look on. One of the goats was christened Mahatma.
Source: *Time*, 2 November 1931, London.

It was not without reason that Gandhi re-christened Madeleine as Mira, after the famous medieval Bhakti saint Mirabai of Mewar, whose *bhajan*s (devotional hymns) Slade grew to love and sing in later life: '[a]s an Indian name had to be chosen the one that best describes Miss Slade's aspirations was chosen'.[102] Her unflinching love and loyalty for Gandhi were similar to Mirabai's passionate devotion to the deity of Krishna.

Eager to prove her loyalty, Mira desperately wanted to please Gandhi. She made her life consonant with his wishes, often at great physical and mental distress. When she decided to take a vow of celibacy, Gandhi warned against it, while also invoking Andrews's way:

> ... a vow means a religious determination to carry out a decision for self-restraint even at the cost of one's life. I ... welcome your desire to take what is perhaps the supremest vow for a man or a woman. But ... let it be taken after the maturest deliberation.
>
> ... But there is the other side, i.e., Andrews's. He says: 'I must ... hold myself free to do the will of God as I discover it from moment to moment.'[103]

Nevertheless, Slade persisted in becoming a celibate Mira, adopting the strictest vows. Communal life was a 'tough job', as she put it, having never attended schools or colleges before. There were frequent minor tempests with other inmates of Sabarmati, including Mahadev Desai, Gandhi's secretary. Trying to follow Gandhi's directions to the extreme, she was

> [i]n continual dispute with Mahadev Desai, the first secretary and right arm of Gandhi. This very proud man, Brahmin, great intellectual – rebels, when Mira (of her own authority), gives him orders: – 'You will do this' – 'You will do that' – 'No! I will not do it!' – 'You will do it' – 'No!' – he goes away, slamming the doors. A short time after, he returns, repenting of his anger.
>
> But Mira, her, does not repent. She stays upright, tough, and proud. – There is only Gandhi whose judgment can break this haughty creature. He knows her, and he is also very harsh on her – in his own way.[104]

Gandhi's reprimands, 'like an old aunt's', would leave Mira distraught and apologetic.[105] While acknowledging the ashram as an inclusive social experiment, Slade's over-identification with Gandhian projects led her to conceive difference as deviance. Her criticism of the Sabarmati Ashram would increase in later years, often leading to serious debates with Gandhi himself regarding the nature of the ashram. Her zealous vision of the ashram as a semi-monastic institution spent in prayer, celibacy and charity was often frustrated.

Ashram and Self-Making

If letters enacted distant self-making, ashrams became the physical site. Both letters and ashrams derived and imparted meaning to each other. In a race-torn South Africa, Andrews found solace in talking about Shantiniketan in his letters to Tagore:

> My whole heart is set on coming direct to the Ashrama before the boys leave and receiving your blessing and offering thanks to God there first of all on my return.... If you only knew the homesickness to get back to India that everyday here brings with it, you would understand! ... I look back to the peace of the Ashrama as a kind of dream or haven of rest, I feed on that picture day by day and it sustains me.[106]

The daily act of writing about the ashram made that space ever more real. From a distance, the ashram acted as a metaphor for a life not yet given. Mira wrote weekly letters to Rolland's sister Madeleine with news from the Sabarmati Ashram. Everyday details of care infused its content, as for instance when Gandhi lost consciousness in Mira's arms due to fatigue.[107] Mira would often massage a bodily tired Gandhi and measure his blood pressure. Her diary gives etchings of this habitual intimacy: 'This morning he slept quite a lot during massage'[108] or the time spent in spinning *khadi*.[109] Moments of bodily weakness brought Mira an opportunity to serve Gandhi. She cherished such moments of caring:

> Bapu took *gur* [jaggery] and water in the early morning and later his breakfast. He looks a little better than yesterday afternoon, but still very worn and pale. He is so sad over Pyarelal, and P's condition

continues to grow worse.... Everything points to its being typhoid
fever. The cholera is also getting worse in the [Segaon] village.[110]

Partaking in daily ashram habits mediated the adoption of new selves. It also
brought to the fore problems and possibilities of this encounter. As mentors,
Gandhi and Tagore pushed for personal affections to be translated into broader
commitments. When the Indian nationalist leader Gokhale suspected that it
was Andrews's 'strong personal love' that was driving him to serve Tagore: 'I
told him that if Gurudev were to die – in that case I should regard the call to
go there as doubly sacred and doubly an act of duty, then he became happy
about it'.[111]

Disciples' intimations of Indian-ness had to be continually proven and
performed through the nation's spectacle. Mira willingly courted political
imprisonment for Gandhian political causes. She courted arrest for aiding the
civil disobedience movement in 1932: 'It seems that the honour will be mine at
last! A notice has been served on me and I expect arrest tomorrow morning.'[112]
She was sentenced to three months in prison along with many 'leading ladies'
of Bombay in C-class cells.[113] Ashram life helped Mira to embrace prison:

> The Ashram discipline stood me in good stead now. I made out a
> regular daily program of work and exercise, which I stuck to strictly.
> So much time for reading, so much for Hindi, so much for spinning,
> so much for cooking, eating and clothes-washing, and so much for
> walking up and down the yard for exercise.[114]

Political imprisonment was cherished in Gandhian movements. Women
followers eagerly spilled onto streets and filled prisons alongside men. Shared
prison life produced a different kind of intimate understanding between Gandhi
and Mira, yoking her deeper within anti-colonial nationalism.

While Andrews never went to jail, given his excellent contacts in high
official circles, Pearson was deported and arrested for his book *For India* which
severely criticised British rule. Written while in Japan, the new Communist
government in Russia translated the pamphlet and distributed it widely. [115]
Pearson was warned severely by British authorities as liable to penalties under
'British Law' before being released. He saw this as *nishkam karma*, a detached
service rendered without any expectation. Andrews continued to lobby and
represent Indian nationalist opinion at home and abroad. Notwithstanding his

immense work for Indian immigrant settlers, allegations followed. In Nairobi, Sitaram Achariar, the editor of the *Democrat* newspaper, attacked Andrews for betraying Indians and alleged him to be an English spy.[116] At home, Indian labourers, whose interests Andrews represented during the railway strike in 1922, were told that he was not to be trusted as he was 'both an Englishman and a spy'.[117] Ashrams legitimised their Indophilia but racial identities could never be dissolved fully.

Within the Ashram

Love for the ashram showed in different ways. While Andrews moved heaven and earth to prove his commitment, Pearson was engrossed intensively in the ashram's daily activities. He learnt Bengali, taught ashram students and set up night schools in adjacent tribal villages as part of Tagore's Sriniketan enterprise. He took ashram boys on local trips for leisure (Figure 2.10):

> We want to go to the river Ajoy for a picnic this afternoon starting at 3 o'clock. Can you let us have your motor lorry? …
>
> If this is not possible could we come to Surul and cook under the trees there? As there are about 40 boys we shall have to use the school bus too which needs attending to by Alu Roy.[118]

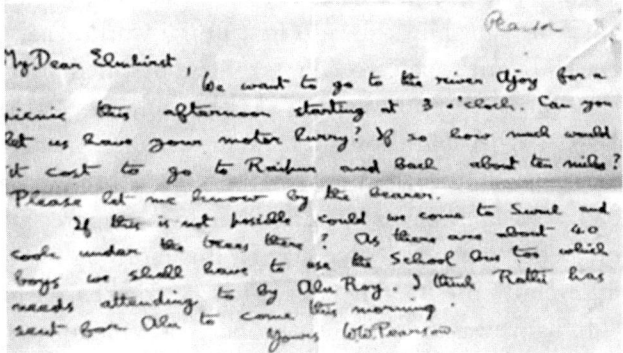

Figure 2.10   Pearson's memo to Elmhirst, asking to borrow his motor lorry for a picnic with students.

Source: Dartington Hall Trust.

Pearson was 'calm, composed and loved to work in his corner of the ashram' while Andrews was mobile and in the thick of things, being more politically connected than the former. As Leonard Elmhirst, another English disciple and associate of Tagore working at Sriniketan noted: 'Andrews arrived back at 8.00 this morning and was cheered lustily for some minutes by the whole school and college.'[119] Tagore jokingly referred to him as 'Sir Charles', given his constant propensity to relieve the 'wrongs' done to Indians everywhere.[120]

Pramathanath Bishi, a student of the ashram, noted this difference while framing them on a high note of exemplary 'self-sacrifice':

> Both of them embraced with easy regard the unused to life of the ashram; they had difficulties, but no one ever saw them unhappy because of it…. There was no outwardly glory in teaching here, no worldly praise for the small responsibilities, yet they performed everything with respect, pride and undiluted pleasure and became part of the ashram – perhaps this is complete self-sacrifice. They have received many offers with attractive pay; yet they have without a second thought, refused them.[121]

In Bishi's words: 'we were devoted to Mr Andrews, and Mr Pearson we loved'.[122] Pearson immersed himself completely in the life of the ashram and its students. His continuous living in the ashram made him fluent in Bengali and brought him closer to its cultural world. Pearson acted in a minor role in Tagore's play *Achalayatan* (The petrified altar), staged in Shantiniketan for a reception given to C. F. Andrews (1914).[123] While Pearson played cricket and football with students and managed ashram affairs minutely, Andrews raised money for Tagore's ashram from distant friends as 'Vice Chancellor' of Visvabharati. Tagore appreciatingly wrote of his devoted efforts: 'Andrews has started this morning for Madras on a Visvabharati errand', presumably a fund-raising trip that yielded 'meagre results'.[124] His name was continuously proposed as a member of the *sansad*, or governing body of the ashram (Figure 2.11).[125]

Voting Paper for Election of 7 ordinary members of the Samsad.

VISVA-BHARATI

NOTICE

The following names have been proposed for election as ordinary members of the Samsad (Governing Body). Sadasyas (members) of the Visva-Bharati are requested to put a X against the names of persons for whom they wish to vote in the column provided for this purpose.

Members are entitled to vote for not more than seven (7) persons. Not more than one vote shall be given to any one candidate.

The voting paper must be signed and must reach the Karma-Sachiva, Santiniketan on or before the 23rd December, 1923.

10, Cornwallis Street.	Prasantachandra Mahalanobis,
Calcutta.	Karma-Sachiva,
22nd November. 1923.	Visva-Bharati.

VOTES

1. Achyutakumar Sarkar, M.A.,
   17, Mohindra Bose Lane, Calcutta.

2. Amiyakumar Chakravarty,
   Santiniketan.

3. C. F. Andrews, M.A. (Cantab)
   Santiniketan.

4. Charuchandra Bandopadhya, B.A. (B) (C)
   33, Simla Street, Calcutta.

5. Charuchandra Bhattacharya, M.A. (B) (C)
   1, Kalu Ghose Lane, Calcutta.

6. Devendramohan Bose, Ph.D. (A) (C)
   92/3, Upper Circular Road, Calcutta.

(A) Member, Finance Committee, Visva-bharati.
(B) Acting Member, Finance Committee, Visva-bharati.
(C) Retiring Member of Samsad.

Figure 2.11   Andrews's name proposed in the governing board
of Visvabharati, 1923.

Source: National Archives of India.

Urmila Devi, an ashram student's mother, recounted her son's fondness for Pearson: 'he loves me very much'. When her son was near unconscious with typhoid, the few words he could barely muster were all about him. Pearson urged her to wire every day about his health, sending twelve prepaid telegram forms so that she would not incur any expense.[126] The personal possessions and services of these disciples were slowly but surely claimed by an ever-encroaching ashram as its own. Neither Pearson nor Andrews resisted such a claim. As Dorothy, Pearson's sister, attested: 'He told me quite recently that all his books had had the School Library label put on them once while he was away so of course they had better be left where they are.'[127] The personal fused with the collective, though not for the sake of any homogenised uniformity. Tagore valued individuality greatly.

Edward Thompson, then a Wesleyan Missionary at Bankura, (near Shantiniketan), as well as a poet and translator, confirmed that both these sahibs were 'immensely popular' and to be considered a friend of theirs earned immediate affection.[128] Both of them wore 'dhoti and punjabi while staying in the ashram'.[129] Often, Andrews would pull the rickshaw carrying Tagore's infirm elder brother Dwijendranath to the ashram.[130] Nathaniel Sircar, the Bengali catechist of the Burdwan church, was surprised at Andrews's dress on his visit there, like 'a Bengali gentleman, with dhoti, shirt, chuddar, and slippers'.[131] Andrews's visits, almost always itinerant for various nationalist causes, were eagerly anticipated moments:

> Gurudev, it is wonderful to be home. I'm quite exhausted! I never want to leave the Ashram again. In fact I just now saw Jagadananda Babu on my way here. I told him I plan to start up my English classes again from next week. I must go now and get rest.
>
> 'Sir Charles!' the Poet jokingly answered.[132]

The ashram journal *Visvabharati News* followed his travels and visits closely: 'Mr C. F. Andrews has come back to India for a few days' hurried consultation and it is expected he will make time to visit us during the coming Utsab.'[133] In 1935, nearly a decade later, Andrews's visits were as enthusiastically heralded:

My Gurudeva

Twentyfive years ago, my whole heart
was given to the poet, Rabindranath
Tagore, and it has remained with him ever
since. He has been my Gurudeva, teaching
me to understand and love humanity in
the East no less than I had learnt, in
earlier years, to love it in the West. By
his love and patience he broke down
within me the narrow barriers of religious
tradition which had confined me before,
owing to my birth, upbringing and education. Nothing but a friendship so deep
and sincere as his could have effected
this. Now looking back, after a quarter
of a century, I can say with truth that
this friendship has grown stronger as the
years have passed and has remained steadfast throughout. It has been a supreme
treasure in my life ; the greatest gift
which God has given me in human ways.

C. F. Andrews.

Southampton,
March 20, 1936.

Figure 2.12 Andrews's poem, 'My Gurudeva', published in the ashram journal on Tagore's birth anniversary, *Visvabharati News*, vol. 4, May–June 1936.

Source: National Archives of India.

C. F. Andrews spending 4 days during the Pous Utsav in Shantiniketan. On 24th morning he gave a short sermon on the life of Jesus Christ and presided over the reunion meeting of ex-students. Expects to be back during summer for a few months. Andrews present at the 34th Foundation anniversary of Shantinketan.[134]

Christianity continued to play a part in his personal motivation, but this was not proselytising. Andrews and Pearson continued to be involved in ashram affairs till their deaths. Pearson's book *Shantiniketan: The Bolpur School of Rabindranath Tagore* was received and circulated widely. It portrayed Shantiniketan in the image of an idyllic Vedic ashram – *brahmachari* (celibate) students coming to learn from wise gurus/rishis who resided in forest schools.[135] Unlike Sabarmati, caste did not form a central aspect of its agenda. Shantiniketan's students were predominantly from upper-caste backgrounds, even though the area itself was primarily tribal, along with substantial lower and untouchable caste presence.[136]

Andrews gave devotional tributes to Tagore's profound influence in breaking down the 'narrow barriers of religious tradition' that had confined him before. Being in the ashram released him from this confinement. On Tagore's birth anniversary in 1936, he invoked and restated his love (Figure 2.12): 'Twenty five years ago, my whole heart was given to the poet Rabindranath Tagore, and it has remained ever since.'[137]

Mira's devotion to Gandhi, while premised on a similar idiom of bhakti, was far more intensely personal: '[f]rom early morning to the last thing at night I lived for the moments when I could set eyes on Bapu. To be in his presence was to be lifted out of oneself.'[138] Living for Gandhi led her to rush into an austere lifestyle, thinking it would make him happy: 'I was myself sufficiently highly strung during at that period and spontaneously joined the ascetic group with not a little fanatical zeal.'[139] This asceticism extended to drastic dietary practices, premised on the wisdom of Gandhian dietetics 'worldly food, worldly dreams':

> Both my mind and body have been troubled especially when spices, ghee etc do get into food. My experience in the last 3 years has invariably been *worldly food, worldly dreams*. And so I am taking drastic steps for the moment … I will eat only roti made by my own hands & vegetables that I have prepared myself, together with milk, fruit etc according to circumstances.[140]

Building 'ashrams in the air', she looked for Gandhi's approval. Following Gandhi's examples in exercising minimalism and *brahmacharya*:

> The next urges that took possession of me were to have my hair cut off and to take a vow of celibacy. This was a very much more serious matter and Bapu held me back for some time, even though these two things were greatly to his own liking.[141]

Finally, Gandhi relented. Mira took to wearing *khadi* sarees and travelling in third-class railway compartments like her adopted master. In the ashram, she along with a group of ascetic-minded followers pushed for stricter austerities.[142]

She took up the practice of fasting with zeal, often up to seven days 'as a spiritual experience'.[143] Bordering on the extreme, these sartorial lifestyle choices did not please Gandhi, who thought them pre-mature. He felt she had not grasped the moral or political significance of the act itself, a cornerstone in Gandhian self-making. Gandhi confided in Kasturba in 1933, when even eight years of discipleship had not dimmed her devotion: 'Mirabehn has only one thought day and night. She doesn't attend any meeting, but spends all her time in keeping things ready for me.'[144] Mira's cherished desire to serve Gandhi personally was also her most vivid moments of self-sublimation. Despite his repeated attempts to thwart her presence, she was, however,

> on the brain. I look about me, and miss you. I open the charkha and miss you.... But what is the use? ... all the time you were squandering your love on me personally, I felt guilty of misappropriation.[145]

Reining in her 'personal love' would remain an unfinished project. Yet, Gandhi's own methods of training were no less severe. Wary of Mira's longing for an intensely personal relationship, he sent her away for long periods of time to other ashrams – Kanya Gurukul in Delhi, Gurukul Kangri at Hardwar and the Bhagavad Bhakti ashram at Rewari, Rajasthan – to cultivate distance or learn Hindustani. Mira felt helpless in her desperation.[146] But distance only heightened her longing. She boldly dared the police: 'when the police came to arrest Gandhi at Bombay, Mira's eyes blazed, and she had insulting words for them'.[147]

Gandhi corresponded in detail with her regarding the moral and material aspects of various ashrams she stayed at. He enquired after her dietary habits, spinning and praying, even bowel movements.[148] Mira continued to seek Gandhi's counsel on the ethics of the smallest habits: should she use soap as it contained animal fat?[149] When a group of women accosted her at a meeting in Delhi insisting that she sing a Mira bhajan – 'a bhajan – a bhajan, we must have a bhajan from you' – she obliged. 'It went off quite successfully and they all beamed with such charming simple delight & started cries of "*Mirabai ki jai*". The name had evidently appealed to them.'[150] Thrilled at the recognition and celebration of this dual register of love and longing – *krishnabhakti* and *deshbhakti* – she learnt more about Mirabai bhajans, anticipating further demands. Halide Edib, a distinguished travel writer from Turkey, wrote in 1935 of how she thought of Mira, as did those close to her, as 'a Hindu of

Hindus' but not in any denominational sense.[151] She was impressed at Mira's Sanskrit chanting during the ashram's 'Morning Prayer', the others repeating after her.[152] She wholeheartedly joined Gandhi's anti-untouchability campaign in Wardha, witnessing first-hand the everyday violence of untouchable life. Having accepted water to wash her hands from an outcaste man (socially inferior to Mahars) in the village of Sindi, Mira was refused permission to use the wells of both caste Hindus and Mahars.[153]

Holding forth Mira's strivings and struggles as emulative, Gandhi forwarded much of her correspondence for general reading by specifically women members of his ashram:

> Mirabehn's life should set all of you thinking…. She does not waste a single moment. I expect such devotion, sacrifice and purity from you.[154]

Mira's letters became spectacles to emphasise personal sacrifice and purity (Figure 2.13). He regularly enclosed her 'perfect letters' as mandatory reading for the ashram girls,[155] commending her as 'the most ideal woman worker among us'.[156] He, however, did not circulate the more critical letters Mira sent him.[157]

Figure 2.13   The Vinoba–Mira Kutir: Mira's room in the Sabarmati Ashram, where she lived from 1925 to 1933. Before her, Vinoba Bhave, another prominent disciple of Gandhi, lived in this cottage from 1918 to 1921.

Source: Photo by author.

Mira's letters illustrate the convergence of the epistolary and the ashramic used to design an ideal community. Several ashrams Mira was sent to live were in direct conflict with some of Gandhi's foundational vows. The pervasive anti-Muslim sentiment at Kanya Gurukul and Gurukul Kangri, founded by the militant Hindu nationalist Swami Shraddhanand (Munshi Ram), perturbed Mira. Shraddhanand's assassination by a Muslim man in 1926 further heightened such feelings. The third – Bhagwad Bhakti ashram in Rewari (in modern-day Haryana) – where she was sent to learn Hindi by Gandhi in 1927, suffered from a '*bhang* problem'.[158] This was a different kind of ashram. Unfamiliar with the habit of consuming *bhang* in the *sadhu* world, Mira was horrified.[159] The all-male members of the Bhagwad Bhakti ashram cornered Mira and her young female companion Gungu Behn, forcing them to consume *bhang*:

> Maharajji chimed in with 'Drink, drink, just a little', and one of the brahmachari taking some bhung in a glass came straight for me – I retired a little way into the room. He then put his hand into the glass and tried to put his fingers to my mouth. I tried to avoid him, but it was no good. I caught him by the wrist; took the bung [*sic*] from his hand and emptied it out of the window....
>
> ... as we descended the stair case I felt some bhung being sprinkled on our backs from above.[160]

Reminiscent of bawdy tavern scenes, Mira was aghast but sought to interpret it as a 'loving joke'. Gandhi expressed disappointment at the fall of yet another ashram in his esteem, and insisted that it was not her place to suggest any reform but to learn Hindi.[161] Nevertheless, he did acknowledge her criticisms of these spaces as 'honest attempts' to lead an ashram life. Reflecting on this time later, she wrote how in her zeal to gain Gandhi's approval, she rode roughshod over her own freedom:

> I was progressively crushing my natural independence ... and putting myself wholly under another's will.... It was the intense reverential love I felt for Bapu which made me discipline myself in that way.[162]

The desire for a closer relationship with her mentor pushed her to undertake extreme practices. The ashram was the prescribed mode for her to attain perfection:

I want you to be a perfect woman ... to shed all angularities....
Ashram is the centre of your home, but wherever you happen to be
must be your home ... you must not cling to me as in this body.[163]

Gandhi believed that differences in the mode and materiality of these ashram
spaces would be an object lesson for Mira. Insisting that she 'must forget what
[she had] been' in her past life, he laid for her the prospective vision of being
proud of the day she would 'be taken for a common village girl'.[164] Gandhi
was relentless in his attempts to uncouple her affections. Gandhi fought against
her attachment; Mira fought for it. If separation became unbearable, she
could however 'come without waiting for an answer or any prompting' from
Gandhi.[165] While accepting their relationship as that of a father and daughter,
her adoration and longing for him was most intense. Separation often resulted
in acute mental and physical distress.

Beyond the Ashram

Intimacies fostered in ashrams often inspired disciples to lay zealous claims on
their mentors' projects. Sustaining Tagore's literary reputation in the West or
propagating the cause of *khadi* for Gandhi represented two such endeavours.
Indian disciples were involved in these projects, but the presence of willing
Western disciples provided valuable international visibility, leverage and access.

Andrews inserted himself extensively in brokering Tagore's translation
contracts with publishers and dealings with prominent Western literary
colleagues. He saw this as a service to Tagore and his ashram, which was always
cash-strapped and needed his book royalties to meet financial ends. Though
himself not a literary critic, Andrews's adoration of Tagore's translated works
skated over its uneven quality. William Rothenstein, an artist and British
associate of Tagore, wrote to Edward J. Thompson that Tagore's 'vanity
ha[d] become ridiculous', blaming 'Andrews, who ha[d] encouraged it'.[166]
Thompson, knowledgeable in English and Bengali literature, would go on
to write several important and sympathetic volumes on Indian literature and
history, a few of which Tagore critiqued devastatingly.[167]

Thompson was present in the ashram the day Tagore received news of his
Nobel Prize. Caught up in the frenzy of Indian students and staff offering
pranam by touching Tagore's feet, he almost did it. Nevertheless, he remembered
he was still 'an Englishman & have a stern contempt for the fools who pretend

they are easterners'.[168] This fundamental difference was at the heart of liberal sympathisers such as Thompson (still a formal Christian missionary) and more Indianised figures such as Andrews or Pearson, who adopted native customs and culture quite openly. Andrews and Pearson freely touched the feet of their guru, an intimate marker accepting Tagore's social superiority. Thompson had approached Tagore with an offer to translate and was thwarted several times, the latter often citing literary and financial considerations:

> Your proposal of translating my stories is a little premature. If you had read at least a dozen of them and felt that they must be translated then I should consider your proposal seriously....

> The next best thing for me is to work with some Englishman who has literary abilities. I have every hope that Andrews will be willing to help me in this work when he comes back [to Shantiniketan] from England in April.... This arrangement will help Andrews to learn Bengali and help me to learn handling English prose with more freedom than I dare do now.[169]

Andrews, however, never really learnt much Bengali. But Tagore's denial of Thompson stung him deeply, particularly as he was a published poet and considered himself well acquainted with contemporary English literature and possessing sufficient knowledge of Bengali. Thompson ranted against Andrews:

> ... beneath contempt as regards judgment (& intellect generally). I can't understand how R[abindranath]. ever got humbugged into his ecstatic exaltation of him ... I have always refused to worship indiscriminately.[170]

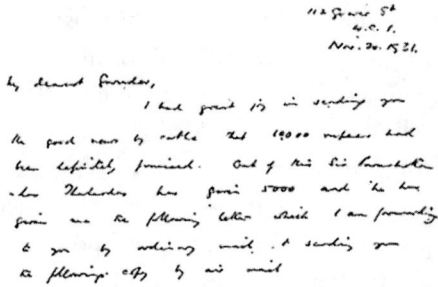

Figure 2.14 Andrews fundraising for Shantiniketan, whose finances were generally precarious, 20 November 1931.

Source: Rabindra Bhavana, Visvabharati.

He saw Andrews's worship of Tagore and the latter's uncritical acceptance as responsible for the stifling atmosphere of adulatory excess and pose in the ashram. Andrews became what the historian E. P. Thompson has called the 'Western door-keeper' of a proliferating Tagore cult.[171] Andrews laid claim to Tagore's literary affairs in a bid to safeguard his legacy and to make the ashram's financial future secure. He remained unaware of the contemptuous asides and reputation he had gained. Rothenstein wryly observed to Thompson that it was 'not to a foul flatterer like Andrews, but to one like yourself from whom we can look for truth about India'.[172] Unaware of the simmering resentment against him and his role in perpetuating a 'Tagore Cult', Andrews asserted to Thompson that 'books like "*Nationalism*", "*Home and the World*", "*Personality*", etc. surely do not fall in with the "Tagore Cult" of the "mystical Orient". He has surely kept his virile nature in his English as well as in his Bengali works.'[173] The proof of Tagore's intellectual 'virility' was taken up with great gusto by Andrews.

Pearson, while less proprietary and possessing a decent knowledge of Bengali, was similarly, if less defensively, invested in preserving Tagore's literary legacies in translation. Tagore had earlier suggested that Thompson could take up translating his novel *Gora* in 1920.[174] Yet by 1922, we find Pearson translating it, serially published in the journal *Modern Review*: 'I have reached Page 220 in "GORA", and at each hundredth page I feel like having a celebration!'[175] Pearson and Andrews's labours in this regard were generally unremunerated, the royalties of these translations used for the ashram's sustenance.[176] It raised their esteem further within the closely knit world of the ashram (Figure 2.14).

Andrews and Pearson's representation of Tagore as a lofty Gurudev chiding the materialistic West reinforced this image. Thompson put it acidly: 'His appetite for flattery has grown to absurdity since his first success. He lives amid incense, and India outside Bengal and the Punjab half resents, half laughs at it.'[177] The avowal of British disciples added to the stereotype of Tagore as a mystical saint dispensing transcendent wisdom. This aura also attributed to Andrews and Pearson a halo of sainthood that made them impervious to external criticism. Proprietary claims to represent Tagore were justified for the sake of preserving his literary integrity, the welfare of the ashram and its upkeep. Andrews would habitually insert himself in editorial decisions, advising on whom to grant requests and permissions, often involving established literary figures in Britain (Robert Bridges for instance).[178] Staking on his intimacy with Tagore, he asserted to Thompson: 'I suffer in no small degree through my ignorance of Bengali but I have had the unique advantage of an intimate friendship with the Poet himself.'[179] Claims to intimacy were repeatedly made to derive authority.

Pearson, now proficient in Bengali, made several translations of Tagore and other Bengali authors' works. He insisted Tagore not abridge his translations to please Western readers: 'Think of what a terrible misfortune it would have been if the novels of Tolstoy, of Turgenev, of Dostoevsky, had been abridged in the way that you abridged for example your "Glimpses of Bengal".'[180] In this, he presciently echoed Thompson's cautions against watering down for the West, which his translations often did: 'I fear that your "careful abridgement" is nearly always more correctly described as "ruthless pruning"!' He advised Tagore not to pay too much importance to some English readers' impatience with detail, but rather heed those who would want to learn about a foreign country in its fullest and finest detail.[181] Both disciples remained wound up in the management of Tagore's literary legacy in the West.

If Tagore was ensnared by the adulation of his disciples, Gandhi remained sceptical of Mira's many attempts to please him. This did not deter Mira from enthusiastically taking up Gandhian causes like *khadi*. Widely held as the 'national fabric', the moral and material economy of *khadi* and *charkha* (spinning wheel) in Gandhian satyagraha was supreme. Wearing *khadi* for those used to donning Western clothes was, in this sense, a supposedly transformative experience, making them visibly 'Indian'.[182] Mira's desire to align with such practices signalled her idealism, but also made her available for nationalist consumption. Mira continued to propagate the All-India Spinning Association's work in Indian villages for more than a decade. 'Spinning wheel and the act of spinning', argued Gandhi, 'would instill truth, purity, peace and a spirit of service in one's life.'[183] At a time when Gandhi's politics and practices were deemed near hegemonic, to be visibly Gandhian was an undisputed way of being Indian.

Hitherto, Mira had been wearing white *khadi* skirts and shirts stitched in London, as 'Bapu seemed rather against [her] taking to Indian clothes'.[184] In her eagerness to win Gandhi's affection and approval, she had learnt how to wear a saree made of *khadi* from Anasuya Sarabhai, a non-ashramite Gandhian belonging to a powerful industrial family in Ahmedabad. Gandhi was displeased but did not prevent her from wearing so. Once her adoption of *khadi* was approved, she now moved towards an active engagement with the cause of *khadi*. Within a year, she began touring villages in the United Provinces, Bihar and Nepal, promoting *khadi*, adopting improvisations and organising demonstration workshops for village women. Gushingly, she wrote to Gandhi that her 'little room [was] adorned with charkhas, ginning machines and carding bows and [she felt] so happy'.[185] Her extensive travels through rural India proved life-changing: 'What I have seen and learned in those villages have been the richest possible education. And it has filled me with infinite inspiration for I now know that I can win the hearts of the peasants and serve and help them.'[186]

Pleased that she was devoting her time to his causes rather than himself, Gandhi began discussing intricate technical details involving the adaptability of various slivers, wheels, yarns, spindles and their suitability to local needs. She shared insights gleaned from her travels across Bihar, which she cherished. Pointing the utter 'uselessness to the peasants of the wheels, spindles and ginning charkhas being turned out at the Udyog Mandir workshop', the crafts workshop within the Sabarmati Ashram, as they were neither simple nor cheap to use, she urged the need to improvise tools that would address these twin problems.[187] *Khadi* – its practice and profession – became a regular concern for Mira in her correspondence with Gandhi. Mira seemed finally able to expand her affections from the personhood of Gandhi to his projects. Yet, after long periods of physical separation, Mira's reunions with Gandhi were emotionally charged affairs. She would burst into tears and Gandhi would chide her, advising the necessity of physical separation.[188] Distance brought home an awareness of the impossibility of intimacy.

Epilogue: Disenchantments

The ashram and its habitus played a central role in mediating the mentor–disciple encounter. The psychoanalyst Sudhir Kakar has noted in Mira and Gandhi's relationship a strong unresolved psycho-sexual desire, which made Gandhi resist her so fervently.[189] In Andrews too (Pearson more guardedly) we find an urge for personal love, but it has not been noted with the same intensity, probably because it was between men. The ashram became a site of sublimation for all such personal desires, a continuous deferral of the potent 'eros' towards more 'impersonal' work. The effacement of physical urges was part of this striving. Both Andrews and Pearson (who died in a train accident aged forty) remained unmarried.

The ashram was, however, not always an enchanted space. When these enchantments broke, it affected their relationships. When Pearson wanted freedom from playing the obedient disciple, Tagore was visibly hurt, pointing out that he had not asked him to:

> You have got into some conventional habits, such as calling me 'Gurudev' and making 'pranam' to me. Drop them. For I know there are occasions when they hurt you and for that very reason are truly discourteous to me. You know I never care to assume the role of a prophet or a teacher; I do not claim homage from my fellow beings....[190]

Pearson resented having to go on long voyages with Tagore, acting as his secretary (having an Englishman as a secretary was both strategic and symbolic). Tagore gauged the extent of this resentment only when he ran away to Boston in the middle of his American tour. Rolland, once again, gives us a first-hand account of Pearson's bitterness:

> What he tells us of Santiniketan is quite discouraging. Tagore's International University (more fictional than real) lacks true organisation.... Chance in part governs the offering of lectures and courses during the year ... pupils come sometimes one or two hours after that indicated. Bengalis are intelligent, very gifted, exuberant in words and gestures like southerners,[191] but are without perseverance, and following that without spirit. They tire as quickly as they enflame themselves.... But they would not be willing to accept anything from a more energetic race. And Tagore is a poet, hardly a practical man. He seems to tire as quickly as his compatriots. He was enthralled for his school for several years; now he barely takes interest.[192]

Pearson relieved his growing disquiet to Rolland, far removed from that world, yet vitally connected to major currents in India. The promise of freedom that had once seduced Pearson had largely eroded. Tagore cautioned him against the 'growing feeling of distrust': 'towards your colleagues in the ashram is leading you astray from the path of charity and love. With very great pain I have been noticing for some time past Andrews also drifting into this hopeless mood of contemptuous mistrust.'[193] Tagore believed Pearson could never reconcile with the small Brahmacharyashrama becoming the international university Visvabharati in 1921: 'Until his last days, Pearson never reconciled himself completely with it. Intellectually, he had nothing to say back to it, but his heart was pained.'[194] Tagore himself had begun to lose some of his initial enthusiasm for Shantiniketan by the 1930s, and his thoughts turned now turned towards safeguarding. Utopian experiments often suffered from the 'high-minded elitism' that characterised their founders' visions, causing irreconcilable differences.[195]

Rolland felt 'melancholy in Pearson's destiny': 'uprooted, who has lost his homeland and not found it again…. And yet he can no longer live anywhere else other than India. He has gotten out of the habits of European life, and can no longer tolerate it.'[196] The ashram that had once seemed home had lost its appeal. He died a tragic death in 1923, falling from a train near Pistoia, in Italy, far from his guru and beloved ashram. Rolland noted a similar sense of dislocation in Mira:

> Mira is happy to be back in India. Her return to England (where her mother died, alone, far from her, a few months ago), instead of awakening affection, made her feel more strongly how much the native land was a foreign land for her.[197]

Figure 2.15   Envelope addressed to Andrews, then residing with Gandhi at Sabarmati. Written in Tagore's hand, 1918.

Source: Rabindra Bhavana, Visvabharati.

Mira yearned to return to India; her 'native land' felt foreign.[198] On meeting Lord Halifax, the former Indian Viceroy in 1934, she almost ventriloquised the 'mythopoeic' divine status Gandhi enjoyed with the peasantry:

> Gandhiraj will mean something more in his stomach, less taxation and a feeling of being cared for.... I further explained how in the villages one rarely hears 'Mahatma Gandhi ki ji [jai]' but Gandhi Maharaj ki ji [jai]....[199]

Ashrams rooted Indophilia within Indian imaginaries. Andrews, claiming dual discipleship to both Gandhi and Tagore, remained devout in his loyalty to both. His connection to Gandhian movements ran the risk of politicising Shantiniketan students, which Tagore remained wary of. Andrews confided in Pearson: 'It has been extraordinarily difficult for me at times because ... in Gurudev's absence, it was absolutely vital not to involve the ashram itself directly in "politics"....'[200]

Andrews felt the political sand shift continually. His presence instigated Shantiniketan members to actively participate in nationalist politics, in sharp contravention to Tagore's wishes (Figure 2.15). Andrews was held responsible by the poet for infusing students with mainstream nationalism, even though the ashram was already exposed to it. On one occasion when some staff and students wanted to go on strike responding to the call to Gandhian non-cooperation:

> Tagore ... immediately called to Charlie Andrews in his room across the passage. 'Charlie', he said, 'this is all your doing. You are responsible. Whilst I was away you turned my school over to politics. You must now help us get out of this trouble. Take Alu [the driver] and the lorry right away. Meet those three boys on the road. Tell them we can on no account have any of them back at Santiniketan. Take Shotyen [striking student] to the station and telegraph his people.'[201]

While Tagore himself never participated in non-cooperation or boycotts, not all ashram members were immune to it. Non-cooperation featured in the ashram life not infrequently, Andrews occasionally rousing passions. Andrews's position on the Mappila riots that broke out on the Malabar in 1921, in which Hindu landlords were attacked by their Muslim peasantry, irked Tagore. Elmhirst, also at Shantiniketan, narrates:

Andrews made continuous appeals to the sentiment and emotions of his student audience. Time and again Tagore tried to pull him up, and kept asking him 'How far do you think you will get towards further progress by appealing to our lowest instincts for revenge?[202]

Tagore was unmoved by Andrews's repeated call for revenge against Muslim perpetrators, addressed to a Hindu audience. Tagore was by then a vocal critic of nationalism, precisely for its capacity to alienate its own people. There was much difference of opinion with Gandhi on this point as Tagore refused to let himself or his ashram follow in the trend of majoritarian nationalism.[203] Andrews's attempt to act as an interlocutor between Tagore and Gandhi left him 'perpetually torn … and swept by deep emotions'.[204] Constantly moving between Gandhi and Tagore's worlds as the 'hyphen', he felt drawn to both, his own convictions restless. In Gandhi's house, he felt 'a Christ-like passion' and an absence of selfishness in his tireless service, compared to the lofty peace and aloof solitude of Tagore.[205] Andrews desired intimacy to both Tagore and Gandhi, in different ways. Andrews never quite mastered vegetarianism though, for we find Mira, a thorough vegetarian, writing 'that CFA eats meat is open knowledge to Bapu'.[206]

Mira's disenchantments with Gandhian ashrams were more serious. Even as Gandhi made public and private declarations of Mira's exemplary discipleship: 'No member of the Ashram has striven more strenuously than Mira Behn to observe the rules of the Ashram and realise its ideals'; she thought Sabarmati had moved away from a life of simplicity and spirituality it was premised on. She came across several small ashram-like institutions (often for promoting *khadi,* also showing the malleability of the ashram form) in Bihar and Nepal whose 'simplicity and village life' appealed to her greatly. She vented to Gandhi about the superficiality of the 'Sabarmati boys': 'with their watches, their torch lights, their bicycles and their glaring white soap washed clothes':[207]

> … nowadays the Ashram is being *run by force.* This force has produced a fine outward appearance … but underneath … much bitterness, backbiting and hypocrisy…![208]

She hauled up Gandhi and Sabarmati children for making serious compromises with modern technology, and more generally, modernity.

Confessing to Gandhi that the return to Sabarmati filled her with dread, she pointed out that the lack of village life and the presence of urban distractions hollowed the spiritual potential of his ashram and its members.[209] Other ashram disciples, like Chhaganlal Joshi, were perturbed to learn of her disagreements. Mira did not hide her disdain: '… my criticism of the ashram is an old story, dating back some two or three years. The only new thing is that one cannot live to oneself in the Udyog Mandir, and I know my nerves would be unable to bear the strain of living there nowadays.'[210]

She felt closer to 'her Bapu's self' in the villages she visited rather than in the simulated atmosphere of the Sabarmati Ashram. This dissatisfaction grew more acute with Gandhi's decision to involve ashram members in his Salt Satyagraha of 1930, Mira doubting the ability of ashramites to participate in it. Gandhi resisted the imposition of a strict ascetic ideal for the ashram, pointing to her that it reflected the vision of a composite society, to be realised through striving.[211]

Disappointed with so many ashrams she passed through, the ideal of the ashram as an aspirational world, however, did not lose its appeal. She continued to build ashrams wherever she went, Sevagram at Wardha (modern Maharashtra) being the most prominent. Sevagram had emerged as Gandhi's last ashram abode, after he vowed in 1930 not to return to Sabarmati till India achieved freedom. Mira threw herself fully into this project. She designed two cottages that served as Gandhi's residence, the Adi Niwas and Bapu Kutir, both novel attempts at fusing Gandhian ideas about space and aesthetics.[212] She carried buckets of human excreta to make the community sanitary and habitable, helping build a Gandhian community. Mahadev Desai remarked how she 'looked a perfect picture of [a] modern sadhu' as someone who 'had more effectively burnt her boats and … worldly ties' than any other disciple of Gandhi. Despite her labours, Gandhi mandated that Mira must live in a village other than Segaon. Building the very cottage Gandhi would live in, she shifted to another village, living with her horse as companion.[213]

Conclusion

The ashram, therefore, emerged as a major mode for Indophile disciples to invest in an idealised India. The ashrams and their founders, in co-opting these disciples, found in them useful 'white' interlocutors for Indian-led projects.

Andrews, Pearson and Mira saw their efforts for Tagore, Gandhi and their ashrams partly as *prayaschitta*, or atonement, performed on behalf of the British nation for its many injustices. Gandhi verbalised this desire aptly in an editorial of the Gujarati journal *Navajivan:*

> Non-violent disobedience can be a holy duty. It is with this thought that Deenabandhu Andrews has often said that he is doing atonement on behalf of the English, that Mirabai has come to live in the Ashram....[214]

Or in Pearson's utterance on his deathbed in Italy, far away from his beloved Shantiniketan: 'My one and only love – India'.[215] Thompson, generally a bitter critic of Andrews, acknowledged (again on deathbed) that Andrews was the 'bravest man on the planet' to go against his own country.[216] Gandhi, in spite of his turbulent relationship with Mira, would attest a decade later that 'Mira behn's faults are negligible, but her merits are worthy of emulation'.[217] There is much heartbreak, but there is redemption too. Ashrams made possible a politics of redemption whose practices could be harnessed for Indianist projects within and beyond the ashram, in Gandhian movements, in anti-indenture discourses or for preserving the literary legacy of Tagore.

Notes

1   Rosenwein, *Emotional Communities*, 2.
2   Gandhi to Mira, 22 March 1927, Suhrud and Weber, *Beloved Bapu*, 42–43.
3   See Gandhi's letter to Romain Rolland, 13 November 1925: 'I shall leave no stone unturned to assist her to become a bridge between East and West' (*CWMG*, vol. 33, 218).
4   Ajay Skaria, 'Gandhi's Politics: Liberalism and the Question of the Ashram', in *Enchantments of Modernity*, ed. Dube, 199.
5   Helen Ralston, 'The Construction of Authority in the Christian Ashram Movement', *Archives de sciences sociales des religions* 67, no. 1 (1989): 54.
6   Ibid., 54–55.
7   Skaria, 'Gandhi's Politics', 207.
8   Ibid.

9   There is a voluminous literature on this since the publication of Benedict Anderson, *Imagined Communities: Reflections on the Origin and Spread of Nationalism* (London: Verso, 1983).

10   Rabindranath Tagore, 'Society and State' (1904), in *Towards Universal Man* (London: Asia Publishing House, 1961), 49–66.

11   Dube, *Enchantments of Modernity*, 1.

12   Ibid., 6–7.

13   Veena Das, foreword to *Enchantments of Modernity*, ed. Dube, xi.

14   Soja, *Postmodern Geographies*, 25.

15   Slade talks about the animosity towards German and Austrian musicians in England during this time while trying to organise orchestra events. Mira Behn, *The Spirit's Pilgrimage* (London; New York: Great Ocean Publishers, 1960), 53.

16   Ashis Nandy explains how Gandhi was against both technicism and technocracy – the hierarchy between those who possess modern technology and those who do not – and how this inequality becomes a logic of power. Ashis Nandy, *Traditions, Tyrannies and Utopias* (Delhi: Oxford University Press, 1987), 136–137.

17   Vegetarianism was also financially more viable as a dietary practice, particularly for Shantiniketan. However, Debendranath Tagore had very clearly laid down the rule (not out of financial considerations) that no meat was to be consumed within the ashram compound. Tagore was not personally a vegetarian and fish was often cooked in the ashram dining hall. See Shivani, *Amader Shantiniketan* (New Delhi: Radha Krishna Prakashan, 2016), 28. After it became Visvabharati, the ashram received students from royal and aristocratic families who often brought their own cooks and made separate cooking arrangements (Shivani, *Amader Shantiniketan*, 12).

18   Thomas Weber, 'Gandhi Moves: Intentional Communities and Friendship', in *Rethinking Gandhi and Nonviolent Relationality*, ed. Debjani Ganguly and John Docker (New York: Routledge, 2008), 83–99.

19   Anna Neima, *The Utopians: Six Attempts to Build the Perfect Society* (London: Picador, 2021).

20   The only study, though not strictly scholarly, that discusses all of Gandhian ashrams within a single volume is Mark Thomson, *Gandhi and His Ashrams* (Mumbai: Indiana University Press, 1993). Individual studies of Gandhian ashrams include works by Skaria, Weber and Kathryn Tidrick.

21   M. K. Gandhi, *Ashram Observances in Action*, trans. Valji Govindji Desai (Ahmedabad: Navajivan Publishing House, 1955), 3.

22   Charles Bower, 'The Gandhian Ashram and Its Contemporaries' (Unpublished Undergraduate Honors Theses 784, 2015), https://scholar.colorado.edu/honr_theses/784 (accessed on 20 October 2018).

23   Charlotte Alston, *Tolstoy and His Disciples: The History of a Radical International Movement* (London: Palgrave Macmillan, 2014), 90–92.

24   Radical Jewish politics also has a complex lineage – particularly in the way it merged with Asian forms of religious and cultural inheritances – which will not be possible to address here.

25   Jonathan Hyslop, 'Gandhi 1869–1915: The Transnational Emergence of a Public Figure', in *The Cambridge Companion to Gandhi*, ed. Judith Brown and Anthony Parel (Cambridge: Cambridge University Press, 2011), 41. Gandhi and Kallenbach's trajectories grew into very different ones. Whether there was any link between the two is only speculative. Kallenbach, a German Jew, later came to be closely associated with the Zionist cause. See Bower, 'The Gandhian Ashram', 44–45.

26   Gandhi, *Ashram Observances*, 3.

27   Hyslop, 'Gandhi 1869–1915', 43.

28   Gandhi, *Ashram Observances*, 4.

29   Charles F. Andrews, ed., *Mahatma Gandhi at Work: His Own Story Continued* (London: George Allen and Unwin, 1931), 322.

30   Nandy, *Traditions, Tyranny and Utopias*, 141.

31   Tanika Sarkar, 'Gandhi and Social Relations', in *The Cambridge Companion to Gandhi*, ed. Brown and Parel, 188.

32   Gandhi cut the long hair of two girl students in an effort to save them from sinful male gaze in the Tolstoy farm. Long hair made them vulnerable to sexualised abuse. Andrews, *Mahatma Gandhi at Work,* 325.

33   Such as Tagore's attraction to the Argentinian poet and litterateur Victoria Ocampo and Gandhi's with the political activist Sarala Devi Chaudharani (also Tagore's niece).

34   As, for instance, Tagore's muse Ranu Mukherjee, a young student of his ashram. Ranu Mukherjee wrote long letters full of romantic longing and pain to Tagore. Letters from Ranu Adhikari to Tagore and Leonard K. Elmhirst, 1924, Dartington Hall Trust Papers. The Bengali author Sunil Gangopadhyay fictionalised their relationship in his novel *Rānu o Bhānu* (Kolkata: Ananda Publishers, 2001).

35   Abha and Manu Gandhi, with whom Gandhi used to sleep naked. The women themselves never raised any concerns about his behaviour or allegations of sexual misconduct. However, there was fierce competition for Gandhi's

attention among ashram women of all ages, as between a guru and his women disciples. See Sudhir Kakar, *Intimate Relations: Exploring Indian Sexuality* (Gurugram: Penguin, 1990), 108–110.

36   Rabindranath Tagore, 'The Problem of Education', *Towards Universal Man* (1906), in *The Oxford India Tagore: Selected Writings on Education and Nationalism,* ed. Uma Dasgupta (Oxford; Delhi: Oxford University Press, 2009), 112.

37   For a discussion on missionary education in India during this time, see Hayden J. A. Bellenoit, 'Missionary Education, Religion and Knowledge in India, c. 1880–1915', *Modern Asian Studies* 41, no. 2 (2007): 369–394.

38   Rabindranath Tagore, 'Tapovan', *Tagore Web*, http://www.tagoreweb.in/ (accessed on 20 October 2018), 10.

39   Rabindranath Tagore, 'Ashramer Roop o Bikash-1', *Tagore Web*, 1.

40   Rabindranath Tagore, 'Ashramer Roop o Bikash-3', *Tagore Web*, 4.

41   Tagore's father Debendranath had advocated a return of the Brahmo Samaj to a more conservative form of Brahminical Hinduism.

42   Rajarshi Chunder, 'Tagore and Caste: From Brahmacharyasram to Swadeshi Movement (1901–07)', https://www.sahapedia.org/tagore-and-caste-brahmacharyasram-swadeshi-movement-1901%E2%80%9307 (accessed on 30 January 2019). Though the ashram had three Christian teachers (high-caste Hindu converts) at the very beginning, including Brahma Bandhab Upadhyay.

43   It was not until Gandhi's visit and intervention in the Shantiniketan ashram that inter-caste dining was allowed in 1915. However, a Brahmin-line continued during meal hours for students who wanted it. For Tagore, forcing them to not follow caste practices amounted to an imposition from above. See Uma Dasgupta, *Rabindranath Tagore: An Illustrated Life* (Delhi: Oxford University Press, 2013), 69.

44   V. Balgangadhara Menon, V. Gopala Reddy and Mrinalini Sarabhai, students who came from staunchly nationalist backgrounds, attest that their 'nationalist commitments were not hampered' but found new cultural expression in Shantiniketan. Uma Dasgupta, 'In Pursuit of a Different Freedom: Tagore's World University at Santiniketan', in 'India: A National Culture?', special issue, *India International Centre Quarterly* 29, nos. 3/4 (Winter 2002–Spring 2003): 34–35.

45   Shivani, 'Anek Bibhutiyon Ka Agaman', in *Amader Shantiniketan* (Delhi: Rajkamal, 2007), 56.

46   Skaria, 'Gandhi's Politics', 212. Belief in the 'universal' of civilisation is typical to almost all Indian (as well as non-Indian) thinkers including Gandhi, Nehru, Ambedkar and Tagore, among others.

47 Hence, the ancient *tapovan* life was not merely circumstantial living in the forest, but a matter of enlightened and conscious choice. He illustrates this difference with living in the African forest, 'where to stay in nature was borne by ignorance'. Rabindranath Tagore, 'Tapovan', *Tagore Web*, 9. Merze Tate was the first African-American woman to have visited Shantiniketan, a decade after Tagore's death and under Rathindranath's tenure. She participated in the pedagogical experiments there in 1950–1951. See Katharina Rietzier, 'Merze Tate and Women's International Thought', https://blogs.sussex.ac.uk/whit/2018/12/05/toward-a-history-of-womens-international-thought/ (accessed on 15 May 2019).

48 Uma Dasgupta, *A History of Sriniketan: Rabindranath Tagore's Pioneering Work in Rural Reconstruction* (New Delhi: Niyogi Books, 2022).

49 Mira to Gandhi, 6 January 1929, Suhrud and Weber, *Beloved Bapu*, 166.

50 Rathindranath Tagore, *On the Edges of Time* (Calcutta: Orient Longman, 1958), 53. Debendranath Tagore had explicitly forbade consumption of meat in the ashram premises. Though a major financial consideration, vegetarianism was idealised, if only to normalise and render its ease in implementing.

51 Though Tucci, an Italian visiting scholar, writes: 'They say that in Santiniketan there is freedom and Ananda [bliss]. Ananda may be, but certainly no freedom; if somebody wishes to speak frankly, he is very often compelled to go.' Andrew Robinson and Krishna Dutta, *Rabindranath Tagore: The Myriad Minded Man* (London: Bloomsbury, 2009), 276.

52 William W. Pearson, *Shantiniketan: The Bolpur School of Rabindranath Tagore* (New York: MacMillan, 2007), 32.

53 Andrews to Tagore, 1 September 1913.

54 Behn, *The Spirit's Pilgrimage*, 71.

55 Lakshmi Subramanian, 'Music for the Congregation: Assembling an Aesthetic for Prayer', in 'Gandhi and Aesthetics', ed. Tridip Suhrud, special issue, *Marg* 71, no. 2 (December 2019): 38–41.

56 Halide Edib, *Inside India* (London: Oxford University Press, 1937), 276.

57 Peter Scriver and Amit Srivastava, *India: Modern Architectures in History* (Glasgow: Reaktion, 2015), 92–93.

58 Ibid., 93.

59 C. F. Andrews, 'The Indigenous Character of Our Work' (Paper presented at National Missionary Society Conference, 12 April 1912), cited in Donald Fossett Ebright, 'The National Missionary Society of India, 1905–1942:

An Expression of the Movement Toward Indigenization within the Indian Christian Community' (PhD thesis, Chicago, Fraser–Tagore Collection, University of Edinburgh, 1944), 147.

60 C. F. Andrews, *Sandhya Meditations at the Christukula Ashram* (Madras: Natesan, 1940).

61 *Young Men of India*, December 1910, 25. In a rather programmatic missionary statement Andrews etches this out:

> ... a body of spiritual Christian men eminently fitted by learning and temperament to pursue a life of study and contemplation, to be like swamis and Paramhansas, fitted to set a new standard of Christian holiness which shall appeal to the New India of the future. Such men would have a mission to Indian Christians as well as non-Christians.

62 Pearson to Tagore, 17 December 1912. Italicised words transliterated in English from their Bangla originals.

63 Andrews to Tagore, 20 December 1912.

64 Andrews to Munshi Ram, n.d., Daniel O'Connor, *The Testimony of C. F. Andrews* (Madras: Christian Literature Society, 1974), 114.

65 Pearson, *Shantiniketan*, 32.

66 Pearson to Tagore, 17 December 1912. Shakuntala is the protagonist of the ancient Indian poet Kalidasa's play *Abhijnana Shakuntalam*, the same poet who inspired Tagore's visions about a *tapovan*-style modern ashram.

67 Andrews to Tagore, 8 March 1913.

68 Pearson to Tagore, 6 May 1913.

69 Andrews to Tagore, 15 May 1913.

70 Andrews to Tagore, 8 March 1913.

71 Andrews to Tagore, 29 May 1913.

72 Ibid.

73 Andrews to Mahatma Gandhi, 13 April [1914?].

74 Andrews to Tagore, 1 September 1913.

75 Pearson to Tagore, 30 July 1913.

76 Pearson to Ajit [?], 8 October 1913, Delhi, Folder 287 (iv), Pearson Misc.

77 There were, of course, very real limits to this. Students of the ashram had to pay the price of its utopia. They had to face the struggles of higher education and jobs after a certain age. Shantiniketan was not taken seriously as a proper educational institution and its students often had to experience the stiff competition that characterised college education and job markets. See Sudhiranjan Das, *Amader Shantiniketan* (Calcutta: Visvabharati 1959), 104–106.

78 Tagore, *On the Edges of Time*, 154. Almost against himself, he sought affiliation with the University of Calcutta in 1926, yielding to the demands of his students who found it difficult to find employment outside without a proper 'degree'.

79 Behn, *The Spirit's Pilgrimage*, 40.

80 Ibid., 46–47.

81 Madeleine Slade to Gandhi, 29 May 1925, Suhrud and Weber, *Beloved Bapu*, 12.

82 14 September 1925, Rolland, *Inde*.

83 A high point in Gandhian mass mobilisation, Chauri Chaura also represented its tragedy. Following clashes between non-cooperation protestors and the police, the former set fire to a police station, killing twenty-two policemen. The colonial government retaliated sharply, sentencing nineteen demonstrators to death, and a further fourteen to life imprisonment.

84 Rolland, *Mahatma Gandhi*.

85 14 September 1925, Rolland, *Inde*, 100–101.

86 Rajmohan Gandhi, *Mohandas: A True Story of a Man, His People, and an Empire* (Delhi: Penguin Books, 2006), 192.

87 Thomson, *Gandhi and His Ashrams*, 107.

88 Romain Rolland, Extracts from Romain Rolland's Diary, September 1925, in *Romain Rolland and Gandhi Correspondences* (Delhi: Ministry of Information and Broadcasting, 1976), 48.

89 Gandhi to Slade, 24 July 1925, 12–13.

90 Behn, *The Spirit's Pilgrimage*, 66 (emphasis added).

91 Ibid., 75. Though he popularised calling Tagore 'Gurudev'.

92 Madeleine Slade to Romain Rolland, 12 November 1925, *Romain Rolland and Gandhi Correspondences*, 50.

93 Behn, *The Spirit's Pilgrimage*, 70.

94 Ibid., 71.

95 Gandhi to Rolland, 13 November 1925, Suhrud and Weber, *Beloved Bapu*.

96 Behn, *The Spirit's Pilgrimage*, 67.

97 Mahadev Desai, 'Our Time a Trust', *Young India*, 26 November 1925, *CWMG*, vol. 33, 260.

98 A 1928 letter from Mira to Desai shows her giving basic French lessons: 'As I know you like to get in a French lesson wherever possible – rue means road; sur means on, pris means near.' Mira to Mahadev Desai, 16 October 1928, Sabarmati Ashram Archives.

99 Notes on Interview with Winston Churchill, 2 November 1934, Writings by Mira Behn, Sl No. 2, Mira Behn Papers, Nehru Memorial Museum and Library (NMML).

100 Mira to [Gandhi?], 17 July 1942, on her meeting with Laithwaite, Secretary to the Viceroy, Mira Behn Correspondence with Lord Halifax (Linlithgow), 5th Instalment, NMML.

101 Mira to Lord Linlithgow, 16 July 1942, Birla House, New Delhi.

102 Gandhi, 'A Silence Day Note', [On or before 24 November 1925], *CWMG*, vol. 33, 247.

103 Gandhi to Mira, 28 February 1927, Suhrud and Weber, *Beloved Bapu*, 39.

104 Rolland, *Inde*, 385.

105 Ibid., 385.

106 Andrews to Tagore, January 1914.

107 Mira to Mme Rolland, 10 September 1928, Rolland, *Inde*, 230–231.

108 20 April 1938, Diary No. 3, Mira Behn Papers, VI inst, Acc. No. 1552, Nehru Memorial Museum and Library, Delhi.

109 Diary No. 4: Daily Notes – 25 August 1938 to 19 September 1938, 6.

110 13 August 1938, Diary No. 3, Mira Behn Papers.

111 Andrews to Gandhi, 5 April 1914, Folder 21, Letters from Andrews to Gandhi (1914–1933), CFA Papers; File 1–26, 28 (ii), RBVB-018, CD.

112 Mira to Rolland, 17 February 1932, *Romain Rolland and Gandhi Correspondences*, 258.

113 Political prisoners in British India were classified into A, B and C types, though this was not necessarily based on the magnitude of crime. C-class cells were reputed to have the worst facilities and food, and generally suggested a punitive edge shown to particular prisoners.

114 Behn, *The Spirit's Pilgrimage*, 156–158.

115 Pearson wrote a pamphlet *For India* while in Yokohama, Japan, severely criticising British rule, exploited by the Japanese propaganda machine.

116 *Democrat*, 11 August 1923, cited in Tinker, *The Ordeal of Love*, 203.

117 Leonard Elmhirst, *Poet and Plowman* (Calcutta: Visvabharati, 1975), 147.

118 Pearson to Elmhirst [undated, seems that the memo-like letter was sent by hand when they lived in the close vicinity of the ashram or between Sriniketan and Shantiniketan, 1922?].

119 Elmhirst, *Poet and Plowman*, 67.

120 Leonard K. Elmhirst, LKE Notes and Articles, Dartington Hall Records, LKE/TAG/3/B, 12–13.

121 Pramathanath Bishi, 'Andrews O Pearson', in *Rabindranath o`Shantiniketan* (Calcutta: Visvabharati, 1944), 88–89. Translation from Bengali by author.

122 Bishi, *Rabindranath o Shantiniketan*, 90.

123 Tagore, *On the Edges of Time*, 101.

124 Tagore to Pearson, 15 May 1922, Santiniketan, Folder 287(i), Letters from Tagore to Pearson.

125 Voting Paper for Election of 7 ordinary members of the Sansad/Governing Body, Roll_00025_File_No_237_A, 1926, PA_Microfilm, National Archives of India, Digitized Private Papers, M. R. Jayakar.

126 Urmila Devi, 'Winstanley Pearson', *Pearson Smriti* (Calcutta, 1923), 14, Folder 287 (viii), Rabindra Bhavan.

127 Dorothy Pearson to Leonard Elmhirst, 10 October 1923 [after Pearson's death].

128 Thompson, *Alien Homage*, 113.

129 Bishi, *Rabindranath o Shantiniketan*, 90.

130 Ibid., 89–91.

131 Butler to Waller, 9 July 1914, Tinker, *The Ordeal of Love*, 95.

132 Leonard K. Elmhirst, Notes and Articles, Dartington Hall Records, LKE/ TAG/3/B, 12–13.

133 The Pous Utsav or Winter Festival, celebrated in Shantiniketan to mark the coming together of the ashram community and villagers from the adjacent tribal areas. *Visvabharati News*, vol. 3, December 1934, Roll_00025_File_ No_237_B, 1935, PA_Microfilm, Digitized Private Papers M. R. Jayakar.

134 *Visvabharati News*, [February?] 1935, 50, Roll_00025_File_No_237_B, 1935, PA_Microfilm.

135 Pearson, *Shantiniketan*.

136 The adjacent Sriniketan project foregrounded the caste aspect more strongly in its interventions. Outcaste families were not only enumerated, but their social, cultural and economic habits also formed a part of its studies. See for instance Kalimohan Ghosh, ed., *Rural Survey: Ballabhpur* (Sriniketan: Visvabharati, 1926). This survey report is reproduced in full as an appendix in Dasgupta, *A History of Sriniketan*.

137 C. F. Andrews, 'My Gurudeva', *Visvabharati News*, vol. 4, May and June 1936, nos. 11 and 12, 88, Roll_00025_File_No_237_B, 1935, PA_Microfilm.

138 Behn, *The Spirit's Pilgrimage*, 69–70.

139 Ibid., 71.

140 Mira to Gandhi, 1 November 1928, Suhrud and Weber, *Beloved Bapu,* 140.

141 Behn, *The Spirit's Pilgrimage*, 80.

142 Mira to Gandhi, 21 October 1928, 126.

143 Gandhi to Esther Menon, 8 August 1926, *CWMG*, vol. 36, 182.

144 Gandhi to Kasturba, 7 December 1933, *CWMG*, vol. 36.

145   Gandhi to Mira, 24 June 1931, Suhrud and Weber, *Beloved Bapu*, 290.

146   Gandhi to Mira, 2 Oct 1927, Suhrud and Weber, *Beloved Bapu*, 97.

147   Rolland, *Inde*, 385.

148   Gandhi to Mira, 9 December 1926, Suhrud and Weber, *Beloved Bapu*, 28.

149   Gandhi assured that she could, as long as she did not eat it, clarifying that 'applying is not eating'. Gandhi to Mira, 15 October 1926, *CWMG*, vol. 36, 408.

150   Mira to Gandhi, 21 October 1928, *Beloved Bapu*, 126.

151   Edib, *Inside India*, 69.

152   Ibid., 276.

153   Behn, *The Spirit's Pilgrimage*, 194.

154   Mahatma Gandhi, Letter to Ashram Women, 13 December 1926, *CWMG*, vol. 32, 438.

155   Gandhi to Maganlal Gandhi, 20 December 1926, 423.

156   Ibid., 439.

157   Gandhi to Mira, 24 January 1927.

158   Cannabis-laden drink, often consumed by religious devotees to produce euphoric effects.

159   Behn, *The Spirit's Pilgrimage*, 95.

160   Mira to Gandhi, 27 May 1927, Behn, *The Spirit's Pilgrimage*, 59.

161   Gandhi to Mira, 3 June 1927, Behn, *The Spirit's Pilgrimage*, 65.

162   Behn, *The Spirit's Pilgrimage*, 88.

163   Gandhi to Mira, 22 March 1927, Suhrud and Weber, *Beloved Bapu*, 42–43.

164   Gandhi to Mira, 13 April 1927, Suhrud and Weber, *Beloved Bapu*, 46.

165   Gandhi to Mira, 25 April 1927, Suhrud and Weber, *Beloved Bapu*, 47.

166   Rothenstein to Edward J. Thompson, 18 May 1932.

167   His biography of Tagore: Edward J. Thompson, *Rabindranath Tagore: His Life and Work* (London: Association Press, 1921). Tagore thought it was a one of the most 'ridiculous' books ever written on a poet's life.

168   Edward J. Thompson's Notebook, Conversations with Tagore Transcript, 6, E. J. Thompson Papers, MS. Eng. C. 5328-9, Bodleian. The Tagore scholar Uma Dasgupta has transcribed this interview in the appendix of E. P. Thompson's *Alien Homage*. Among other observations, Thompson notes that Tagore had scruples about Brahmins being ridiculed, that came up when discussing the Bengali novelist Saratchandra Chattopadhyay's works (himself a Brahmin), often sharp parodies of Brahminism (Thompson, *Alien Homage*, 6–7).

169   Tagore to Thompson, 18 February 1914, Edward J. Thompson, General Correspondence – Tagore, E. J. Thompson Papers, MS. Eng. C 5318, Fols 1–40.

170 Thompson to Canton, 14 August 1917, Thompson, *Alien Homage*, 33.

171 Thompson, *Alien Homage*, 33.

172 William Rothenstein to Edward J. Thompson, 1 June 1932, MS. Eng. C 5311, E. J. Thompson, General Correspondence – Rothenstein-Rust.

173 Andrews to E. J. Thompson, 26 March 1921, E. J. Thompson Papers, General Correspondence – Abbott – Bayley, MS. Eng. C 5273.

174 Tagore to E. J. Thompson, 17 November 1920: 'Can you take up "Gora" yourself or find some competent person who can undertake to translate it?' Thompson Papers, MS. Eng. C 5318, fol. 112.

175 See Pearson to Tagore, 15 June 1922, Folder 287(ii), Letters from William W. Pearson to Rabindranath Tagore, where he cautions against abridging his translation of *Gora* for the sake of foreign readers.

176 When the first two volumes of Tagore's short stories were published in English translation, *Hungry Stones and Other Stories* (1916) and *Mashi and Other Stories* (1918), only Andrews was alone acknowledged as the translator of seven stories; Thompson was mentioned as having assisted in the work. The latter took it badly, and the next time Tagore sought Thompson's translations, he promptly refused. See Uma Dasgupta, ed., *A Difficult Friendship: Letters of Edward Thompson and Rabindranath Tagore, 1913–1940* (Delhi: Oxford University Press, 2003), 19.

177 Thompson to Rothenstein, 14 May 1932, MS. Eng. C 5311, E. J. Thompson, General Correspondence – Rothenstein-Rust.

178 This seems to have created a rumour that Andrews ghost-wrote some of Tagore's translations. Tagore was on the defensive when such allegations reached his ears: 'There are people who suspect that I owe in a large measure to Andrews' help for my literary success, which is so false that I can afford to laugh at it.' Tagore to Rothenstein, 4 April 1915.

179 Andrews to Thompson, 26 March 1921.

180 Pearson to Tagore, 15 June 1922.

181 Ibid.

182 Rahul Ramagundam, *Gandhi's Khadi: A History of Contention and Conciliation* (Delhi: Orient Blackswan, 2008), 7.

183 M. K. Gandhi, 'Speech to Students', Dimapur, 21 May 1925, *CWMG*, vol. 27 (1925), 141.

184 Behn, *The Spirit's Pilgrimage*, 80.

185 Mira to Gandhi, 13 November 1928, 151.

186 Mira to Brother [?], 28 April 1929, Chhatwan, Sabarmati Ashram Archives.

187 Mira to Gandhi, 4 November 1928, 143.

188 Behn, *The Spirit's Pilgrimage*, 92.

189 Sudhir Kakar, *Mira and the Mahatma* (Delhi: Penguin, 2005).

190 Tagore to Pearson, 13 December 1920, Folder 287 (i).

191 Matteo Mazzamurro assures me that 'southerners' here indicate Italians and possibly the Spanish.

192 September 1923, Rolland, *Inde*, 47.

193 Tagore to Pearson, 16 May 1915, Folder 287(i), Letters from Tagore to Pearson, Rabindra Bhavan Archives.

194 Tagore to Romain Rolland, 21 February 1924, March 1924, Rolland, *Inde*, 60.

195 Anna Neima notes this insightfully in her chapter on Shantiniketan, 'Life in Its Completeness', in *The Utopians*, 41.

196 Rolland, *Inde*, 49.

197 Ibid., 342.

198 Ibid., 342.

199 Notes on interview with Lord Halifax, 1 November 1934, Writings by Her, S. No. 1, Mira Behn Papers, NMML.

200 Andrews to Pearson, 22 February 1921.

201 Elmhirst, Notes and Articles, Dartington Hall Records, LKE/TAG/3/B, 11.

202 Elmhirst, *Poet and Plowman*, 118.

203 See Sabyasachi Bhattacharya, ed., *The Mahatma and the Poet: Letters and Debates Between Gandhi and Tagore, 1915–1941* (Delhi: NBT, 1997).

204 LKE Notes and Articles, Dartington Hall Records, LKE/TAG/3/B, 12.

205 Andrews to Rolland, 22 March 1924, Rolland, *Inde*, 65.

206 Mira to Rajkumari Amrit Kaur, 15 September 1937, Sabarmati. The letter was dictated by Gandhi to Mira. A few lines were scribbled at the bottom of the same letter by Mahadev Desai. Multiple authorship was not uncommon in Gandhi's letters to his disciples, often for the sake of convenience.

207 Mira to Gandhi, 29 October 1928, 136.

208 Mira to Gandhi, [?] January 1930, 167.

209 Mira to Gandhi, 2 November 1928, 142.

210 Mira to Chhaganlal Joshi, 5 December 1928, Sabarmati Ashram Archives.

211 Gandhi to Mira, 20 April 1933, 364.

212 Venugopal Maddipati, 'Architecture as Weak Thought: Gandhi Inhabits Nothingness', *Marg* 71, no. 2 (December 2019): 45.

213 Tridip Suhrud and Thomas Weber, 'A New Ashram and New Problems', in *Beloved Bapu*, 409.

214 M. K. Gandhi, 'We Are All One', *Navajivan*, *CWMG*, vol. 43 (16 March 1930), 82.

215 Dorothy Pearson, 'Willie Pearson's Last Days, before His Death in Pistoia, Italy', Folder 287 (viii), RBVB.

216 Thompson to Tagore, 15 November 1935, Dasgupta, *A Difficult Friendship*, 194.

217 Gandhi to Jamnalal Bajaj, 21 May 1936, Krishna M. Gupta, *Mira Behn: Gandhiji's Daughter Disciple, Birth Centenary Volume* (New Delhi: Himalaya Seva Sangh, 1992), 10.

CHAPTER 3

India, Indophiles and Indenture

Cultural Politics of a Transnational Discourse, 1911–1931

This chapter examines how indenture became a site for Western disciples to merge their ideologies and intimacies, cultivated around the guru-figures of Gandhi, Gokhale and Tagore. It focuses primarily on the doings of three individuals in the campaign against indenture: the English-born Jewish lawyer/journalist Henry Polak, and the English missionaries C. F. Andrews and William Pearson. Inspired by their mentors, Western Indophile engagements with indenture affirmed their conviction to create a more egalitarian empire. At the same time, these relationships enacted notions of race, caste, class and gender as integral to the politics of respectability that preoccupied Indian nationalist discourse. Western Indophiles became useful interlocutors to ventriloquise nationalist priorities and their divergent trajectories.[1] This is not to argue that Indophiles wilfully participated in a hegemonic schema designed by a cross-section of the Indian nationalist elite, but rather to underline that such politics and practices had distinct exclusionary effects, particularly for marginalised groups like Dalit women (and men) migrating to indentured colonies.

Introduction

The history of indenture is well-charted territory.[2] The abolition of slavery across the British Empire in 1834 witnessed a massive surge in the demand for cheap labour. This was supplied from the Indian subcontinent, China and West Africa. Between 1834 and 1860, the British consensus for indenture was justified in the name of anti-slavery and free trade.[3] This consensus posited indenture as civilising 'primitive' Indian labour and rescuing them from a life of poverty and caste atrocities. Liberal economic and demographic theories were invoked to argue that the supposed failures of slave emancipation could be corrected through the system of indenture.[4] Indentured labour became a synonym for 'free labour', pitted against the unjustness of slave or 'unfree' labour. The scale of this regulated labour regime was vast, spreading rapidly across different imperial colonies.

Indian indentured labour was well integrated within this globally expanding labour market.[5] Supplied through a system of recruiters, middlemen and government agents, labour from colonial India was eagerly sought by planters across the Indian Ocean littoral, starting with Mauritius, Fiji and South Africa, spreading significantly by the latter decades of the nineteenth century to East Africa. Recruited mostly from labour-surplus rural Indian provinces, particularly the United Provinces and Bihar, more than 3 million Indians emigrated as indentured labourers between 1834 and 1920 to work in British, French, Dutch and Portuguese colonies. They were hired through a system of debt bondage and shipped from Indian ports in Calcutta, Bombay and Madras to work on plantations, primarily sugar, but also coffee, railways and other industries. An elaborate chain of recruiting agents liaised between various government institutions in India and European planters. Exploitative and fraudulent practices were rife in recruitment. Shipboard mortality was high, even though successive Emigration Commissions sought to exercise a degree of government control in the selection of immigrants.[6] Historical opinion differs on whether coolies were mere victims of an oppressive labour regime[7] or sought (and often found) better lives through work overseas. Outcaste and tribal communities constituted a major share of emigrating labourers, often desirable as they had fewer injunctions on travel and food than upper-caste Hindus. Lower-caste women also emigrated in substantial numbers, often seeking to escape the harshness of the marital home or better opportunities for work.[8]

The historian Adam McKeown has argued that overall Asian labour migration experiences to sites of plantation, mining and industrial capitalism were at par with European labour migrations, subject to comparable forms of coercive regulation and contract regimes.[9] Yet, this ignores the sharp racial hierarchies that generally determined the difference in experiences of imperial migration. Ethnic British migration, even with its internal stratifications, to the 'British World', was not the same as Indian or Chinese labour migration to that world.[10]

Indenture and Its Wider Context

Settler colonies like South Africa, New Zealand and Australia hired indentured labourers extensively. Interlinked to the indentured movement was also the steady emigration of mercantile and artisanal communities from India's Western seaboard. They took the advantages afforded by British imperial expansion and contributed to the opening of internal and external trade between various parts of the Indian Ocean world. These gradually expanded to lower-level bureaucrats and administrative staff in which Indian presence increased from the early 1900s.[11]

The introduction of a significant community of Indians – indentured and non-indentured – in British African colonies posed a major problematic in the racial ordering of difference. Indians were preferred by white planters over Afro-Caribbean workers, the former deemed more pliant and suitable as cheap agricultural labour.[12] However, Indians threatened to destabilise the binarised status quo of 'native Africans' and 'settler Europeans'.[13] Neither white European nor native African, existing racial categories struggled to accommodate their intermedial identity. The co-existence of a relatively affluent, mercantile class of Indians alongside poor indentured labourers further complicated this identity work.[14] The figure of the unsanitary Indian 'coolie' became a conflated cultural marker to signify both ends of a diverse community.[15] In white settler discourse, this became a precipitating node against any kind of Indian immigration. Indian nationalist discourse came to castigate indentured migration as a source of 'moral evil', impeding the free and equal mobility of respectable Indians within the empire.

The conjoining of Indophiles and indenture is distinctive for several reasons. As European men, they were particularly well positioned to comprehend and embody the privileges that 'imperial' endowed on white subjects.[16] Indians, educated or not, did not escape the stigma of racial inferiority or move freely like Andrews, Polak or Pearson across all parts of the British Empire. Indenture exposed the inequality of imperial citizenship few discourses in India had before. Spectres of Indian honour being at stake haunted Indian leaders like

Gopal Krishna Gokhale, an early representative of the abolitionist cause in the Indian National Congress.[17] Indophile critique resonated with nationalist anxieties around the way India and Indians were perceived abroad. Indophile figures became embroiled in mobilising against indenture, and after abolition, articulated the right of respectable Indians to free imperial emigration, while repatriating indentured labourers from various plantations. Indophile interlocution of indentured migration drew deeply from an earlier generation of abolitionist arguments, couched in a language of humanitarian appeal.[18]

Andrews's and Pearson's increasing involvement with the anti-indenture movement coincided with their own self-transformations via personal encounters with Gandhi, Tagore and their ashram communes. Andrews gives a sense of this overlap when soliciting Gandhi's advice on his choice of work:

i) I can stay on in India and possibly visit the Punjab and above all get some real writing done

ii) If we are of real need I could visit South Africa

iii) I could pay my provincial visit to Malaya and tackle the labour problems there

But what would you wish?[19]

A skilled lobbyist, Gandhi believed Andrews was particularly suited to address the issues of overseas Indian settlements. Almost all major commissions, reports and papers referenced and/or involved Andrews, Polak and Pearson in deliberating issues arising out of indentured migration.[20] This was hardly a coincidence. From 1913 to 1917, Andrews, Polak and Pearson's incessant lobbying and propagandising helped abolish the system of indenture. This consensus was then harnessed to support free imperial emigration for respectable Indians – predominantly upper-caste Hindus engaged in middle-class professions – representing and restoring Indian 'honour' abroad. Culture talk often masked the intense economic rivalry between Indian and European businesses. Racialised legislation provided an important foil to prevent Indian settlers from overtaking European economic interests, especially in South Africa.

Gandhi and South Africa

The gradual emergence of an autonomous Dominion government in 1909, under the Union of South Africa, represented a key moment in consolidating a unified white identity after the Anglo-Boer wars. Nationalising white settler dominions into self-governing polities was increasingly a way to control the imperial mobility of non-white populations.[21] The opposition to Indian entry into South Africa exemplified this move.

As a lawyer, Gandhi had been involved in opposing discriminatory legislation passed by the Natal government since the 1890s. While representing both indentured and non-indentured Indians (comprising Hindu and Muslim communities), he, however, argued for controlled immigration:

> British Indians do not desire an indiscriminate influx of their countrymen into the Transvaal ... by a judicious administration of the Immigration Act, all but a few – say six highly educated Indians per year – may be prevented from entering the colony.[22]

The trope of the 'highly educated Indian' featured prominently in middle-class Indian representations on imperial emigration, prompted in response to white settler stereotypes of the 'uncultured and unsanitary Indian'. They constructed the indentured coolie as the undesirable emigrant, arguing that the disabling provisions that applied to 'coolies' should not be applicable to 'respectable' Indians.[23]

Gandhi's first commune experiments – Tolstoy Farm and Phoenix Settlement – provided key bases for his activities. His associate and follower Henry Polak close-lived with him since 1906. Polak left his well-paid legal career to take up the editorship of Gandhi's *Indian Opinion*. Both Polak and his wife Millie shared Gandhi's household in Durban and Johannesburg. Gandhi assumed the role of his 'elder brother' and served as his best man. At his wedding, Polak referred to himself and his circle of Indian associates as 'we Indians', causing the registry office to withhold his wedding, pending enquiries about whether it was a mixed marriage.[24]

Together, they later launched the Phoenix settlement, one of Gandhi's earliest experiments in community living. Gandhi wrote comforting letters to Millie when Polak felt upset:

Henry is a tender flower. The slightest breeze ruffles his spirits. You and I divide him. When he is in such a mood, you can make him happy and to a lesser degree I. But alas! He can just now have neither you nor me.[25]

Polak canvassed wide support against discriminatory legislation introduced by the South African government. In 1909, he published his first pamphlet on the issue: *The Indians of South Africa: Helots within the Empire and How They Are Treated*, observing that 'the real Indian nation [was] being hammered out in South Africa'.[26] Gandhi sent him to plead support for South African Indians with Gokhale and the Indian National Congress. His knowledge, Gandhi believed, 'of the different questions affecting British Indian settlers and Asiatic legislation ... is almost unrivalled'. Polak's public campaigning in India for thirteen months, with the help of the Servants of India Society (founded by Gokhale) in 1909, imploring moral and material support for Gandhi's movement, was hugely successful. At Gokhale's behest, the Congress passed a resolution supporting the Indian struggle in South Africa at its Lahore session in 1909.

For the first time, South African Indian grievances became a 'central feature of the session', particularly their disenfranchisement and prohibitions against property ownership in Natal.[27] The appointment of a new liberal viceroy, Lord Charles Hardinge – who was sympathetic to the Indian cause in South Africa – greatly strengthened the nationalist campaign led by Gokhale. In growing recognition of the South African Indian problem, Gokhale himself visited Natal in October 1912, meeting prominent white South African politicians and ministers to push for a repeal of discriminatory laws.

In essays written throughout the 1900s, Gokhale, a formidable liberal nationalist and a firm believer in constitutional methods, appealed to the 'righteous' conscience of the British: 'The bitter mockery of the assertion that we are British subjects ... was never made plainer than by this Natal business.'[28] Gokhale had returned on an optimistic note, assured by the Union Government of their desire to abolish indenture and other discriminatory laws. Instead, the Immigration Regulation Bill that limited indentured immigration to South Africa was passed in 1913. Gandhi sought help from Gokhale and the Indian National Congress. Gokhale asked Andrews; the latter roped in Pearson and both visited South Africa as personal envoys to help broker truce.[29]

Andrews and Pearson had by then already come under the charismatic influence of Tagore. They were eager to prove their self-worth to be able to serve in his idyllic ashram at Shantiniketan. Both saw this as an opportunity to build their relationship with Tagore and his ashram, while gradually distancing themselves from their missionary work. Pearson reflected:

> The very thought that I go to South Africa as a messenger from the ashram will strengthen me and help me to mend the broken threads of my life's purposes in that service of love.
>
> All through our voyage my chief endeavour will be to preserve the peace and quietness of mind which came to me in such full measure during my stay with you [Tagore].[30]

Neither of them had joined Shantiniketan formally, yet they already conceived themselves as 'messengers of the ashram'. Offering their services for the Indian cause in South Africa was a 'service of love' to mend the 'broken threads' of their lives.

As missionaries who found their own vocations morally limiting, the pull to serve a cause that bound them to India beyond the ashram was deeply affirmative. Andrews's Mission Secretary Dr Stanton dismissed the attention he received from Indian figures such as Tagore as 'mere selfish bias' and pointed out that he was 'being less than just to [his] own countrymen'.[31] Andrews feared being an outcast in missionary and Anglo-Indian circles but was desperate to liberate himself. Pearson, similarly, could not wait to finish his Baptist missionary engagement in Delhi, and be free to join Tagore's side fully, trying to 'give up thinking of the poverty and failures of [his] own life'.[32] Aboard the ship to visit indentured plantations, the men reminisced: the 'greatest time when we are tired is to talk about you and to turn our minds back to our home at Shantiniketan'.[33] Tagore and his ashram became an embodied memory that moved his disciples to embrace Indianist causes beyond India. From afar, Tagore affirmed: 'You know our best love was with you while you were fighting our cause in South Africa.'[34]

Andrews and Pearson reached South Africa in January 1914, when the movement was nearing final negotiations between General Smuts and Gandhi. Though Andrews believed their arrival was timed 'just when the deadlock was most critical',[35] Gandhi remembered it as a time when the 'worst was over'. Yet, in these brief two months, they managed to etch themselves firmly in South African Indian discourse. Andrews tended to overshadow Gandhi's longstanding associates Polak and Hermann Kallenbach, much to the latter's resentment. In summing up the three major causes that contributed to the elaborate defence of the anti-indenture bill in the Parliament, Gandhi accounted for Andrews' 'mission of love' as a major factor.[36] Gandhi understood the strategic value of white collaborators, even though this was not their only importance.

On their first encounter at the Durban port, Andrew had 'instinctively' touched Gandhi's feet. Andrews's letter to Tagore gives us a sense of the reactions it espoused:

> The struggle has begun and all the turmoil you expected and warned me about has already been realised. The English in Natal are far worse than the English in Calcutta. What was exercising them at present is the fact that I took the dust of Mr Gandhi's feet – the feet of an Asiatic – on landing. I am afraid I shall never be forgiven. They boil over with indignation that I, an Englishman, – an *Englishman* mind you! – should have touched the feet of an Asiatic.[37]

White South African opinion was scathing, his 'feet touching' was seen as race betrayal. He was ridiculed for socialising with Indian friends and warned not to 'do these things in this country' for the 'bad effect it ha[d] on the kaffirs!' Feeling stifled, Andrews was heartened to spot Tagore's book of poems *Gitanjali* in Durban that had recently won the Nobel in Literature:

> I cannot tell you what living water that was to my parched spirit! The whole aspect of life was changed in a moment and I took heart again! … I found that very many had been reading it. Those who had were enthusiastic and if ever I was able to strike a sympathetic note and get right past the racial barrier it was through your writings. And you know, I can be very enthusiastic when I begin to speak of them to you, and my enthusiasm carries conviction with it![38]

Excitedly, he conveyed to Tagore that talking about him made white listeners 'change wholly their view of India and Indians'.[39] Andrews preached at two cathedrals in Durban and Pretoria quoting from his poems. The sense of jubilation was momentary. His own belief in Christianity suffered a great blow when Gandhi and other Indians were not allowed to enter the church in Natal where he was invited to sermonise.[40] However, his sensational act of obeisance to Gandhi won him lasting popularity in Indian circles. Premised on the symbolic enactment of subservience, it evoked a powerful transgression. In almost every article that Gandhi wrote thereafter in the *Indian Opinion*, Andrews's name was invoked warmly. Gandhi appraisingly wrote of this interweaving of intimateness and official work: Andrews 'entirely lives the Indian life and loves to live among and with Indians. He had a two-hour interview (private) with the Governor-General [Botha] and he preached at the Cathedral here last Sunday.'[41] And again: 'Mr. Andrews is moving forward. He has got a wonderful grasp of the central position and he is pushing it forward with all the spiritual force he possesses.'[42]

At Andrews' insistence, Gandhi agreed to stay for a week at the Phoenix ashram with him.[43] Offering his son Manilal to accompany Andrews as secretary on his Natal tour, Gandhi advised that 'he should have no shame about doing any work for Mr. Andrews. You may even massage his calves; polish his shoes and tie up his laces.'[44] Having massaged Andrews's calves before, Gandhi found that he 'liked it'. The act of massage was rooted in meaningful reverential service. Some of Gandhi's fondest memories of his father involved massaging his legs every night shortly before his death. Indeed, his greatest regret was that he was not by his father's side 'massaging him' when he passed away, but in a 'grip of lust' towards his wife. Being deprived of the privilege of his father dying in his arms continued to haunt him long after his death, not insignificantly shaping his attitude to sex.[45]

Several of Gandhi's intimate relations with male associates (often but not exclusively white) border on the homoerotic. He considered himself Polak's second wife, for 'he would pour himself out only before' them.[46] A more intimate (and possibly romantic) relationship was struck between Gandhi and Herman Kallenbach, with whom Gandhi had jointly started the Tolstoy Farm, about the same time. Gandhi left his wife to live with him during this period, and despite earning comfortable incomes, both participated in shared strictures to lead simpler lives. As an earlier chapter on letters has shown, Gandhi didn't shy away from acknowledging the depth of this intimacy with Kallenbach.

Andrews's ability to identify with Indians rested significantly on the ease with which he could adopt their sartorial and culinary habits.

Gandhi remarked how Andrews 'dressed in dhoti' and 'is full of India'.[47] Pearson remained busy studying the conditions of indentured labourers away from the high political lobbying at Cape Town. He was far less in the political limelight than Andrews, what with the latter's penchant for lobbying. Gandhi thanked Gokhale for this deputation:

> Indians feel deeply grateful for deputation of Messrs Andrews and Pearson. Many Europeans, including Ministers, have expressed sincere satisfaction at the results of the visit. Mr. Andrews spread a spirit of sympathy and love all round and has contributed much towards speedy settlement.[48]

Gandhi was pleased with Andrews's 'wonderful work' and his 'main topic of conversation being always India and Tagore or the Indian question here'.[49] Munshi Ram, another Indian guru-figure whom Andrews adored, assured Andrews that his South African venture made him more popular:

> Your work in South Africa has endeared you to the Indian masses and I hope that you will in future have found opportunities of serving the motherland – for [have] you not become an adopted son of the land?[50]

Andrews derived great comfort in such intimations. It deepened his older affections and determined new ones. Though love for Gandhi did not come 'immediately, instinctively' as it had for Tagore, Andrews hoped [through] his 'overflowing love of India to find that love running freely between us'.[51] Love for Gandhi continued to grow and by the time he left South Africa:

> I have been thinking so much about you on this voyage – more even, I think, than on my voyage from the Cape. It is the coming closer to India that brings me even closer to you.... I do so long to keep very close to you and now I feel I shall. You have been with me, drawing nearer to me, not receding from me, during all these weeks of absence, and this has taken place amid distractions and anxieties which might have taken me from you, if our love had not taken deep root. What I have known and felt is that your love has brought me really closer to you, in your absence or in your presence, for I have quite constantly turned to you in spirit ... and I have quite constantly clung to you in times of anxiety and trouble.[52]

'Coming closer' to Gandhi was coming closer to India. Within months, Andrews and Gandhi had become Charlie and Mohan, and their intimacy matured:

> ... you have been to me in South Africa what no one else ever could be and are now a part of my life as Mahatmaji and Gurudev ... are – and when I saw you on the wharf standing with hands raised in prayer and benediction I know as I had not known, even in Pretoria how very very dear you had become to me. And I gazed and gazed and the sadness grew up in me and even the thought that I was on my way to India could not overcome it.

> Somehow I did not quite know how much you had learnt to love me till that morning when you put your hand on my shoulder and spoke of the loneliness that there would be to you ... and when again you told me you had kept those hurried letters I had sent you – then I knew....[53]

Through letters, Andrews could imagine Gandhi's hand on his shoulder and experience his love and loss. The conceptual unity that bound Andrews's love for India with Tagore, Gokhale, Munshi Ram and others now embraced Gandhi and his causes too as part of the same imaginary. Andrews and Polak continued to be involved in the abolition/emigration cause, especially after Gandhi left South Africa to enter Indian politics permanently.

Representing 'Indian Honour'

Andrews's many lectures on Tagore, some published in major dailies such as 'Cape Times', emphasised how 'the personality of Tagore was' an example of how 'India had developed perhaps far above other parts of the British empire in civilisation and efforts to attain higher life'.[54] This evocation of a 'real', exalted and enlightened India, exemplified through personalities such as Tagore, Gokhale or Gandhi, was a common contrasting rhetoric when countering the stigma of 'coolie labour'.

Indians engaged in medical, legal, clerical or mercantile professions resented the 'coolie' stereotype. Polak lamented, in his 1909 book on *The Indians of South Africa* that the great Indian languages, with their wonderful literatures, are not recognised; and thus a learned pundit, deeply versed in Sanskrit and the profound philosophy of his race, but possessing no knowledge of English or any other European language, would be prohibited from entering Natal ... except as visitors.[55]

Terms like 'coolie doctors' or 'coolie lawyers' to refer to Indian men, and 'coolie Maries' for Indian women, were common. Often upper-caste and middle-class Hindu Indian immigrants were eager to produce a discourse of difference that portrayed themselves as distinct representatives of a high cultured India. Honour was enmeshed within a particular intersection of race, caste, class and profession in Indian claims for equality with whites (the Black African as the common other). In South Africa, Gandhi repeatedly underlined Indians' superior difference from 'aboriginal Natives'.[56]

From London, India Office reports attested to the inferior status that indentured work imparted on European opinion of Indians, fuelling segregationist policies:

[T]he system created a false impression abroad of India's status; it gave no opportunity for the settlement of the good types of Indian agriculturist; India came to be regarded merely as a reservoir of the lowest kind of unskilled labour. This kind of objection operates now to make unpopular, not only the old indenture system, but any kind of emigration based merely on the labour requirements of the country of immigration ... that the term coolie became synonymous with Indian in the West Indies and with Hindu in South Africa.[57]

The 'good type' of agriculturist was pitted against the 'unskilled' labour immigrant, responsible for stoking anti-Indian policies. Across the 'British World' that included Canada and Australia, the trope of the 'good agriculturist' dominated labour immigration discourses, especially in settler colonial contexts.[58] Adam Mckeown has argued that the institutions and paperwork forged at the borders of these great migration macro-systems were originally designed to exclude Asian immigrants, ultimately coming to define the relationship of all mobility and international borders.[59] As Radhika Mongia notes, the racialised nature of the passport-control regime was aimed at restricting the mobility of Asian immigration on the basis of the 'colour-bar'.[60] Indian nationalist opinion chafed against the imposition of the colour bar, despite the Government of India trying to argue for equal mobility in various imperial councils.[61]

The aspirations of middle-class Indian emigrants fitted neatly with Moderate nationalist rhetoric for equal rights and representation within a multi-ethnic British Empire. As an emergent Indian nationalist elite sought to reclaim a cultural sovereignty that was absent politically, white Indophiles performed the useful task of representing Indian honour. As Andrews's reporting of the South African satyagraha reveals:

> 'Isn't it simply a question of Indian honour?' His eyes flashed into mine and I shall never forget his look, as he said quickly, almost vehemently – 'Yes! That is it! That is it! That is the real point at issue.' As far as I was concerned, this answer ended the whole matter. For it did not need even a day's residence in Natal to understand, that for an Indian leader to give up honour meant to lose the whole position....[62]

And Andrews's complete self-effacement as he assumes the Indian position as his own:

> My own intense love for India made me able to see the real issue with their eyes ... we might surrender our reputation in the eyes of the world: we might be misrepresented and even slandered: we might surrender the immediate abolition of the 3£ tax. But one thing we could not surrender (I am writing as one of themselves) – we could not sacrifice our Indian honour.[63]

Within months of his involvement, Andrews was able to identify with and vocalise 'Indian honour', confidently 'writing as one of themselves'. Written for a largely middle-class and upper-caste English-educated reading public in India, they further vindicated his representative claims. Andrews's reports emphasised that Gandhi had grasped the absolute notion of Indian honour and had yoked 'the poorest and humblest men and women, just out of indenture' to rally around 'this one intangible thing – *honour*'.[64] Indenture was increasingly cast as an example of bad emigration, while mercantile and other non-indentured emigration was of the desirable kind. Indian nationalist politics became entangled in an intensifying campaign for the abolition of indenture in the Indian Ocean world. Their articulations for uniform citizenship rights across a unified imperial space spoke to growing nationalist concerns about India's place in the empire and world.

India's South African moment, and the insertion of the white Indophile figure thereof, came to represent strategic transnational convergences. Embodying both white privilege and the idea of 'imperial', Indophile association strengthened the rhetoric of free and equal access for India. It brought, for the first time, the issue of imperial emigration to the fore of Indian nationalist discourse in the decades following the 1900s. The Indian National Congress and its leadership, by officially recognising such bodies as the Natal Indian Congress and the Transvaal Indian Congress as legitimate affiliates, reinforced an expansive axis that unified Indians at home and abroad. The South African moment ushered a new phase of 'transnational' in Indian politics.

Fiji: Reporting Moral Panic

As John Kelly and Martha Kaplan have noted, 'being coolies anywhere' was perceived as a 'threat to Indians everywhere', in their quest for 'cosmopolitan respect and full citizenship'.[65] Immediately after their South African debut, the Indian National Congress requested Andrews and Pearson to visit Fiji. Andrews wanted to delay the visit, but 'Pearson ... decided it' for him.[66] Fiji had come into sharp focus after the publication of two tracts: Totaram Sanadhya and Banarsidas Chaturvedi's *Fiji Dwip Mein Mere Ikkis Varsh* (My twenty-one years in Fiji Island),[67] a narrative account of indentured labourers in Fiji, and James McNeill's official report on indentured labour in the four British colonies.[68] Banarsidas Chaturvedi, a Gandhian nationalist, ran the journal *Vishal Bharat* from Calcutta.[69] In him, Andrews found a Brahmin disciple obsessed with national purity and the dangers of contagion that emanated from the unregulated morals of indentured societies. Missionary and nationalist disgust converged in the making of a 'moral panic'. Criticising the McNeill report, Andrews fulminated to Viceroy Hardinge, with whom he was on close terms:

> I have seen these wretched, frightened, quivering, cowering Indian
> coolies with the haunted look in their eyes. I have heard their stories
> from their own lips. McNeill has evidently not. If he had, his pages
> would burn with fire.[70]

In his portrayal, the coolie became a mute, dumb cattle-like creature, with no one to represent them. Pearson wrote about the suffocating racism that characterised Fiji sugar plantations and society. When they had gone to meet a hotel manager

> who has 50 Indian servants under him and treats them abominably. We went into his office and in two minutes were bundled out again by his offensive rudeness.... Our discomfiture was witnessed by several delighted white men, and I have no doubt that they thought we had been rightly served.[71]

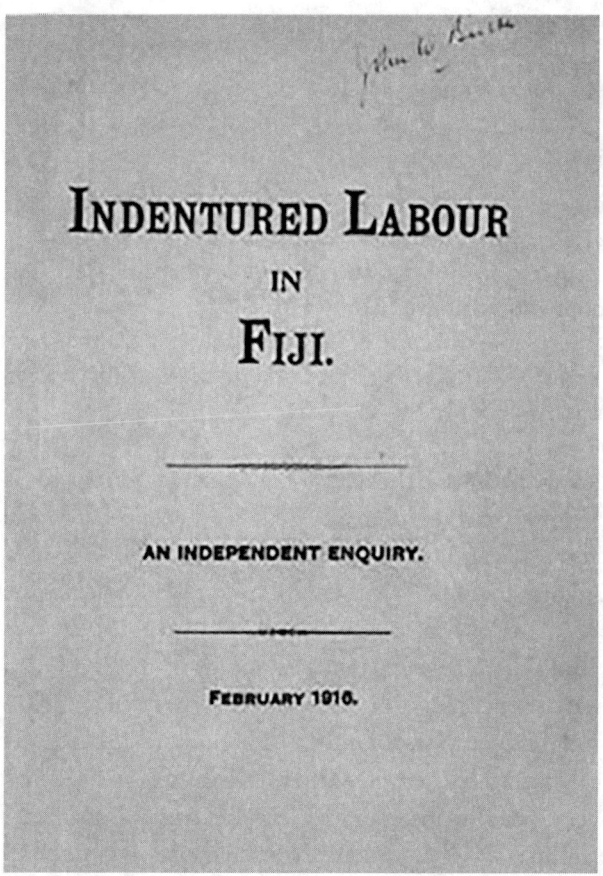

Figure 3.1   The *Fiji Report*, authored by C. F. Andrews and W. W. Pearson and dedicated to Gokhale.

Source: National Library of Australia.

Based on their findings, Andrews and Pearson published a comprehensive *Report on Indentured Labour in Fiji* in the *Modern Review* journal in 1916 (Figure 3.1). The Andrews–Pearson Report or *Fiji Report* became a key moment in precipitating nationalist opinion against indenture. The India Office seemed less impressed at their feat. Thomas Holderness, the Undersecretary, conceded that the system is 'morally bad' but remarked: 'Mr. Andrews saw precisely what he had meant to see when he planned his visit, and has returned confirmed in his original opinions.'[72]

The *Fiji Report* became the basis for Indian nationalist demand to abolish indenture across the empire. The language of the report reproduced the caste presumptions of India's Hindu nationalist elite:

> *A Madrasi of very low caste* and low features came to us for protection against a sardar [coolie manager] who had locked him up ... and beaten and starved him....

> *A Hindustani girl of good caste and respectable Hindu parentage* was deceived by a neighbouring woman in her village.... On board ship her honour was assailed and only with the greatest possible difficulty had she been able to retain it. Now her only hope is that her father and mother will think that she is dead, because she has brought disgrace to her family.[73]

Both missionary men were shocked at high-caste Hindu boys put out to hard field labour and low-caste Hindus made to cut 'meat with other Muslim butchers'. They opined to the Fiji authorities that Hindus, however low in caste, should not be asked to slaughter animals.[74] Meat consumption by Hindu labourers disturbed the caste expectations of Andrews and Pearson, who considered vegetarianism as the ideal Hindu diet: 'It was a strange sight for us to see a butcher's shop in Suva, where beef as well as mutton was being sold, crowded with Hindus waiting eagerly to obtain their purchases of meat.'[75] The authors' association with Tagore, Munshi Ram, Gandhi and their extended ashram circles, comprising upper-caste Hindus with a preferred vegetarian diet (for different reasons) had led them to consider vegetarianism as the normative Hindu dietary regime.

If meat-eating disturbed their ashram-attuned missionary sensibilities, the issue of women, their bodies and moral status absolutely horrified them. They disapproved 'respectable' women mixing with 'abandoned women' aboard the ship: 'Temptation to evil was ever present.'[76] In a narrative worthy of descriptions of the Black Atlantic's middle passage, the report detailed the misery and death caused by the voyage from India to Fiji.[77] It argued that the hugely skewed male-to-female sex ratio often resulted in a high incidence of (un)'regulated prostitution on the estates'. Planters opposed female labourers as they considered them less profitable than male labour.[78]

Troubled at the 'moral evil' festering in Fiji and the 'unmistakeable tale of vice' that marked the men, women and young children in the coolie lines exposed to it, the authors thought 'the moral disease … was eating into the heart and life of the people'.[79] In this, Andrews followed Gandhi's opinion on how this contagion spread back to India, threatening its vitality:

> Indians who return to Madras and Behar and UP disseminate new vices among the simple village peasants of India. Mr Gandhi says they have acted like plague spots on certain districts in Tamil country. Secondly, Government by entering into the system at all gives it a prestige and thus itself becomes a recruiter. Each wretched recruiting agent uses the name of Sarkar. I have written to the Viceroy fully on with these points.[80]

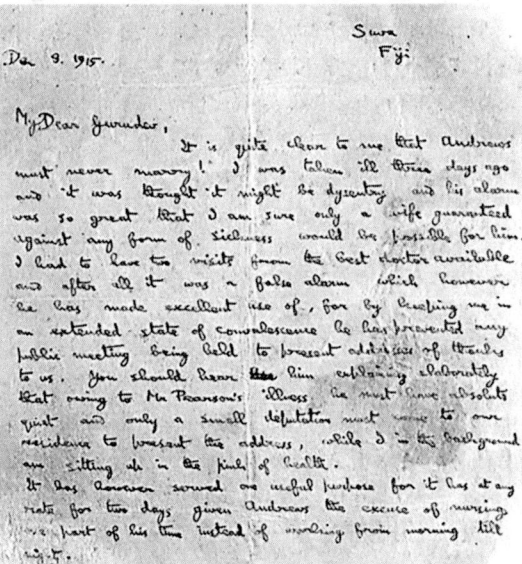

Figure 3.2   Pearson's letter to Tagore from Fiji, 1915.
Source: Rabindra Bhavana, Shantiniketan.

Andrews and Pearson recorded that fathers sold their daughters many times to different men in marriage. Divorces were common and

> women left their husbands for the sake of jewellery and went to live with other men. They seemed to do just what they pleased, and to live just as they liked. Castes and religions were mixed in a common jumble. Hindu girls were sold in marriage to Muhammadans and vice versa; sweepers' children were sometimes married to Brahmans.[81]

The caste dystopia appalled Andrews and Pearson. The report bemoaned the contagion spread by coolie line habits in Hindu marriage practices: 'The tragedy of it all was this, that the whole Hindu fabric had gone to wreck on this one rock of marriage, and there were no leaders to bring the people back into the right paths. The best Hindus we met were in despair about it.'[82] Of particular alarm was the profligacy of Hindu women, fallen from culture and grace:

> The Hindu woman in the coolie 'lines', having no semblance, even of a separate home of her own ... and divorced from her old home ties, has abandoned religion itself. The moral ruin is almost pitiful on this side. Though there are beautiful and stately rivers in Fiji, no women are seen making their morning offerings: no temples rise on their banks; there is no household shrine. The outward life which the Hindu women in the 'lines' lead in Fiji, appears to be without love and without worship, – a sordid round of mean and joyless occupations.[83]

The report idealised a pristine state of female piety, from which Fiji Hindu women had fallen. Andrews and Pearson's reports were widely cited, translated and invoked in a range of nationalist texts. Within the Hindi public sphere, where the abolitionist discourse was strongest, indenture was conflated with prostitution. The women's journal *Stri Darpan* argued that indentured women were 'prostitutes-in-waiting'.[84] As Charu Gupta has argued, emigrating women's identities (generally low or out caste) as labourers were vilified, casting them as immoral sexual subjects.[85] Nationalist expectations of respectability portrayed Dalit women's bodies as either unfit for representative purposes or sites of passive victimhood. Debates in India reflected anxieties like that in Britain around 'assisted passage' schemes involving the emigration of lower-class white women to dominion colonies.[86]

Andrews and Pearson's report on Fiji and indenture was an indictment on how 'everything that could be recognised as Hindu ha[d] departed'.[87] At the centre of this moral propaganda were 'Hindu women' and their bodies, displaced from fulfilling their nationalist function as passive sites of religion and morality. Indentured sexual mores were regarded as little more than 'legalised prostitution … of chaste and pure Indian women being inveigled out'.[88] The demand for abolition was presented as a moral argument to recover Hindu Indians in Fiji.[89] They were convinced that

> when the present indenture system has been abolished and the present recruiting system stopped, we have every hope that a rapid recovery of the morals of the Indian population will ensue. With the improvement in morals, other changes will follow their turn.[90]

The emphasis on Hindu values in the report showcased the enduring influence of the modern ashrams of Tagore, Munshi Ram and Gandhi (Figure 3.2). The influence of ashram values, ideals and memories on their investigations was fully acknowledged:

> The memory and inspiration of the Ashram, and of those who dwelt there, was with us through all our long journey. The freedom of its life made us the more sensitive to the misery which we witnessed in the coolie 'lines'.[91]

The new kinds of conjugality fostered in indentured societies were seen as marked departures from those of idealised ashram communities or village family units. Missionary understanding of sin combined with nationalist anxiety about representation. Andrews urged Hardinge, warning that the 'Fiji question would lead to far worse resentment than the South African trouble if it continued much longer unchecked'.[92]

The refrain on the loss of Hindu values fed the broader nationalist rhetoric of 'Hinduism in danger'. The *Fiji Report* was eagerly taken up by the Hindu nationalist leader Madan Mohan Malaviya, who mobilised a resolution in the Legislative Council, calling upon the Government of India to abolish the indenture system. Hardinge, acknowledging the influence of the report and its validity, wrote back to Andrews:

I have been reading your pamphlet on indentured labour in Fiji.
It is very good, and its contents did not astonish me, the Pundit's
[Malaviya] resolution comes up on the 20th [March] and I am going
to speak on it in Council. You will probably see my speech in the
Press ... hope you ... think it satisfactory.[93]

Malaviya urged Andrews to commit to the anti-indenture campaign at
the Lucknow session of the Indian National Congress (1916), which Polak
too was attending. Polak's campaign against indenture, primarily from an
African Indian perspective, explicitly referenced the *Fiji Report* to argue that
indentured emigration was acting against 'free' Indian emigration in general. In
his pamphlets, he pointed out that India was widely seen as a 'coolie country'
that its aspirations of racial equality:

This danger is bound to militate against closer relations between
the people of India and the white inhabitants of the colonies and
dominions, ... I know, of my own experience in South Africa, how
the whole Indian population, including those Indians who are born
there, are classed alike as 'coolies' by the average white citizen of the
Union, a fact that is an unceasing cause of heart burning amongst
the Indian settlers' who resent this 'contemptuous designation' as
impeding their civic and political progress.[94]

It resonated well with Indian nationalist agendas that sought equality of status
with British settler colonies. In an emotionally charged speech, Gandhi invoked
the *Fiji Report*'s dire findings and spelt out what was at stake:

[E]ither Mr. Andrews' harrowing picture of the conditions of life
in Fiji is true or it is untrue. We believe it to be true, and it has
never been seriously attacked.... Substitute or no substitute, we are
entitled, for the sake of our motherhood [motherland?], for the sake
of our own honour and reputation, and indeed that of the Empire, to
the unconditional abolition of this last remnant of slavery.[95]

Abolition was argued as possible within, and indeed for, the sake of empire.
Andrews and Pearson's report powerfully enabled this projection. Their fervent
reporting on plantation life focused on women's sexual promiscuity to shock
and guilt the moral sensibilities of upper-caste educated Indians. Every monthly
issue of the Calcutta-based journal *Modern Review* contained a sordid exposé

on plantation life by Andrews and his disciple Banarasidas Chaturvedi. They portrayed in great detail the proliferation of 'whore houses', venereal diseases and sexual assault in Fiji: 'every indentured Indian woman has to serve three indentured men, as well as various outsiders'.[96]

Within a year of the report's publication in 1915, and the mobilisation of nationalist outrage and political lobbying, indenture was 'officially' abolished in May 1917.[97] However, by this time, official recruitment had already fallen to about 10,000 to 13,000 annually, suggesting that the issue's appeal far outstripped actual numbers.[98] The *Fiji Report* was cited by both Indian and government members in the Indian Legislative Council when moving the abolition motion. Within two years of its publication, therefore, the *Fiji Report* managed to intensify a political momentum that led to its abolition.

After Abolition: 'The Indian Question'

Post-abolition work was difficult and painstaking. After abolition, the Overseas Indian Association was formed by Indian mercantile and artisanal interests to represent them in India and Britain. Henry Polak was made responsible for the campaign against racial legislations in London, while Andrews was invited to lobby for Indian settlers in Fiji, Mauritius, East and South Africa, Malaya and British Guiana.[99] He followed up on the 'early termination' of indentured contracts, alongside resolving and representing issues faced by emigrant Indian communities.

Indophile investments now moved to normalise the Indian emigrant as a desirable entity in the empire, enabling imperial ethics and expansion. This was not easy as European associations pushed back fiercely against any kind of concession to Indians. Andrews anxiously telegraphed Gandhi from Nairobi in 1919:

> East African situation now most critically dangerous because united attempt made by European associations to close door against future immigration and stop Indian Franchise Chief reason stated through Indian contact but advance under Christian Western civilisation Government economic commission report recently published takes same attitude mentioning specifically Indian moral depravity

and approving South African exclusion policy intense indignation expressed here by Indian Congress gathering which was remarkable for its weight and numbers. I have decided on urgent request to stay till January here.[100]

An Imperial Conference in 1921, comprising Indian leaders such as V. Srinivasa Sastri and the then Colonial Office Secretary Winston Churchill, adopted resolutions to improve the status of Indians in the empire. It supported the 'entry of educated Indians', improvement of their sanitary conditions and the adoption of policies to make them 'good citizens' of whatever country they were domiciled in.[101] These moves aligned perfectly with what Andrews, Pearson and Polak, along with Indian nationalists, had hoped for. The indentured labourer slipped away, appearing only in debates on repatriation or contract termination. Five years after abolition, 'batches' of repatriated labourers came to visit Andrews at Shantiniketan, asking to be sent back:

> Nothing on earth will make these people settle down in India, if only they can get away, anywhere, out of the country.… They always answer me "Either shoot us and get rid of us or send us back. We shall commit suicide if you force us to remain in this country.[102]

It revealed the bias of representation, and how the needs of the 'respectable' Indian emigrant overwrote the demands of labourers themselves, justified in the name of morality, religion and nation. Difficulties of reintegration, given strictures of caste, class and religion in rural Indian society, was particularly acute. Used to a more fluid form of social mobility and life, repatriation was hard, given that most of them came from lower or untouchable castes (for example, Pasi and Chamars).[103]

The 'Indian Question' evolved into a demand for settlement rights and political representation. In a *Report of the Economic Commission of the East Africa Protectorate*, convened by members of the Allied Nations in Paris in 1917, a new ruse came up: the 'welfare of the native African'. The commission felt that due to the intimate contact and introduction of an intermediate race of Indians between Europeans and Africans, 'the African of this country is at present receiving [influences that] are mainly imparted to him by the Asiatic, and are predominantly Indian rather than British'.[104] The Indian emigrant continued to be cast in white settler discourse as a figure steeped in crime, violence, squalor and moral depravity against whose influence the child-like native African needed protection. Andrews's initial defence of Indians, however, recycled existing stereotypes of the savage native African and justified Indian occupation and settlement:

> East Africa is really what we may call a test case for Great Britain. If Indians cannot be welcomed [?] as equals in a vacant, or almost vacant part of the world, where they did all the pioneering and where they were first in occupation … it means that they can only be tolerated, even in their own tropical belt of the world, as inferiors, and that the so-called freedom of the British Empire is a sham and a delusion. This is what I mean by a test case.[105]

Andrews, along with many others, including Gandhi, believed in an essential difference between Indians and Africans. In line with hierarchised notions of civilisation, this reproduced a logic of superiority that often obstructed effective solidarities between Indians and Black Africans.[106] Andrews' complete identification with the Indian cause precluded for a long time his understanding of the exclusionary racial politics that cast mercantile Indians in sub-imperialist roles against African lands and communities. He justified that Indians would only continue the work initiated by European interventions to 'civilise' Africans:

> I have seen the African in his raw and savage state, – the state wherein cannibalism was practised as a matter of course. I have no illusions … about the kind of existence which used often to be led before the European intervened.[107]

Overseas Indian organisations and local Indian Congresses repeatedly invited these white interlocutors to broker agreements and disputes on their behalf in various international councils and commissions. Both Indian and white settlers claimed rights over Kenyan land and resources, often causing deadlocks in imperial policy-making. Representing the Indian side, Andrews and Polak argued against a white monopoly in the British Commonwealth: 'this assumption, if once finally accepted and endorsed, would change the whole structure of British Rule abroad'.[108] Realising the impossibility of racial or political equality for Indians within the empire, Andrews and Pearson would soon come to advocate Indian independence. By 1921, however, East African Indians had abandoned their sub-imperialist claims, embracing broader equality for all colonised subjects, prodded by the 1919 Jallianwala Bagh Massacre and collaboration with the

Kenyan nationalist Harry Thuku who founded the East African Association.[109] Hereafter, Andrews fought against Indian sub-imperialist impulses in Africa (such as the demand for a special zone in Tanganyika).[110]

By 1920, Andrews felt keenly the hardening of 'the "White Race" idea everywhere among the British all over the world', a realisation brought on by post-war British nationalism and erosion of any residual belief in imperial munificence.[111] Polak converged with Andrews to issue a joint statement that the government and people of India unite to fight for the rights of overseas Indians and oppose the Colonial Office policy of acceding to white settler demands in pushing Indians out of those countries.[112] Andrews's identification with the Indian cause led him to be assaulted twice by white mobs, on his way to Nairobi on 26 November 1921, who tried to haul him off the train. He had to be hospitalised and travel under police protection on his way back. Winston Churchill, then Colonial Secretary, smugly replied to the Governor of Kenya that it 'would have been a source of satisfaction to [him] … if the offender had received the punishment he deserved'.[113]

Conclusion: Becoming National Icons

The association with indenture transformed Andrews, Polak and Pearson's public legacies. In a moving account, Andrews recounted meeting groups of Indian men, women and children while travelling along the Nile in East Africa. They wistfully greeted him at railway halts in remote locations. In a darkness broken only by dim lantern lights, he gave impromptu addresses in broken Hindustani.[114]

In a discourse that spanned multiple contexts, colonies and continents, and sharply split along race, gender, class and caste lines, the presence of rare white figures to speak for Indian interests provided a critical impetus to the politics of representation. Indeed, this also gives us a glimpse into the fraught nature of their interlocution. Indentured labour migration and its conditions represented a radically different kind of India and Indians from the rarefied icons they coveted: Tagore, Gandhi or Gokhale. Indenture became a discursive site to evidence that representative claim.

Western Indophiles were spectacularly deployed against notions of imperial whiteness. As the honour of these Indian leaders, India and the causes they led formed part of a composite logic, defending one generally meant a defence of the other. In this, their racial identity acted both for and against them. This tense deployment of racial privilege was central in legitimising their investments for Indian audiences. Nationalist Indian dailies commended Polak's representation of 'South African Indians': 'Mr. Henry Polak has been all within his power to keep before the preoccupied public mind the problem of the position of Indians in South Africa.'[115] Gandhi publicly hailed Andrews' service (Figure 3.3). At Kheda (in Gujarat) in 1918, where peasants had offered civil disobedience or satyagraha due to their inability to pay high taxes, Gandhi introduced Andrews:

> … as a rishi for he has all the qualities of a holy sage. He has recently returned from Fiji, where he went on a mission that concerns us. While in Fiji … he lived among the labourers, in their own houses, and studied their manner of living. We have, at present, the Kheda affair at hand…. I am sure you will be glad to hear that Mr. Andrews has taken it up as his own for the time being. He is leaving today for Bombay to see his Excellency the Governor. He will, on my behalf, place certain facts before him and also convey my request. If anything comes of this, all right; otherwise he will be in Nadiad on Sunday next. Thus he has started working for our cause as well.[116]

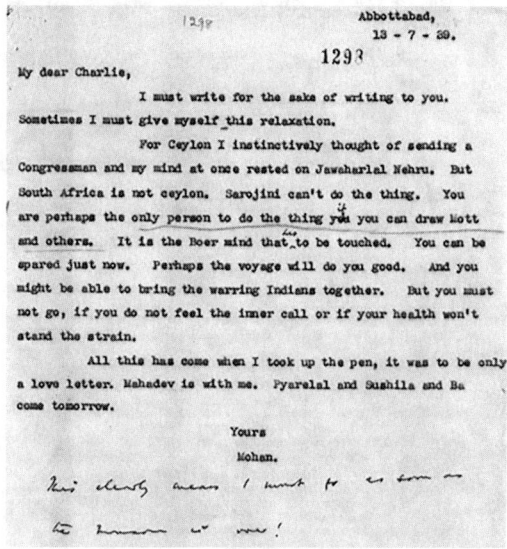

Figure 3.3   Gandhi requesting Andrews to visit South Africa, on the 'Indian Question', July 1939.

Source: Rabindra Bhavana, Visvabharati.

Andrews emerged as a *rishi* in public discourse, a sage who 'sacrificed' his privileges for Indian nationalist causes (Figure 3.4). It prefaced his public investments in and around India. One *Bharatiya Hriday* [An Indian heart], referring to a particular instance in Fiji where 150 Indians were convicted owing to their strike against repatriation measures after abolition, argued: 'Mr. Andrews is returning from South Africa and certainly he is the best person to do this difficult task [of investigating]'. Owing to Andrews's illness, however, he suggested one 'Pandit Tota Ram of Firozabad' whom Andrews had approved for his work in Fiji. Andrews's service, 'sacrifice' and sincerity emerged as a gold standard in public life, to be invoked and emulated.[117]

For The Special Congress, Calcutta.

Proposed General Resolution Concerning Indians Abroad.

That this Congress demands that in all Colonies and Protectorates within the British Commonwealth the principle of equal status of Indians with all other subjects of the King-Emperor be recognised by the Colonial Office and by the local colonial and protectorate administrations; and that in all self-governing dominions the same principle be accepted by the different dominion governments, on the understanding that reciprocal action in India may follow its refusal.

Special Resolutions.

(1) That Lord Milner's proposals with regard to franchise, land purchase and race segregation for Indians in East Africa are incompatible with equal status.

(2) That the principle of a property and literacy test incumbent on all races be recommended as a solution of the difficulties concerning franchise.

(3) That complete freedom of land purchase both in the lowland and upland areas of East Africa can alone satisfy Indian legitimate claims.

(4) That the segregation of Indians in separate town locations in East Africa is unnecessary and undesirable.

(5) That an immediate guarantee be required from the Tanganyika administration not to use against Indians for political purposes the "Undesirables' Ordinance."

(6) That any administration of the South African Indian Relief Act, of 1914, for political ends, which may involve pressure, bribery, or compulsion in order to induce repatriation, be condemned.

(7) That this Congress protests against the colour bar in the South African Union Assembly which prevents any Indian from holding a seat.

(8) That the Fiji Government proposal to allot two seats by election to Indians on the Fiji Legislative Councils is inadequate.

(9) That in the light of recent events in Fiji, including the deportation of Mr. and Mrs. Manilal and others, and in view of the dissatisfaction of Indians on the spot with local conditions, the resumption of labour recruiting in India for Fiji is not advisable.

(10) That no action be taken with regard to the renewal of labour immigration from India to other Crown colonies, such as Demerara and Surinam, without full popular consent, both of the Indian people as a whole and of the province which might be required to supply such labour.

Figure 3.4   Proposal tabled by C. F. Andrews at the Special session of the Indian National Congress, 1930. The manifesto for the non-cooperation movement, the first national movement launched by Gandhi in India, was adopted at this session.

Source: Sabarmati Ashram.

The sacrificial mode framed Andrews, Pearson and Polak's services. Their movements were continuously reported in public media, giving them an audience and aura few white British figures could ever achieve. Their work was not without its critics on the Indian side, but their representative abilities were never questioned, given their 'sacrifices'. British official opinion differed on the role they fulfilled. Andrews was considered 'one of those who always sees the virtues of other nations and only the faults of his own'.[118] Most of them however acknowledged the important place they had come to occupy in Indian public imagination, even if it meant a critique of official British politics and policies. Ramsay Macdonald, then British Prime Minister in 1932, attested to the usefulness of Andrews and his close links to Gandhi: 'I have myself seen Mr. Andrews personally in connection with recent events and he is in regular touch with the India Office.'[119] While 'disliked and mistrusted by most Englishmen in India', his endorsement was seen as carrying greater authority in India than many prominent nationalist leaders. It occasionally led to his being used unknowingly by the British imperial bureaucracy. Recommending his usefulness in the matter of Indian emigration to Kenya, the British Governor of Nigeria remarked to his colleague:

> [M]ore than anyone else he is in a position to deliver the goods as far as Indian opinion is concerned. If Shastri were to consent to a settlement it would not follow that Indian opinion would endorse it: if Andrews were to say that it was just and fair there is a big probability that he would carry India with him.[120]

The association of Western Indophiles in a transnational discourse such as indenture helped open mainland political discourse to that of its diasporas. Whether India would be equal and free in the larger empire was put to test as much in India as through Indians elsewhere: in Africa, Australia and the Indian Ocean world. To this end, Andrews regularly tabled proposals on 'Indians Abroad' for consideration at sessions of the Indian National Congress. Supporting the right for Indians to equal citizenship and mobility within a unified Commonwealth, he critiqued the racist politics of the white community in dominion colonies:

> This assumption – that the White Community alone can represent the British Commonwealth, and that citizenship in that Commonwealth must never be extended beyond the White Race – this assumption, if once finally accepted and endorsed, would change the whole structure of British Rule abroad.[121]

Only by realising the exclusions practised at its margins, they argued, could nationalist discourse harness a wider geopolitical axis. Indophile reports, essays and books crucially enabled the realities of this geopolitical imagination. Almost every issue of the journal *Modern Review* from 1914 to 1940 had an article on indenture or emigration. The Imperialist Citizenship Organisation sponsored their visits to Indian communities settled abroad. Polak lobbied for better pay and work conditions through the Overseas Indians Association in London, 'allay[ing] public feeling in the Indian community in Fiji and also in India'.[122]

Indophiles became valuable resources in high-profile negotiations, providing access to audiences and spaces that hitherto no (or few) Indian individuals or institutions were privy to. This was exploited most skilfully by nationalist politics at home and abroad. Indophiles helped establish a particular category of Indians as phenotypes of high culture and civilisational inheritance. Representations of the ideal Indian emigrant in imperial migration discourses invariably reflected the caste–class–race presumptions of the Indian nationalist elite. The ideal Indian emigrant was to be in the image of a Tagore, Gandhi or Gokhale, educated and enlightened, spreading civilisation in British colonies everywhere, their communities upholding respectable values and an ideal family life wherever they settled.

Notes

1   However, to see these engagements as only an epiphenomenon of that desire would be limiting.

2   A selective representation of this historiography include, but are in no way limited to: Hugh Tinker, *A New System of Slavery: The Export of Indian Labour Overseas, 1830–1920* (London: Oxford University Press, 1974); David Northrup, *Indentured Labor in the Age of Imperialism, 1834–1922* (Cambridge: Cambridge University Press, 1995); Kay Saunders, ed., *Indentured Labour in the British Empire, 1834–1920* (London: Croom Helm, 1984); Marina Carter, *Voices from Indenture: Experiences of Indian Migrants in the British Empire* (London: Leicester University Press, 1996); more recent works include Sunil S. Amrith, *Crossing the Bay of Bengal: The Furies of Nature and the Fortunes of Migrants* (Cambridge, MA: Harvard University Press, 2013); Kumar, *Coolies of the Empire*. Recent studies have suggested 'Coolitude' as a shared identity that commemorates the experiences of the Indian labour diaspora, based on

the lines of Negritude: Marina Carter and Khal Torabully, *Coolitude: An Anthology of the Indian Labour Diaspora* (London: Anthem Press, 2002). Black thinkers such as Aime Cesaire within the Francophone tradition pioneered the concept of Negritude.

3   Jonathan Connolly, 'Indentured Labour Migration and the Meaning of Emancipation: Free Trade, Race and Labour in the British Public Debate, 1838–1860', *Past and Present* 238 (February 2018): 85–119.

4   Ibid., 103–109.

5   Michael Mann, 'Migration-Re-migration – Circulation: South Asian Kulis in the Indian Ocean and Beyond, 1840–1940', in *Connecting Seas and Connected Ocean Rims*, 109.

6   Carter, *Voices from Indenture*, 46–47.

7   This is the line taken by Tinker and many of his influential followers.

8   Charu Gupta, '"Innocent" Victims/"Guilty" Migrants: Hindi Public Sphere, Caste and Indentured Women in Colonial North India', *Modern Asian Studies* 49, no. 5 (2015): 1352.

9   Adam McKeown, 'Global Migration, 1846–1940', *Journal of World History* 15, no. 2 (June 2004): 173–174. For an excellent overview of the main debates within the global history of migration, see Amit Kumar Mishra, 'Global Histories of Migration', in *Global History, Globally: Research and Practice around the World*, ed. Sven Beckert and Dominic Sachsenmaier (London: Bloomsbury, 2019), 195–214.

10 For how the British moved around and across their 'World', see Gary B. Magee and Andrew S. Thompson, *Empire and Globalisation: Networks of People, Goods and Capital in the British World, c. 1850–1914* (Cambridge: Cambridge University Press, 2010).

11 Bill Guest, 'Indians in Natal and Southern Africa in the 1890s', in *Gandhi and South Africa: Principles and Politics*, ed. Judith Brown and M. Prozesky (Pietermaritzburg: University of Natal Press, 1996), 9–13.

12 Madhavi Kale, 'Indian Labour in Trinidad and British Guiana', in *Nation and Migration: The Politics of Space in the South Asian Diaspora*, ed. Peter Van Der Veer (Philadelphia: University of Pennsylvania Press, 1995), 80.

13 Sana Aiyar, *Indians in Kenya* (Cambridge, MA: Harvard University Press, 2015). Though, of course, mercantile connections with South Asia had existed much before European colonial rule in eastern and southern Africa.

14 By 1900, the emergence of a well-to-do mercantile community of Indians in Natal threatened white business interests, who actively lobbied for a restriction of franchise rights and Indian economic activities to less threatening roles such as that of indentured labourers. Kathryn Tidrick, *Gandhi: A Political and Spiritual Life* (London: I. B. Tauris, 2008), 53.

15   While Gandhi was considered an exceptional Indian, at par with white counterparts, most white-run papers would note that the average Indian in South Africa was a creature of 'bestial habits, given to malingering and dishonest practices. 'Natal Witness, 29 Dec 1894', cited in Ramachandra Guha, *Gandhi before India* (London: Allen Lane, 2013), 79.

16   The position of Jewish figures must be understood cautiously, especially in relation to other 'white communities', for they reveal how stratified whiteness was internally as a project. While European Jews faced various forms of exclusion in settler colonies from more categorically 'white' settlers (Anglo-Saxon Protestant or Boers, for instance), this was not the same as more non-white communities like Indians. Racial hierarchies are shifting, but they tend to congeal sharply in the face of significantly non-white others, flattening differences, if only provisionally.

17   The Indian National Congress (1885) was the premier nationalist organisation run by mostly English educated Indian elite members, hailing from upper-class/caste backgrounds. It was predominantly Liberal and moderate belief in the munificence of the empire till at least the 1900s, when a more radical faction emerged that split the organisation till at least 1916. The Imperialist Citizenship Association and Indian Overseas Association were founded by Indian merchants and industrialists to represent the interests of mercantile emigration in the empire.

18   As Mrinalini Sinha observes, indentured abolitionism was seen as politically backward and elite led, even though it actually predates the age of Gandhian mass nationalism, and was a widely popular movement in agrarian north India. Mrinalini Sinha, 'Premonitions of the Past', *Journal of Asian Studies* 74, no. 4 (November 2015): 828–829.

19   Andrews to Gandhi, 16 July 1919, Folder 21, Letters from CFA to Gandhi (1914–1933), CFA Papers; File 1–26, 28 (ii), RBVB-018, CD. Henceforth MSS/F/RBVB/F/21.

20   See Indians Overseas Papers, India Office British Library. Andrews, in particular, is continually jutting around the globe at requests of Indian communities settled in Fiji, Guyana, South and East Africa, New Zealand and so on. See Tinker, *The Ordeal of Love*, for a rather appraising discussion of Andrews and others.

21   Sinha, 'Premonitions of the Past', 826.

22   Mohandas K. Gandhi, 'Summary of Enclosed Statement' (Papers relating to Indian Struggle in South Africa, File No. 5, 1904, Servants of India Society Papers, NMML, Delhi), 9.

23   It was, therefore, the franchise rights and trading interests of the Indian merchants that Gandhi attempted to secure first, arguing that it was unfit to bracket prestigious, educated Indians to the same restrictive regulations as that of their uneducated, labouring countrymen.

24   Thomas Weber, *Gandhi as Disciple and Mentor* (Cambridge: Cambridge University Press, 2006), 60. However, Gandhi's reliance on white associates (Henry Polak, Hermann Kallenbach, Albert West and so on) did not go uncriticised by several Indian contemporaries in South Africa, most notably M. C. Anglia, Dada Osman and P. S. Aiyar. Ashwin Desai and Goolam Vahed, *The South African Gandhi: Stretcher-Bearer of Empire* (Delhi: Navayana, 2020), 179–180.

25   Gandhi to Millie Polak, 24 April 1910, *CWMG*, vol. 11, 18.

26   Henry Polak, *The Indians of South Africa: Helots within the Empire and How They Are Treated* (Madras: Natesan, 1909).

27   C. F. Andrews, 'Mr Polak's Visit to India', in app. VII, *Mahatma Gandhi at Work*, 392.

28   Gopal K. Gokhale, 'British Indians in South Africa', in *Speeches and Writings of Gokhale*, vol. 2, *Political* (London: Asia Publishing House, 1966), 400.

29   Though Hardinge sent a British ICS Officer – Benjamin Robertson – as an official representative of India, it was Gokhale's personal emissaries, the Reverend C. F. Andrews in particular, and Willie Pearson, both Englishmen who played a signal role in the mediations that resulted in the Gandhi–Smuts Agreement of 1914.

30   Pearson to Tagore, 14 December 1913, MSS/WP/RBVB/F 287(ii). All letters from Pearson to Tagore are from this series unless otherwise stated.

31   Andrews to Tagore, 28 July 1913, MSS/CFA/RBVB/F/ 4–11.

32   Pearson to Tagore, 6 May 1913,

33   Pearson to Tagore, 19 October 1915.

34   Tagore to Andrews, [undated] 1914.

35   Andrews to Tagore, 6 January 1914.

36   'A Historic Debate', *Indian Opinion,* 17 June 1914, *CWMG*, vol. 14, 182.

37   Andrews to Tagore, 6 January 1914 (emphasis in original). On landing, Andrews greeted Polak and asked: 'Where is Mr. Gandhi?' Polak turned to a slight ascetic figure, dressed in a white dhoti and kurta of such coarse material as an indentured labourer might wear. Andrews bent swiftly down and touched Gandhi's feet. Charles Freer Andrews, *CWMG*, vol. 14, footnote 20.

38   Andrews to Tagore, 6 January 1914.

39   Ibid.

40   Tinker, *The Ordeal of Love*, 88.

41   Gandhi to Hermann Kallenbach, 14 January 1914, *CWMG*, vol. 14, 32.

42   Gandhi to Hermann Kallenbach, 18 January 1914, *CWMG*, vol. 14, 37.

43   Gandhi, Cable to Gokhale, 3 January 1914, Servants of India Society Papers, F. No. 45, National Archives of India (NAI).

44   Gandhi to Manilal, 28 January 1914, *CWMG*, vol. 12, 341.

45   M. K. Gandhi, 'My Double Shame', in *The Story of My Experiments with Truth* (Ahmedabad: Navajivan Publishing House, 1927), 73–79.

46   Weber, *Gandhi as Disciple and Mentor*, 62. A comparable instance can be found in C. Rajagopalachari's admonitory letter to Gandhi, when he was romantically drawn towards Sarala Devi, noted poet, singer and niece of Rabindranath Tagore. Urging Gandhi that his love for him was no less than a woman's, he warned him to refrain from straying if he truly loved him: 'There are no more ... women, – certainly no more than me, ... who simply dote on you as no woman ever loved man.' C. Rajagopalachari to Gandhi, 16 June 1920, Gopalkrishna Gandhi, ed., *My Dear Bapu: Letters from C. Rajagopalachari to Mohandas Karamchand Gandhi, Devadas Gandhi and Gopalkrishna Gandhi* (Delhi: Viking, 2012). Throughout his life, there are several such instances of male intimacies that borders on the romantic.

47   Gandhi to Chhanaganal Gandhi, 18 January 1914, *CWMG*, vol. 14, 38.

48   Gandhi, Cable to G. K. Gokhale, 24 February 1914, Cape Town, *CWMG*, vol. 14, 76.

49   Gandhi to Hermann Kallenbach, 17 February 1914, Cape Town, *CWMG*, vol. 14, 70.

50   Munshi Ram to Andrews, 31 January 1914.

51   Andrews to Tagore, 14 January 1914, Tinker, *Ordeal of Love*, 86.

52   Andrews to Gandhi, 13 April [1914], MSS/CFA/RBVB/F/ 21. All letters from Andrews to Gandhi from this series unless otherwise stated.

53   Andrews to Gandhi, 26 February [1914?].

54   Cable to G. K. Gokhale from Gandhi, 19 February 1914, Cape Town, *CWMG*, vol. 14, 73.

55   Polak, *The Indians of South Africa*, 22–23.

56   Desai and Vahed, *The South African Gandhi*, 42. However, the fundamentally racialised nature of law and polity in South Africa encouraged a language of competitive racialisation, which Gandhi, as a lawyer, strategised when arguing for Indian rights. In his later life Gandhi moved away from many of these positions and developed excellent relations with several African-American intellectuals. Faisal Devji draws attention to all of these in his sharp piece on 'Gandhi's Racism', *Asia Dialogue*, 2 October 2019.

57 Indians Overseas: Note by Mr J. C. Walton, IOR/L/PO/1/22 (ii), Fol. 105, India Office Records, British Library.

58 Kent Fedorowich, 'Restocking the British World: Empire, Migration and Anglo-Canadian Relations, 1919–30', *Britain and the World* 9, no. 2 (2016): 244. See also Somak Biswas, 'Approaching Migration in World History: How to Use Primary Sources', in *Research Methods Primary Sources* (Marlborough: Adam Matthew Digital, 2021).

59 McKeown, 'Integration and Segregation in Global Migration', 63.

60 Mongia, *Indian Migration and Empire*, 2–6. Radhika Singha reminds us that there were also other geopolitical considerations and the management of labour flows in the Indian Ocean region. Singha, 'The Great War and a "Proper" Passport for the Colony', 290.

61 Singha, 'The Great War and a "Proper" Passport for the Colony', 291.

62 C. F. Andrews, 'Mr Gandhi and the Commission', *Modern Review*, July 1914, 97.

63 Ibid., 98.

64 Ibid.

65 John Kelly and Martha Kaplan, 'Diaspora and Swaraj, Swaraj and Diaspora', in *From the Colonial to the Postcolonial*, ed. Dipesh Chakrabarty, Rochona Majumdar and Andrew Satori (New Delhi: Oxford University Press, 2007), 321.

66 Andrews to Munshi Ram, 27 September 1914, Tinker, *The Ordeal of Love*, 113.

67 Written by Pandit Totaram Sanadhya in collaboration with Banarsidas Chaturvedi, *Fiji Dwip Mein Mere Ikkis Varsh* (Agra: Rajput Anglo-Oriental Press, 1914).

68 Tinker, *The Ordeal of Love*, 107. James McNeill, Indian Civil Service, and Chimman Lal, India, *East India (Indentured Labour) Report to the Government of India on the Conditions of Indian Immigrants in Four British Colonies and Surinam* (London: H. M. Stationery Off., printed in India, 1915).

69 See Ruth Vanita, 'Introduction', in *Chocolate and Other Writings on Male Homoeroticism*, xxii–xxiii.

70 Andrews to Hardinge, 28 June 1914, Tinker, *The Ordeal of Love*, 108.

71 Pearson to Tagore, 8 December 1915, MSS/WP/RBVB/F 287 (ii).

72 Tinker, *The Ordeal of Love*, 123.

73 Andrews and Pearson, *Report on Indentured Labour in Fiji*, 395 (emphasis added).

74 Ibid., 393.

75 Ibid., 400–401.

76 Ibid.

77 Ibid., 401.

78 Ibid.

79   Ibid., 402.

80   Andrews to Tagore, [early October?] 1915.

81   Andrews and Pearson, *Report on Indentured Labour in Fiji*, 516.

82   Ibid., 519.

83   Ibid.

84   Cited in Gupta, '"Innocent" Victims', 1368.

85   Ibid., 1367. Kunti, a Chamar woman from Gorakhpur, had written a letter alleging rape by a white overseer in Fiji in April 1913, that sparked widespread outrage (Gupta, '"Innocent" Victims', 1357).

86   Biswas, 'Approaching Migration in World History', 12. Britain routinely used assisted passage schemes to transfer some of its 'excess stocks' to the empire, as well as relieve domestic distress (unemployment, crime) at home.

87   Andrews and Pearson, *Report on Indentured Labour in Fiji*, 518.

88   Andrews to Susil Rudra, 12 January 1917, Tinker, *The Ordeal of Love*, 133.

89   Nationalists also made a case for presumed labour shortage within India to stop indentured emigration.

90   Andrews and Pearson, *Report on Indentured Labour in Fiji*, 617.

91   Ibid., 623.

92   Andrews to Hardinge, 27 September 1914, Tinker, *The Ordeal of Love*, 113.

93   Hardinge to Andrews, 14 March 1916, Tinker, *The Ordeal of Love*, 125.

94   *Indian Emigration – Problems, Memorandum of Mr H. S. L. Polak on The Colonial Emigration Conference* (Madras: Sons of India, 1918), 4.

95   Mahatma Gandhi, 'Statement on Abolition of Indentured Labour', [after 7 February 1917], *CWMG*, vol. 15, 308.

96   Tinker, *The Ordeal of Love*, 142–143.

97   There were also other contributing factors such as wartime shortage of shipping and the need to mobilise military labour, often recruited from the same regions. The government line was that it would be stopped once suitable alternatives were found. Resuming briefly under only exceptional circumstances after the war, the last shipment of indentured labour took place in 1925: see https://www.coolitude.shca.ed.ac.uk/abolition-indentured-labour-migration (accessed on 26 March 2022).

98   Abolition had little effect on the supply of unskilled Indian labour in other global markets, including the profitable Bay of Bengal trade region, as shown by Radhika Singha. Cited from Sinha, 'Premonitions of the Past', 831.

99   Aiyar, *Indians in Kenya*, 78.

100 Andrews to Gandhi, 4 December 1919, Nairobi, MSS/F/RBVB/21.

101 'Supplementary Memorandum by the Government of India on the Position of British Indians, containing certain detailed suggestions arising out of the Report of the Asiatic Enquiry Commission and Sir. B. Robertson's Statement before the Commission', *Imperial Conference 1921: Resolution Regarding Position of Indians in the Empire*, IOR/L/E/7/148.

102 Andrews to Banarsidas, 10 April 1922, Tinker, *The Ordeal of Love*, 193–194.

103 Oddvar Hollup, 'The Disintegration of Caste and Changing Concepts of Indian Ethnic Identity in Mauritius', *Ethnology* 33, no. 4 (Autumn 1994): 297, www.jstor.org/stable/3773901.

104 The report argued how British control of Uganda (after World War I) and the employment of Indian labour led to a substantial increase in labour and capital costs in the building of Uganda Railway projects compared to the hiring of African or that of white labour in South Africa. Cited from C. F. Andrews, *The Indian Question in East Africa* (Nairobi: Swift Press, 1921).

105 Andrews to Rathindranath Tagore, 6 September 1920, Tinker, *The Ordeal of Love*, 168.

106 Desai and Vahed illustrates this well in their book *The South African Gandhi*.

107 C. F. Andrews, Final Report, Part I, of the Economic Commission of the East Africa Protectorate, 1917, *The Indian Question in East Africa*, 74.

108 Andrews, *The Indian Question in East Africa*, 25.

109 Sana Aiyar offers an excellent analysis of this collaboration, contestation and shifting ideological underpinnings. Sana Aiyar, 'Empire, Race, and the Indians in Colonial Kenya's Contested Public Political Sphere, 1919–1923', *Africa: Journal of the International African Institute* 81, no. 1 (2011): 141–142. While African opposition to Indian presence continued, this was sharply split across generational lines. Older chiefs and headmen, often middlemen involved with white settler interests, distanced themselves from Thuku's movement. Indeed, Thuku's pro-Indian collaborations were used to discredit him.

110 Tinker, *The Ordeal of Love*, 162.

111 Andrews to Gandhi, 4 September 1920, MSS/F/RBVB/21.

112 Tinker, *The Ordeal of Love*, 194.

113 House of Commons Debates, 14 June 1922, 'Question from Josiah Wedgwood to Colonial Secretary Winston Churchill', cited in Tinker, *The Ordeal of Love*, 189.

114 C. F. Andrews, 'Railway Journey: Indian Settlers in Africa', *Modern Review* 1 (June 1920).

115 'The South African Indians', *Times of India*, 6 November, 1911, 7, accessed from ProQuest Historical Newspapers: Times of India.

116 Speech at Ahmedabad meeting, 21 March 1918, 'Prajabandhu', translated from Gujarati, *CWMG*, vol. 14 (October 1917–July 1918, Delhi, 1965), 274.

117 Letter to the Editor, 'Ek Bharatiya Hriday', *Bombay Chronicle*, 8 April 1920, Indians in Fiji, IOR/L/PJ/6/2705.

118 Chelmsford to Clare, 5 March 1918, Tinker, *The Ordeal of Love*, 138.

119 Ramsay Macdonald to Lord Maclay, 20 October 1932, MSS EUR/D1113/1–3, C. F. Andrews Collection, British Library. This was during the impasse caused by the Poona Pact due to Ambedkar's demand for a separate electorate for Dalits/depressed classes.

120 Oldham to Lugard, 22 May 1923, MSS EUR/D1113/1–3.

121 Andrews, *The Indian Question in East Africa*, 25.

122 Polak, Secy of the Indians Overseas Association, London to the India Office, 14 February 1921, Indians in Fiji, IOR/L/PJ/6/2705, British Library.

Part III

CHAPTER 4

Practices of Discipleship

Vivekananda and His Women Disciples, 1890–1910

Introduction

Unlike Gandhi or Tagore, Vivekananda (1863–1902) did not have female Indian disciples. Vivekananda's female disciples were British, American or European. They did not live monastic ashram lives, and their experiences of discipleship diverge significantly because of that spatial difference. While a product of late nineteenth-century cultural nationalism, Vivekananda himself predated the decades of 1910s and 1920s, a period that saw the intensification of Indian political nationalism and defined the activities of Gandhi and Tagore's Western disciples.

Ramakrishna, the nineteenth-century Bengali mystic, was famous for his aversion to women and gold (*kaminikanchan*) – unless they were amply maternal or daughterly, both forms that negated or transcended their sexuality. The initiation into conventional monasticism meant a withdrawal from the world; overcoming attachments to women was key to that process. His disciples inherited and practised such an approach rigorously. Male disciples' access to Sarada Devi's household (Ramakrishna's wife, regarded as the Holy Mother by disciples) was tightly bound by purdah rules. The Ramakrishna Math and Mission, established by Vivekananda with his community of brother-monks, made important departures from conventional monasticism through an active role in social service, or *seva*.[1] However, the mission did not allow for the equal co-presence of women monks.[2]

Vivekananda intended to institute schools for Hindu women's education. The immediate lack of female takers within India accorded Western women (and workers in general) a special place in his projects.[3] In this, he followed the precedent set by the Brahmo Samaj and other reformist societies in Bengal, Madras and Bombay, that freely enlisted the intervention of white women inspired by a zeal to educate their Indian 'sisters'.[4] His wish to have 'heaps of other English workers out here' for different initiatives such as a farm colony in Bihar remained unfulfilled.[5] Those who followed him to India and sustained an interest even after his death became important figures in the larger history of Western Indophilia, helping produce forms of India and Hinduism for both universalist and nationalist consumption.

Following on from the earlier examination of letters and ashrams, this chapter continues to explore and expand on the theme of self-making across a range of intimate sites. Western women who enlisted themselves in the cause of Vivekananda and Vedanta came from a well-educated class of non-conformist but spiritually inclined women with access to important social, cultural and economic resources. For them, Vivekananda was both *deeksha* and *shiksha* guru, providing ritual initiation as well as instruction in the modes of Hindu devotion. These encounters came together to constitute a language of spiritual domesticity that evoked and sustained their practices of discipleship. This chapter looks at Western disciples' entry into the cultural world of Hindu devotion and moments of enchantment, education and failure that became part of their realignment. They encompass a series of spatial, material and physical experiences that brought disciples closer to the life and world inhabited by Vivekananda and his wider community.

This chapter argues how the claim to intimacy became a cause for change. To be able to love the India that Vivekananda represented was to immerse themselves in their guru's world – of spiritual mothers, fellow godmen, holy shrines and rituals – full of novelty and wonder. It also unsettled, often fundamentally, their own cultural certainties. Both everyday and extraordinary experiences produced in these disciples a love for the guru, his community and the idea of a glorious Hindu civilisation. They shed valuable light on the affective aspects of their discipleship, routinely harnessed for public projects that took Vedanta as an open signifier. A focus on personal relationships helps reclaim the seemingly distant discourse of Vedanta through everyday sights and sensations. Vedanta, an abstract and monist form of Hindu philosophy, greatly appealed to heterodox Western audiences for its ability to render itself on rational, universal and scientific terms, without negating their belief in other religious systems. The personhood of Vivekananda was influential in moulding these affections into concrete discipleships.

The disciples' desire to be part of Vivekananda's life and work involved lengthy periods of training and travel across sacred landscapes of Hinduism. These experiences were often characterised by bitterness and mutual incomprehension. Noble's British pride, for instance, was relentlessly disabused by Vivekananda. Initiation by Vivekananda was replete with tensions and transgressions. Despite differing thrusts, there was a constant re-education and cultural realignment in disciples. Each small training was part of a larger self-making.

Disciples' residence in picturesque retreats and camps, or travels across sacred Himalayan landscapes formed a continuum of spaces suffused with intense spiritual presence. Ashram-like spaces, much like ashrams, came to embody the qualities and experiences of their own differences and their possible dissolution. As the strictly monastic and celibate ashram of Ramakrishna Mission did not allow for the co-residence of white women disciples, the household of Sarada Devi or their own small household by the Ganges came to fulfil that aspiration. They created a series of aestheticised spiritual landscapes, performing gestures of meaningful inclusion. Unlike the (semi-)formal ashramic structures or disciplines that regulated Tagore, Gandhi or Vivekananda's ashrams, these spaces were informal; not always definite yet resembled them in experience.

Populated by a cast of holy characters that ranged from Vivekananda, his *gurubhais*/brother-disciples[6] and Sarada Devi, the Holy Mother of the Mission, these ashram-like spaces, their landscapes and mundane artefacts provided the spatial, affective and material loci of deep discipleship. It produced the idea of a spiritual–domestic world for women disciples to identify with. It framed their encounters, spatialised their affections and translated their love and loyalty within an idiom of *guru-shishya* discipleship.

The desire to be intimate also produced its own tensions. MacLeod felt deeply discomfited at the prospect of touching Sarada Devi's feet. Bull and Noble struggled with the notion of complete submission their guru required of them. MacLeod flatly refused to do so, seeking to contain her relationship within the trope of 'friend'. While travelling in north India, they came across places that prohibited Vivekananda from dining with his white disciples. On the other hand, in orthodox Hindu temples, these disciples found themselves denied entry owing to their outcaste (*mlechcha*) status, something they tolerated without any open resentment. For white women, negotiating a new, unfamiliar idiom of relationship with their guru was not beyond racialised affective structures. They understood not only the difference they embodied but also its instrumental value, utilised amply in taking Vivekananda and Vedanta to the 'world'.

Encountering Vivekananda

Vivekananda's personality exercised a great pull over his women followers, who were spellbound by his oratory and physical appearance. It was an attraction that rested partly on the non-resolution of personal desire and its continual sublimation. Christine Greenstidel, who adopted Vivekananda as her guru and later became Sister Christine, felt overwhelmed by the 'forceful, virile figure which stepped on the platform ... a powerful saint':

> He stood on the platform of the Unitarian Church pouring forth glorious truths in a voice unlike any voice one had ever heard before, a voice full of cadences, expressing every motion, now with a pathos that stirred hitherto unknown depths of tragedy, and then just as the pain was becoming unbearable, that same voice would move one to mirth only to check it in a midcourse with the thunder of an earnestness so intense that it left one awed, a trumpet call to awake. One felt that one never knew what music was until one heard that marvellous voice.[7]

Like Mira's first encounter with Gandhi, it had a *darshan*-like quality; a devotee struck by the vision of her deity. The awe of his voice and its power was shared by MacLeod, who never tired of pointing out

> the beauty, the charm, and the attractive power that beamed from him. An athletic force, that united him to grace. An energetic jaw and fiery eyes. A wonderful voice that in part ensured his success. A beautiful voice like a cello, a bit serious, absorbing, moving

(very different from Tagore's – which is higher), without éclats, but whose deep vibrations filled the room and the hearts, and knew how to quieten gradually to the level of an intense *piano* when the audience was captivated, thus training its audience to the intimacy of the soul....[8]

MacLeod spoke admiringly of his 'athletic body and jet-black eyes'[9] to European literary figures such as Romain Rolland and Nikos Kazantzakis. Several private and public accounts, particularly those of women admirers, remark on the pull of his physical appearance. Noble noted that even as she remained sceptical about the novelty of his message, she was 'deeply attracted by his personality'.[10] His sonorous voice, lofty eloquence, 'liquid eyes' and a blatant disregard for chivalrous codes made him a forceful, if unconventional, 'manly' figure to followers. Reeves Calkins, an American Christian missionary, acidly remarked that it was more his eyes than his ideals that 'were leading captive silly American women'.[11] Greenstidel recounts that Vivekananda would provocatively blow cigarette smoke on his women followers' faces, arguing that at the heart of all chivalrous performance lies sexual desire.[12] While visiting Paris, the French Satanist Jules Bois apparently encouraged the famous French operatic singer Emma Calve to secretly seduce Vivekananda, to test his strength of celibacy.[13]

The presence of cultured white women and their adorations served to buttress the spectacle of his own hetero-masculinity, not only in America but also elsewhere. In turn, Vivekananda praised the beauty, energy and intelligence of American women and commended them to his fellow countrymen. The erotics involved in crowds of white women adoring a celibate brown guru served to delineate the power of his own masculinity and self-control, seemingly impervious to any sexual temptation. Turiyananda, an Indian disciple of Vivekananda, asserted: 'Look at Swamiji! What was his power? He was free from lust. He lived among beautiful women, yet there was dispassion in his heart'.[14] Hagiographies of Vivekananda have faithfully reproduced this narrative: the ability to transcend his sexual desire was what made him a powerful and manly spiritual figure. In a Foucauldian move, they frame Vivekananda's success in relation to his being a sexual subject, if only to deny it.

Figure 4.1   Swami Vivekananda; the folded-hand pose iconised nationally and internationally.
Source: http://vivekananda.net/photos/1893-1895TN/pages/chicago-1893-september-harrr.htm (accessed on 20 January 2022).

The transnational recognition of Vivekananda's masculinity magnified its allegorical power. He became the idealised masculine figure in Hindu cultural discourse, idolised in the famous cross-armed pose (see Figure 4.1) that circulated widely after 1905 with the spread of political extremism in India.

Vivekananda demonstrated the performative aspect of guru-dom with great panache to curious audiences. In a West End drawing room in London, Noble reports:

> ... he sat amongst us, in his crimson robe and girdle, as one bringing us news from a far land, with a curious habit of saying now and again 'Shiva! Shiva!' and wearing that look of mingled gentleness and loftiness, that one sees on the faces of those who live much in meditation....[15]

The chanting of strange Sanskrit hymns in a near mystifying atmosphere, clad in a Hindu monk's habit, slipping in and out of meditation, produced great theatrical effect. For Noble it was a feeling that 'great music wakes in us, grows and deepens with its repetition'.[16] Vivekananda's first words came to MacLeod as truth and 'for seven years whatever he uttered was ... truth'. So complete was this immersion that '[w]hen Swamiji started speaking ... I lifted my eyes and saw with these very eyes.... Krishna himself standing there and preaching the Gita. That was my first wonderful vision. I stared and stared.... I saw only the figure, and all else vanished.'[17] This effacement and merging between Vivekananda and Krishna invoked and deepened the experience of bhakti in followers like MacLeod. But her Krishna was the eloquent prophet uttering the Gita, not the philandering romantic who flirted with *gopis* (milkmaids). In disciples' projections, we already see the incipient 'patriot-prophet' figure that would intensify in subsequent cultural nationalist discourse. Later hagiographies in the Ramakrishna–Vivekananda tradition developed the claim of their being avatars or reincarnations of Hindu deities and saints (*saptarshi*) to great popular effect.

These soul-stirring performances of a lofty yet enchanting guru made lifelong disciples out of several curious spiritual seekers. It birthed the desire to love and serve India, bringing them forever closer to their guru's world. It derived out of their attraction to Vivekananda but was not bound by it. Disciples' derivations of their guru, particularly after his death, existed in a relationship of tense ambiguity, in the kind of investments they sought to identify with. But the memory of Vivekananda remained a moving factor, the power of his speech a continuous source of inspiration. As Greenstidel recalls, many years later:

> Our love for India came to birth, I think, when we first heard him say the word, 'India', in that marvellous voice of his. It seems

incredible that so much could have been put into one small word
of five letters. There was love, passion, pride, longing, adoration....
It had the magic power of creating love in those who heard it. Ever
after, India became the land of heart's desire. Everything concerning
her became of interest – became living – her people, her history,
architecture, her manners and customs, her rivers, mountains,
plains, her culture, her great spiritual concepts, her scriptures. And
so began a new life, a life of study, of meditation. The centre of
interest was shifted.[18]

Noble, Bull and MacLeod – as well as other disciples – felt similarly.
MacLeod recalls how Vivekananda instilled in her a desire to love India.
Encountering Vivekananda was a sensory revelation.

In the early years of their relationship, Western disciples were not
forced to renounce their national or religious identities to be able to love
Hinduism or India. Indeed, Noble was led to think that not 'only has the
New Hinduism found its first firm foothold in the USA and in London,
but everyone who has joined it actively is passionately loyal to England'.[19]
The desire to serve India could sit very well with a belief in British imperial
munificence. However, these early beliefs soon came under severe strain, as
discipleships deepened. Noble underwent a complete transformation, through
her complete identification with anti-colonial nationalism and disavowal
of British privileges. Vivekananda considered Noble a 'real acquisition',
an asset for his Indian work. He was sure that 'she will soon surpass Mrs.
[Annie] Besant as a speaker'.[20] Within two years of her stay, Noble wrote:
'... my whole soul is in India. I am more and more convinced that there is
nothing to be done outside.'[21] In Vivekananda's rousing rhetoric, disciples
found a new love for India that manifested itself through different religious,
political and cultural projects. Indophilia emerged as a central condition and
consequence of their discipleship.

Vivekananda, however, struggled to create an impersonal language of
discipleship. He struggled to demarcate the propriety of disciples' affections,
fearing that the personal would hinder their grasp of the spiritual. Entirely
new to the paradigm of Indian guru-hood, Western women found their
negotiation of discipleship remarkably fraught. The struggle to reconcile their
deep affections into impersonal practices also had to consider the immense
power hierarchy of Indo-Western encounters. The relationships thus forged

were not impervious to the truth of such power. That most of these Western disciples were patrons providing critical material sustenance recreated the symbolism of that hierarchy, if not always the substance. Acknowledgements of Vivekananda and Vedanta's moral superiority unsettled that material hierarchy but the relationships themselves had to be reconstituted and renamed in different terms. Varieties of filial, maternal and fraternal love were regularly invoked to render these affections acceptable. Vivekananda coined nicknames like Yum and JoJo for MacLeod, Saint Sara for Bull or Margot for Noble. Vivekananda was variously referred to in exalted terms as Master, Swami, Prophet and even King.

Not all followers were captivated by his enthralling power. Mrs Ashton Jonson, an early British disciple who grew disillusioned, criticised the 'cult' and culture that grew around Vivekananda. She castigated Vivekananda's lifestyle in the West as un-monastic and opulent for a *sannyasin* (monk), a charge that others such as E. T. Sturdy and Henrietta Müller made as well, before abandoning Vedantic activities in 1899. Jonson felt absolutely disgusted by Noble's 'worship at the Swami's feet', a gesture she considered 'so deplorable as to be quite unspeakable from an English woman's point of view'.[22] 'Feet-touching' remained a transgressive act, one that absolutely polarised racial differences across a variety of contexts. Submitting oneself at the feet of their Indian guru was common to the self-effacement practices of Andrews, Mira and Pearson. It earned them much respect among lay Indians.

Henrietta Müller had been a major benefactor of Vivekananda's British work. She had housed and hosted his retinue of Indian monks and followers in London. But their domestic arrangement was tense, where Müller seemed to have earned the epithet of 'old maid' in Vivekananda's circle. Mahendranath Dutta, Vivekananda's brother, who was staying in the same house with Swami Saradananda, recounts Vivekananda's comments (made in Bengali):

> That mad hag [*khyaptan magi*] is making me restless. Look Sarat [Saradananda], in this country women who do not get married end up in two ways when they age. Some women fatten up; they remain nice gentle people. Some women shrivel up; they become querulous.... Listen you all, you must be very careful when dealing with the old hag. Get up immediately when she comes in the room,

ask her how she is, don't put your hands in your pantaloon pockets, don't put them on your chest. As long the old maid [*buri*] is standing, you guys must not sit.... Satisfy her by all means.[23]

Framed in strongly racialised and gendered terms, it also revealed the compulsions of outward reverence that financial obligation brought towards Western patrons. In later life, Müller alleged deception against Vivekananda (and Hinduism in general) and returned to Protestant Christianity, assuring Noble: 'Oh you won't love him [Vivekananda] long!'[24] Indian disciples were privy to frictions between Vivekananda and Western associates the latter did not always register.

Even as several disciples felt disenchanted with the Vedantic cause or found fault with Vivekananda, there remained others whose faith and investments deepened. Sara Bull became a maternal figure for the fledgling brotherhood of the Ramakrishna Mission. She was addressed by Vivekananda and many of his Indian and Western disciples as the 'American Mother', who in turn, referred to the latter as 'my dearest child[ren]'.[25] While in matters spiritual, Vivekananda remained superior, she remained influential in managing the administrative work and finances of the early Vedanta Societies in the US.

Yet, assumptions of motherhood and guruhood did not always sit together comfortably. There were bitter clashes over decisions taken regarding Vedanta Societies' work in the initial years of their relationship. Bull would reprimand Vivekananda for his occasional loss of temper. After a particularly sharp exchange between Vivekananda and a Presbyterian priest at a parlour talk in New York in 1895, Vivekananda fretted, in a vein similar to his guru Ramakrishna, on attachments to women:

> The last fight with the Presbyterian priest and the long fight afterwards with Mrs. Bull showed me.... [That] ... [a]ll friendship, all love, is only limitation. There never was a friendship, especially of women, which was not exacting.[26]

In times of friction, particularly with women disciples, Vivekananda was wont to invoke metaphors of bondage. His wish to break free of limitations ran counter to the deep obligations his work sustained. Being a guru did not absolve him. The claim to guruhood was continually, if often implicitly, contested by the presence of other claims, both personal and material. Unlike disciples like Henrietta Müller or

Edward Sturdy, however, Bull never broke away. After her death, she bequeathed most of her massive fortune to causes and people affiliated with Vivekananda.[27] Noble and Greenstidel became *brahmacharinis*, or initiated monastic disciples, adopting the severest asceticism regarding diet, dress and company. Several others, including Bull, accepted initiation as lay disciples. MacLeod referred to herself as a friend, accepting Vivekananda's authority as teacher, her 'idol and her passion'.

I take the term discipleship in a wide sense, to refer to people who adopted Vivekananda as their direct spiritual mentor and his exposition of Vedanta. There were, of course, important individual differences in the way these discipleships were negotiated. While there was no uniformity in method, there was a unity in the way they gathered under Vivekananda's tutelage:

> With some, it was an incessant hammering. The severest asceticism was imposed with regard to diet, habits, even clothing and conversation. With others his method was not so easy to understand, for the habit of asceticism was not encouraged. Was it because in this case there was spiritual vanity to be overcome and because good had become a bondage? With one the method was ridicule – loving ridicule – with another it was sternness. We watched the transformation of those who put themselves into line with it. Nor were we ourselves spared. Our pet foibles were gently smiled out of existence. Our conventional ideas underwent a process of education. We were taught to think things through, to reject the false and hold to the true fearlessly, no matter what the cost.[28]

Nivedita fitted easily within the framework of ascetic training and 'loving ridicule' that nearly broke her; for MacLeod and Bull, asceticism was never advised. Notions of *seva* (social service) and *sadhana* (spiritual exercise) played a crucial role in Vivekananda's training.[29] He constantly propelled them to the wider cause of philanthropic service, a mode through which they could merge and identify with things larger than themselves.

Mapping Spiritual Domesticity

The world of Vivekananda's monastic ashram life remained opaque to women disciples. In its absence, they came to inhabit ashram-like spaces – simulations of ashrams – that determined their own sense of belonging to India. This is perhaps an awkwardly termed category to denote a range of socio-spiritual spaces that were not formally ashrams. Ashram-like spaces entitled them to a sense of community marked by intense spiritual striving. It provided a shared space to indulge in the emotional and material practices of discipleship. Many of these landscapes were mobile, in the sense of not always being fixed or territorially rooted. They included camps and retreats organised in the presence of Vivekananda or his brother-disciples. Functionally similar to ashrams, they were organisationally more flexible. It nurtured a spiritual community of belonging.

It is revealing that Vivekananda's Western work was organised under the sign of the Vedanta Society, while in India, it proliferated as the Ramakrishna Math and Mission.[30] This dual move signified the universalist and cultural nationalist registers to which they laid claim, reflecting anxieties of respectability and authenticity. Vivekananda's global operations relied crucially on his Western disciples' travels to and from India, and close collaboration with Indian disciples, both lay and monastic.

In India, disciples' training involved long periods of travel, stay and instruction in spaces and places sacred to Hindu religious geography. This string of aestheticised spiritual landscapes forged a geography of belonging – making 'homes' out of hitherto unfamiliar spaces – that produced an essential Indian-ness for disciples to relate to. Disciples visualised spectacular moments through their guru, even though much of that meaning remained elusive. The elusiveness was, however, also its effect; the density of experience necessitating the need for a guru who embodies and elaborates.

Retreats and camps were used to create a sense of spiritual (be)longing. Vivekananda visited the picturesque Camp Percy by Lake Christine, New Hampshire, at Francis Leggett's invitation (MacLeod's brother-in-law) in 1895. One morning, he seemed to have lost consciousness while meditating under a pine tree. He was not breathing and the 'Gita had fallen from his hand and the front of his robe was wet with tears'.[31] MacLeod, on witnessing this, thought he had passed away. When Leggett assured her that he had fallen into a trance and attempted to shake him out of it, MacLeod stopped him, remembering that 'Swamiji had once said that when he would be in deep meditation one should not touch him'.[32] The trance-like spectacle of *nirvikalpa samadhi*[33]

(Absolute Transcendence) remained beyond the grasp of his Western disciples, yet this inaccessibility impressed Vivekananda's spiritual power and became a lesson to those witnessing.

MacLeod felt as if the days in the camp 'passed in a dream'. Vivekananda's presence wrought a colossal change on her. She felt herself living and breathing a 'tremendous, wonderful ... dream'. All externalities dissolved into Vivekananda: 'She saw only him, illumined.... From that moment everything began, from that moment everything would go on for eternity and [her] with it.'[34] Being with Vivekananda – listening to him – produced the effect of suspending space and time. At Ridgely Manor, the Leggetts' residence, Vivekananda's eloquence left his audience in a heightened spiritual state (Figure 4.2):

Figure 4.2   Vivekananda discoursing at the Ridgely Manor, New York, 1899.
Source: Vedanta Society of Southern California.

[W]e were all spellbound by his eloquence – such thoughts I have never heard expressed by mortal man such as he uttered for two and a half hours. We were all deeply affected. Swami was inspired to a degree that I have never heard before. He leaves us soon and perhaps we shall never see him again, but he will leave an ineffaceable impression on our hearts that will comfort us to the end of our earthly careers.[35]

Draped in 'flame-coloured silks', his 'splendid' demeanour enthralled the imagination of those gathered. However, he was not only a lofty guru. He mingled easily with the MacLeod–Leggett family, partaking in everyday domesticity. The family came to revere Vivekananda as a 'Prophet'. At Ridgely Manor, Vivekananda and his brother-disciples Turiyananda and Abhedananda stayed as guests in July 1899, along with Noble and Bull. The stay subsequently came to be referred to as the 'Great Summer' by his hosts.

Vivekananda struck deep bonds with MacLeod and her family. He reciprocated gestures of affection and inclusion. MacLeod fondly recalled his love for chocolate ice cream: 'because, "I too am chocolate and I like it," he would say'.[36] Maud Stumm, a young artist and admirer of Vivekananda, who frequently visited the Ridgely Manor recounts:

As he was landing from the steamer he was carrying most carefully a big bottle wrapped in papers that were torn and ragged; this precious bottle which he refused to relinquish before reaching Binneswater contained a wonderful sauce like curry, brought by hand from India. 'For Joe,' he said.[37]

The feelings evoked around 'chocolate ice-creams' to 'sauce like curries' continued to bind them. He attended MacLeod's sister Betty and her husband Frank Leggett's marriage in Paris. So pervasive was the presence of Vivekananda in their everyday lives that Frank would write to Betty, after proposing marriage: 'and I long for you and love you with the ardour of *our Hindu* and I go along repeating the comforting words "Betty is mine, Betty is mine"'.[38] MacLeod wanted to name Betty and Frank's daughter 'Nalini' (The Blue Lotus),[39] regarding her as spiritual child of the Swami and herself. Frank, who seemed to have been unmoved in this regard, named her Frances.[40] Assumptions of spiritual matrimony shed light on the spiritual language emerging through the relationships between Vivekananda and his female followers, particularly Noble and MacLeod (Figure 4.3).

Figure 4.3   Vivekananda and his women disciples at a picnic, Pasadena, 1900.

Source: Vedanta Society of Southern California, US.

Greenstidel writes of a similar joyful experience in the Thousand Islands Retreat in the same year, living with Vivekananda:

> Of the wonderful weeks that followed, it is difficult to write. Only if one's mind were lifted to that high state of consciousness in which we lived for the time could one hope to recapture the experience. We were filled with joy. We did not know at that time that we were living in his radiance. On the wings of inspiration, he carried us to the height which was his natural abode. He himself, speaking of it later, said that he was at his best in Thousand Islands.[41]

Being in the company of their mentor uplifted them. The deep silence of his meditations invited those around him to share in that lofty mode of being. Surrounded by dense woods and deep solitude, the atmosphere of the retreat emulated ancient *tapovan*s, an ashram-like space where disciples received instruction from the guru amidst open nature. It was here that Vivekananda 'reached some of his loftiest flights, there he showed us his heart and mind. We saw ideas unfold and flower. We saw the evolution of plans which grew into institutions in the years that followed. It was a blessed experience.'[42] Experiences such as these determined their own moral and spiritual transformations. Disciples felt a sense of one-ness with their guru, sharing in his teachings and presence in these special places.

'Feeling Blessed': Belur Math, Sarada Devi, Himalayas

In India, experiments in spiritual domesticity continued to develop through disciples' travels. Vivekananda clarified to his disciples about the general lack of material comfort, poverty, heightened race and gender segregation, class and caste prejudices that characterised Indian life:

> Europeans and the Hindus ... live as oil and water. Mixing with Natives is damning to the Europeans ... dirt and filth everywhere, and brown people, though plenty of people to talk philosophy with.[43]

His disciples persevered in spite of Vivekananda's warning. Bull did not find the poverty she encountered to be particularly 'painful as anticipated' and was struck by the sense of self-respect among Indians she met despite their colonised status.[44] She thought of Indians as 'a healthy, handsome race, even the poorest, with bodies beautiful enough to be models'.[45] Their physical appeal to Bull (echoed by MacLeod, Nivedita and Christine) suggested an openness to non-Western bodies and beauty.

The spiritual commune of Belur – where Vivekananda, his brother-disciples and Sarada Devi resided – mesmerised them. It was also their first encounter with Indian monastic communes, places where a guru and his community of disciples' lodge and train together. Starkly different from the elegant retreats and well-furnished drawing rooms they knew, it represented a new world of sights and sensibilities. They witnessed monks who were half-clad, widowed women wearing the simplest of white cotton sarees, a life of dire material poverty but potent with spiritual possibilities. Outside the monastic community lay the city of Calcutta, whose 'mass of humanity' – loin-clothed men, thinly draped women and unclad babies – was a novel sight. To be able to enter this world represented a new episode in their lives.

Bull, MacLeod and Noble had converged in Calcutta in early 1898 to meet Vivekananda. Unable to stay in the same place as Vivekananda and his brother-disciples, Bull and MacLeod refurbished a nearby abandoned cottage by the Ganges that was in ruins. The cottage was part of the plot purchased through the Bull's munificence, where the Belur Math would be later built (Figure 4.4). Bull and MacLeod restored the house and redecorated it with old mahogany furniture bought from Calcutta. The drawing room was redesigned in Indo-Western style; half of it was Indian and the other half Western.[46] Vivekananda marvelled at the 'Yanks' industriousness: 'It is wonderful how they accommodate themselves to our Indian life of privation and hardship.... After the luxuries of Boston and New York to be quite content and happy in this wretched little house.'[47] Suffering was seen as a mark of sacrifice, a necessary spiritual striving. MacLeod remarked to Rolland about her first meeting with Noble, in Calcutta: her face was swollen, 'devoured by mosquitoes but glowing with joy'.[48]

The little cottage became a home for the three women. Vivekananda visited them almost every morning for tea, breakfast and discourse in the subsequent months. He loved their little villa by the Ganges, finding 'that little house of Dhira Mata [Bull, the Steady Mother] like heaven, for it is all love, from beginning to end'.[49] He lectured them every morning on Ramakrishna, his own life before Chicago, and commentaries on Indian religion, mythology and history: 'with his stories of Uma and Siva, of Radha and Krishna, and his fragments of song and poetry'.[50]

Figure 4.4   Old Belur Math building on the left and Vivekananda's house on the right; the River Ganges flows in the background.

Source: https://belurmath.org/ (accessed on 20 March 2023).

The backdrop of the Ganges – a river central to Hindu sacred geography – and the location of the Kali Temple on Dakshineshwar on the other side of the riverbank, where Ramakrishna served as a priest, enabled the cottage and its inhabitants to partake in its sacred spatiality. MacLeod felt:

> It was perhaps the most beautiful time we ever had with Swamiji. He loved our living at the riverside cottage and he would bring all those who came to visit him to see what a charming home we had made of this house which he had thought uninhabitable. In the afternoons … we used to give tea parties in the front of the house, in full view of the river, where always could be seen loads of boats going up-stream, we receiving as if we were in our drawing rooms. Swamiji loved all that intimate use we made of things, which they took, as a matter of course.[51]

The cottage and its scenic setting evoked spiritual domestic feelings. The placemaking on the banks of the wide-flowing Ganges was as much a spatial negotiation as material. The house, its material artefacts, arrangements and attachments came together to constitute an intimate home.[52]

In this 'heaven', Vivekananda passionately discoursed a wide range of subjects, ending always on the 'note of the Infinite'. The spatial ordering of the houseboats coming to shore in their drawing room – aided such projections. Noble writes:

> Indeed I do not know that our Master's realisation of the Advaita Philosophy has been in anything more convincing than in this matter of his interpretation of the world. He might appear to take up any subject, literary, ethnological, or scientific, but he always made us feel it as an illustration of the Ultimate Vision. There was, for him, nothing secular.[53]

His disciples struggled to grasp the abstract ideas but 'by his burning enthusiasm it was possible to enter into these things, and dimly, even then, to apprehend their meaning'.[54] He would chant poems on Radha-Krishna bhakti, a common Vaishnavite practice in India to instil in listeners and imbue them with an affection for spiritual love and divine communion. It worlded their Indophilia within a dense web of human and spatial relationships, inspiring mystique.

Even as they sought to grapple with ideas and practices that were not readily accessible, gestures of affection by Sarada Devi and her companions brought home practices of transcultural identification meaningfully. Sarada Devi and her widowed female companions led their lives in strict seclusion and caste orthodoxy. They lived in a household separate from male monastic disciples in Calcutta. The seclusion of Sarada, however, did not render her role secondary; rather, after the death of Ramakrishna, she was acknowledged as the highest spiritual authority by his disciples, and her word was considered superior to that of Vivekananda.[55]

Meeting the matriarch of the young sect was therefore a much-anticipated event. Vivekananda took his disciples to meet Sarada on 17 March 1898, the occasion of Ramakrishna's birth anniversary celebrations. Noble noted that it was also St Patrick's Day, part of her constant search for Christian equivalences. She accepted MacLeod's invitation to have food with them, despite all the caste restrictions that bound her. It was considered a rare transgression, a remarkable gesture that moved the women deeply. Noble referred to it as a 'Day of Days' in her diary:

> ... 'my daughter' she calls me. She has been terribly orthodox, but all this melted away the instant she saw the first two Westerns – Mrs. Bull and Miss MacLeod, and she tasted food with them! Fruit is always presented to us immediately, and this was naturally offered to her, and she to the surprise of everyone accepted. This gave us all a dignity and made my future work possible in a way nothing else could possibly have done.[56]

Sarada, however, later justified her dining with foreigners as not breaking any Brahminical caste stricture: 'I did not take rice – I took only fruits and sweets. I did not violate the rules of Hindu scriptures in spirit.'[57] Yet, the outward gesture of commensality for these women was sufficient to indicate acceptance. Bull wrote proudly to Max Müller the famous Orientalist scholar and philologist at Oxford: 'We are the first foreigners to have received permission to see Sarada.'[58] Though they considered the gesture of commensality a sharp contrast to her 'terribly orthodox' strictures, Sarada's caste practices, while outwardly rigorous, were never absolute. There were past instances in her life where she had served food with her own hands to Amjad – a lower caste and class Muslim construction worker at her village Jayrambati (in Bengal) and accepted fruit offerings from him.[59]

These transgressions, however, were kept as clandestine as possible, largely due to fear of scandal. They also visited Gopaler Ma (Gopal's Mother), a companion of Sarada Devi and disciple of Ramakrishna, in her thatched mud cottage on the banks of the Ganga in Dakshineshwar. She fed them puffed rice (*muri*), some of which MacLeod expressed a desire to take back with her to America.[60] In spite of cultural barriers, the disciples were touched by the simplicity of their living and gestures of affection.

Though Bull and MacLeod never relocated to India, all of them continued to hold Sarada Devi in high regard. MacLeod observed: 'Sarada was still capable of interesting herself in the toilette of her European friends with a childlike joy.'[61] MacLeod saw her as a representative of Indian women, whom she held in 'high esteem' and 'superior to men in general' for their 'dignity, an abnegation and an activeness that cannot be denied'.[62] Bull turned to Sarada for advice on her relationship with Vivekananda. She felt guilty for defying him as a guru when their opinions differed sharply. Sarada put her disquiet to rest by suggesting that while the guru's directives are supreme in things spiritual, she could use her discretion on temporal matters, 'even if at times it were not in agreement'.[63] Sarada Devi and Noble grew extremely close in later years, notwithstanding the social and language barriers that separated them. Noble felt at home in 'the Mother's room':

> When the hot weather came, it was by her express command that I returned to her better-arranged house, for sleeping-quarters. And then I occupied no room apart, but shared the cool and simple dormitory of the others, with its row of mats, pillows, and nets, against the polished red earthenware of the floor.[64]

Her 'deep self-abnegation' amazed Noble. Despite this growing intimacy, however, Noble saw Sarada and her household of women as essentially 'creatures of feeling', incapable of 'educated thought'. This was, as Noble thought, due to lack of formal education:

> For in thought, outside the range of practicality and experience, these ladies have no range; it is in feeling that they are so strong. You see, they have never had the education that would enable her to frame a thought that would appeal to a stranger.[65]

Noble's outcast status dissolved in this close mother–daughter relationship. At her insistence, Sarada formally inaugurated her primary school for girls in November 1898, a place that she continued to visit and enquire about.[66] Noble's admission and acceptance in her home displaced orthodox caste strictures of Hindu widowhood. Even as she entered Hinduism from an outcaste location, Noble herself was never critical of the caste system, knowing it might threaten her own uncertain claim as a Hindu nun. She would often defend its merits, leading to heated exchanges with reformist friends and leaders such as Jagadish Bose and Bipin Pal, both part of the Brahmo Samaj.[67]

Even as Sarada came to be embraced as the 'spiritual mother' of the Mission by Western and Indian disciples, Bull too became a near-beatified figure, elevated as Saint Sara. Being older than Vivekananda and his brother-disciples, she eagerly adopted this maternal position, treating male monastic disciples as her sons. Vivekananda, acknowledging this maternal bond, wrote: 'Ere this I had only love for you, but recent development proves that you are appointed by the Mother [Shakti, a deified force of Nature] to watch over my life; hence faith has been added to love!' This maternal side was, however, not without its material effects; she continued to dispense huge sums of money to Vivekananda's Indian and American projects until her death.[68]

Saradananda, the brother-disciple of Vivekananda and the first secretary of the newly founded Mission, kept only two photographs in his austere room at the monastery, that of Sarada Devi and Bull. Bull used to fondly refer to Vivekananda and Saradananda as her two sons, their tempers comparable to the sun and moon.[69] Saradananda took care of the women's belongings in the Belur cottage when they went to tour the Himalayas with Vivekananda. Saradananda also distributed their material possessions when the cottage had to be disbanded for Math-related construction work:

> I have taken as many of them as I could manage in my little room: viz.: the guest room bed-stead, your wash stand and bowls … the little tea-table for keeping my books, two clothes horses, and two carpets; also the writing pad of Jojo, and some little things … I have taken so many of them in my little room for I thought I would be able to take better care than the others.[70]

Small things became part of larger enactments. Personal artefacts such as washstands, bowls, books and carpets formed sites of material attachment.

Objects and the everyday material culture built through them came to embody the absent selves of their owners. Their re-use and care enacted a recreation of that relationship. For a renunciate monk supposed to possess minimal belongings, this re-materialisation affirmed the potency of these relationships and how material forms could become sites to script personal attachments. Saradananda fondly referred to Bull as 'Grannie' throughout his life.[71]

Traces of this material relationship entered more spiritual practices such as meditation. Swarupananda, a monastic disciple of Vivekananda, helped women disciples understand its practice and power and the material circumstances that influenced it. Nivedita found a skin rug helpful to focus: 'it isolates one and increases the magnetic power in some way'.[72] Material things became interfaces for accessing a new world of spirituality. Sara sought a rosary bead specifically blessed by Sarada for her daily prayer.[73] It mediated the vestiges of her touch, far yet near.

Initiation and After

Alongside spatial practices lay more didactic methods of instruction. Ritual initiation by the guru was of utmost spiritual significance. Rites of monastic initiation, or *mantradeeksha*, spelt the moment of rebirth for a disciple, marking a 'new life' as the older self is symbolically cast away. Vivekananda's initiation of his disciples, in particular Noble, shows how this process was a fraught task. Assumptions of racial and cultural differences were not subverted simply by formal acknowledgements of the guru's authority. For Western disciples, this was an entirely new idiom with a set of practices whose broad thrust was submissive. In effect, the acceptance of Vivekananda as guru would flip the racial relationship on its head, and no disciple was impervious to its strain. There were lengthy and difficult exchanges involved in the remaking of disciples' interiority.

On the morning of 25 March 1898, Vivekananda took Bull, Noble and MacLeod to the Math for an initiation service. Noble was initiated into the rites of a *naishtik brahmacharini*, the first step in a Hindu nun's life of strict celibacy.[74] A year later, Noble reflected:

> I fancy he made me a Brahmacharini for life partly for the sake of
> reviving the old order of Naishtik Brahmacharini, and partly because
> I am not really ready for anything higher in his eyes.[75]

That Vivekananda made her only a *brahmacharini* and not a *sannyasini* suggests that the decision was not taken lightly. *Sannyasa* takes years, sometimes decades, and the initiation into *brahmacharya* indicated the beginning of a life-long process whose end was nowhere near. Bull was initiated as well, while MacLeod bore witness to the service, not taking any vows herself. All of them were bestowed with new Sanskritic names – Noble became Nivedita (the Dedicated), Bull was christened Dhira Mata (the Steady Mother) and MacLeod, Jaya (the victorious one).[76] It marked their new births, in line with Hindu monastic traditions of adopting new names that signified symbolically the beginning of a different life. The Christian Feast of the Annunciation fell on the same day, the Biblical day when Mary was informed by the angel Gabriel of her conception of Jesus, the 'Son of God'. It mattered to Noble that her consecration occurred on a doubly auspicious day. She related to these experiences in the affirmative:

> ... Friday, the Christian feast of the Annunciation, – he took us all three back to the Math, and there, in the worship-room [of Belur Math] was held a little service of initiation, where one was made a *Brahmacharini*. That was the happiest of mornings. After the service, ...[t]he Swami put on the ashes and bone-earrings and matted locks of a Siva-yogi, and sang and played to us – Indian music on Indian instruments – for an hour.[77]

Vivekananda's elaborate performance – donning matted locks and a face smeared with ash – like the deity of Shiva as a *yogi,* impressed the sensory revelation of his guruhood upon enthralled disciples. The initiation ceremony went beyond a spiritual service to become a spectacle, evoking awe and devotion in his disciple-spectators.

Initiation rites were only constitutive rather than conclusive in processes of cultural realignment. This was borne out by the bitterness that followed between Nivedita and Vivekananda. Her autobiographical account *Notes of Some Wanderings with Swami Vivekananda* (1913) testifies to these tribulations. Curiously written in the third person, she was desperate to create through her writing an impersonal distance from a relationship that was already excessively personal for her. Acknowledging the extent of her own belief in English pride, she wrote:

> The youngest of the Swami's disciples at this time, it must be remembered, was an English woman, and of how much this fact meant intellectually, – what a strong bias it implied, and always does

imply, in the reading of India, what an idealism of the English race and all their deeds and history, – the Swami himself had had no conception till the day after her initiation at the monastery.[78]

Vivekananda had naively assumed upon her initiation as a Hindu *brahmacharini* that her British loyalties would cease to exist. When Vivekananda asked after her initiation as to which nation she belonged to, he was 'startled to find with what a passion of loyalty and worship she regarded the English-flag, giving to it much of the feeling that an Indian woman would give to her Thakoor[deity]'.[79] An annoyed guru had then let it pass, but matters came to a head during their travels across sacred Hindu pilgrim sites in Nainital, Almora and Kashmir in 1898. Around this time, Nivedita was still seeking Anglo-Indian introductions from friends and believed it to be the dream of her life 'to make England and India love each other'.[80] Nivedita had not expected her patriotism to be called into question. This kind of paternalist approach characterised much contemporary British liberal thinking, including that of E. J. Thompson and, at one time, both Andrews and Pearson. It visualised a kind of egalitarian relationship under the enlightened tutelage of Britain. These aspirations co-existed in a tense relationship until they dissolved completely by the end of Nivedita's life.

The stress of negotiating discipleship continued throughout this period of travel and training. The difference in American and British identities is perhaps also best illustrated in these episodes. The absence of a direct colonial relationship with the United States allowed Bull and MacLeod to escape much of the bitterness that characterised Nivedita's experiences. This did not, however, mean that American disciples were critical of British rule already. Indeed, as the Mother India controversy in 1927 showed, there was wide American support for the continuance of British rule in India.

Vivekananda chastised Nivedita for what he saw as her unbending British pride:

> [Vivekananda] insulted in every way he could Nivedita's proud and righteous English character. And perhaps also he wanted to protect himself from the adoring fondness that Nivedita showed for him…. He chided her sharply without consideration. He found fault with everything she did. She sometimes returned in tears, seeking consolation in the arms of Miss MacLeod.[81]

It pained Nivedita to see 'the dream of a friendly and beloved leader falling away from me, and the picture of one who would be at least indifferent, and possibly, silently hostile, substituting itself instead'.[82] Extreme in form, this virulent self-excision almost broke Nivedita but Vivekananda saw this as a pre-condition for her new life.

Unable to bear her agony, Bull and MacLeod interceded on Nivedita's behalf against what they felt was excessive severity. A reconciliation followed, Vivekananda blessing her on a new moon day, Nivedita kneeling before him. In Vivekananda's blessing touch, Nivedita realised the 'importance of destroying a personal relationship only to bestow the Impersonal vision in its place'.[83] She felt her older relationship was broken, and not yet anticipating 'that a new and deeper life was being given to it, knew only that the hour was strange and passing sweet'.[84] Even though it was a 'terrible experience' for Nivedita, and Vivekananda dropped this aggressive method, she felt the swami never dictated any opinion or creed, it was 'never more than emancipation from partiality'.[85] In hindsight, she justified his actions as necessary preparation for the effacement of personal attraction into an impersonal ethic of service.

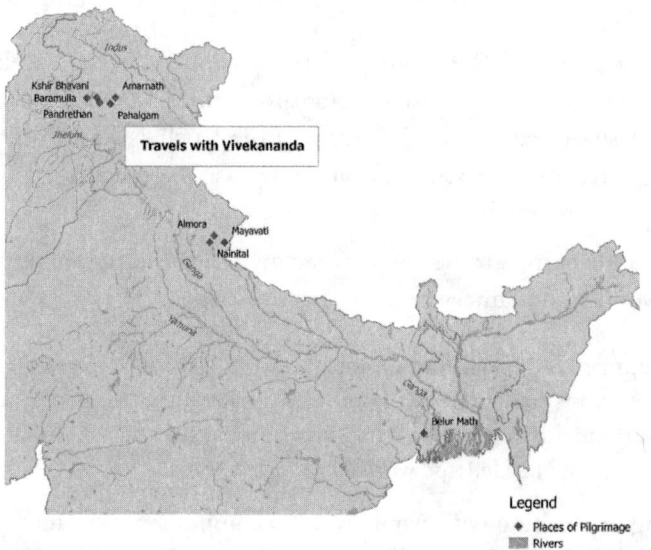

Figure 4.5   Holy Geographies: Vivekananda and his Western disciples' travel across the Himalayas, 1898.

Source: Courtesy of Matteo Mazzamurro.

Note: Map not to scale and does not represent authentic international boundaries.

'Going-to-school'

Negotiating discipleship was inextricably wound up in the cultural politics of race and gender. Practices of discipleship provoked and remade those hierarchies. Replete with moments of affection and alienation, their travels with Vivekananda formed a crucial testing site. Living and travelling with their guru across the Himalayan landscape felt like 'going-to-school' (Figure 4.5). It took the form of morning talks, prayer and visits to holy shrines and Hindu archaeological sites. Staying in picturesque mountain village homes was inspiring: 'You never knew anything so "blessed" as this little home amongst mountains with its utter love and generosity and simplicity.'[86] Here too we find the pursuit of homing – reflecting anxieties of identification in their guru's home-world.

In these settings, morning talks 'took the form of assaults upon deep-rooted preconceptions, social, literary and artistic, or of long comparisons of Indian and European history and sentiments':

> He was always testing his disciples, and the manner of these particular discourses was probably adopted in order to put to the proof the courage and sincerity of one who was both woman and European.[87]

Being a woman and European were both points of stress. Vivekananda's provocative observations on Western colonialism and racial prejudice frequently pre-empted sharp exchanges. Western cultural beliefs and loyalties were repeatedly tested in such sessions, pitted against the exacting claims of an Indian form of discipleship.

Vivekananda narrated tales from Indian mythology, initiating them into its world of wonder and fantasy to draw lessons:

> Sometimes all through the summer he would sit for hours telling us stories, those cradle-tales of Hinduism, whose function is not at all that of our nursery fictions, but much more, like the man-making myths of the old Hellenic world.[88]

Storytelling or teaching with parables was a common and intimate narrative mode for Indian gurus. Ramakrishna was famous for his parable-like teachings, where a popular story was recounted in the simplest of languages, followed by a philosophical gleaning. Vivekananda would tell them of his own visions, the romantic legends of Krishna or the life stories of his guru Ramakrishna. He made the geographies come alive:

… as we journeyed across the Terai, in the hot hours of an afternoon near the beginning of the rains, we were made to feel that this was the very earth on which had passed the youth and renunciation of Buddha. The wild peacocks spoke to us of Rajputana and her ballad lore. An occasional elephant was the text for tales of ancient battles, and the story of an India that was never defeated, so long as she could oppose to the tide of conquest the military walls of these living artillery.[89]

Stories of gallantry reclaimed a greatness for India that was no longer available. It contrasted sharply with the discriminatory treatment meted out to Indian monks at various 'Europeans only' places for food and lodging. It brought home the truth of European conquest and colonisation in ways Western disciples did not encounter before. Despite this, journeying with the Swami was 'delightful'. At times, the disciples took turns to drive with Vivekananda in his *tonga*: 'we were always sorry to reach a destination'.[90] They lived and travelled through scenic places of 'indescribable beauty' on their way to Kashmir – hamlets, frozen rivers, mountain springs and deep woods – mingling with sadhus, peasants, people of many faiths and pilgrims at various holy places. These became part of a moving but unbroken landscape that territorialised their affections for India and Hinduism, evoking in them a love for the land and its people. It induced in them the feeling of living an unfettered 'Vedantic' life.

Figure 4.6   Martand-Sun Temple, Kashmir, 8 CE.

Source: Aadil939, 9 September 2018, https://commons.wikimedia.org/wiki/File:Martand-Sun_temple.jpg (accessed on 10 December 2022).

Vivekananda repeatedly broke caste orthodoxy and religious taboo during his journey, partaking in food and shelter with lower castes and Muslims. In Pahalgam, a small shepherd-village in Kashmir, they halted to observe *ekadasi* (a day of ritual fasting following the Hindu lunar calendar). Vivekananda took Nivedita to be blessed, 'which really meant to distribute alms' to pilgrims gathered there. The party also visited the holy shrines of Takt-i-Suleiman, Kshir Bhavani and the derelict Martand temple in Pandrethan (Figure 4.6). Vivekananda waxed eloquently on the history of Kashmir and Shiva worship, and the 'Hindu genius' in temple-building. Shiva became a frequent benediction for his disciples, a blessing aimed at imbuing them with divine energy and intervention. Staying on the *dunga*s, or houseboats, on the river Jhelum in Srinagar, Bull felt: 'I have found enough to make me hope that the coming months of this quiet life with nature will bring an inner strength that I needed.'[91] In his presence and that of nature, they felt themselves 'brought face to face with the invisible and absolute'.[92] These small observations, benedictions and dedications became constitutive of the emotional practice of discipleship. While aspects of this cultural experience remained opaque, the physical act of participation created a space for attachments to form.

Kashmir constituted the high point of their travels. At Amarnath, the sight of the Shiva lingam made of ice in a mountain cave overwhelmed Vivekananda: 'To him, the heavens had opened. He had touched the feet of Siva.'[93] Vivekananda dedicated Nivedita to the deity, an elusive moment she held in deep regard. Shiva symbolised the benevolent yet furious destructive force in the Holy Trinity of canonical Hinduism. Nivedita believed this to be a moment of rebirth though she herself could barely grasp the meaning of the *darshan* and dedication, a culturally specific experience that eluded her Anglican sensibilities:

> ... it is such terrible pain to come face to face with something which is all *inwardness* to someone you worship, and for yourself to be able to get little farther than externals. Swami could have made it live – but was lost.[94]

The 'inwardness' or interiority of the moment remained vague, she could only appreciate the grandness of its external beauty and Vivekananda's revelatory delight. Still, the physical experience itself seemed to perform for Nivedita what she wanted it to. She felt herself 'growing Hindu in taste with alarming rapidity' immediately after. It also exposed the impossibility of accessing a near-intuitive experience beyond rational knowledge. Vivekananda's revelations became their revelations, even as much of it was lost in translation.

Amarnath, along with other Hindu shrines, became part of a sensory learning for disciples. Even as they were unable to enter or understand them, Vivekananda reassured them that having 'made the pilgrimage … it will go on working.... The effects will come'.[95] A similar but more powerful revelation ensued in the Kshir Bhavani (literally, Milk of the Mother) temple, the Divine Feminine in the form of Shakti (Nature). The darshan pushed Vivekananda into a state of ecstasy, who had gone alone. From Shiva, his mood shifted distinctively to that of Shakti. He came back 'transfigured and inspired', filled with the searing presence of the 'Mother'. Nivedita felt her words were too inadequate to even begin to describe this experience:

> He simply talks like a child of '[T?]he Mother' – but his soul and voice are those of a God.... He is all love now. The mingled solemnity and exhilaration of his presence have made me retire to the farthest corner, and just worship in silence all the time.
>
> 'Patriotism is a mistake. Everything is a mistake' – he said when he came home. 'It is all Mother.... I am never going to teach any more....'
>
> He is all love now. There is not an impatient word, even for the wrongdoer or the oppressor, it is all peace and self-sacrifice and rapture. 'Swamiji is dead and gone' were the last words I heard him say.[96]

This was a transformation that his disciples had never witnessed before – the ability to be completely absorbed and intoxicated by a powerfully divine vision. It laid bare the versatile world of Hindu bhakti, one form of devotion could easily segue into another. Vivekananda's disciples saw him consumed by thoughts of the Goddess Kali, singing devotional songs of Ramprasad, imagining himself as her child.[97] He filled his disciple-companions with a sense of this elusive mother:

It was always his habit to speak simply and naturally of 'Mother', and some of the older members of the party caught this, so that such phrases as 'Well, well! Mother knows best!' were a constant mode of thought and speech amongst us, when, for instance, some cherished intention had to be abandoned.[98]

Deep discipleship manifested in this unselfconscious way Kali or Shiva were constantly invoked in everyday conversations. The constant exposure to various deities throughout their travels initiated them to the breadth of the Hindu pantheon and its specific sensibilities. Kali and Shiva became interlinked states of mind, tethered to their own identities. Nivedita came to regard Kali as the 'Vision of Shiva' in later life, an embodiment of both the maternally affectionate and terrifying aspects of Nature. She saw the worship of Kali as commemorating a primal instinct of love and loss, of sacrifice and self-realisation, of the benevolent and the violent that created and defined human life. In a character sketch of Nivedita, Bipin Chandra Pal, the Extremist Congress leader and Brahmo preacher, commented how she struck him as 'a child of nature ... a pagan of pagans ... born by some mischance among Christian peoples'.[99] For Nivedita, Kali became, as the literary scholar Elleke Boehmer suggests, a 'legitimation of her Hindu self', a motif of cultural de-anglicisation.[100]

At work around the notion of Kali or the 'Divine Mother' was a constant spiritualisation of the female body. Motherhood was the safest form of relationship with women as it did not pose any immediate temptation to male ascetics. Occasionally, even the position of motherhood was not beyond the reproach of 'female shortcomings'. An exasperated Vivekananda would comment after bitter fights with Bull that '[a]ll friendship, all love, is only limitation'.[101] However, motherhood remained the exalted mode. In Srinagar, Vivekananda worshipped the daughters of a Muslim boatman and a Brahmin pundit as the 'Divine Virgin' in front of his disciples. Both were pre-pubescent virgins, or *kumaris*, yet to achieve sexual maturity.[102] This spiritualising helped contain a potently risqué female sexuality that seemed to inhere in the bodies and selves of women disciples. At one remove, it seamlessly connected all womankind to an indigenist but also universalist trope of idealised maternity. Shakti, Kali, Sarada, Bull, the Virgin Mary could all be fused into one.

Motherhood also made available a conjoined category of sisterhood – of single young women disciples such as Nivedita and Christine (or Mira for Gandhi) that could be harnessed for service in a variety of 'national awakening' projects. Nivedita's identification with sisterhood aided her own de-sexualisation, making her body available as a spectacle for nationalist politics to appropriate. Yet, the attainment and acceptance of a celibate state of sisterhood remained tortuous. Past selves had to be continually emptied out before new selves could be assembled. Romain Rolland, who knew both Nivedita and Mira, found in their experiences a similarity of adoration:

> Sister Nivedita was treated very harshly by Vivekananda during the early days…. Maybe in this way he defended himself against the worshipful passion Nivedita had for him. Because it seems she had for him the *lover's adoration* which our friend Miss Slade showed for Gandhi. But between Gandhi and Miss Slade there was a distance of thirty years; between Vivekananda and Nivedita there were only five or six. And though the sentiment of N had always been of absolute purity, maybe Vivekananda understood the danger. He rebuked her without sparing her and would find fault with everything she did…. He was not a man to tolerate the passions people had for him nor to treat them with fatherly compassion as Gandhi did.[103]

Any hint of 'lover's adoration' was suppressed or harnessed into a trope of spiritual love. Both Nivedita and Mira exemplified the tragedy of such negotiations, their 'passions' potently threatening to exceed the acceptable boundaries of discipleship. Bound by the claims of celibate sisterhood on one hand and the struggle to efface past cultural selves on the other, Nivedita's and Mira's sacrifices became inextricably tied to how Indian nationalist discourse saw itself etched on the bodies of Indophile women.

Conclusion: New Selves

Nivedita grew into the life of celibate sisterhood envisaged by Vivekananda. He disapproved of her (initially) indiscriminate socialising with all classes and sections of people (for instance the Brahmo Samaj or Tagore) fearing it might impede her acceptance in orthodox Hindu society. To consolidate Nivedita and her work for Hindu women, her Hindu identity needed to

be stabilised. Ritual strictures were enjoined. Nivedita's body became a site
of control and discipline. Vivekananda advised her to give up all socialising
and live in strict seclusion:

> ... to eat only of approved foods, and to do this with the fingers, to
> sit and sleep on the floor, to perform Hindu ceremonies, and bind
> oneself strictly by the feelings and observances of Hindu etiquette,
> were all, to his thinking, means of arriving at that Indian consciousness
> which would afterwards enable one to orientate oneself truly to the
> Indian aspects of larger questions. Even so trifling a matter as the use
> of lime-juice and powdered lentils, instead of soap, appeared to him
> worthy of thought and effort.[104]

The emphasis on different kinds of practice was absolute. Vivekananda and
Sarada Devi were 'constantly working to make a place for [her], as a foreigner,
in Hindu society'.[105] She ate with her hands – 'à la Hindu' – at home in
the white (later ochre) monastic robes of a Hindu nun. Vivekananda would
ask her to cook a dish and share it with fellow Hindus to break their caste
taboos towards her. Sarada Devi would let her stay in her household, breaking
conservative Hindu convention. This spatial and ritual inclusion was premised
on her becoming a chaste Hindu nun, an austere process that un/re-settled
her race, caste and gender identities. The ideal of celibate Hindu widowhood
was advised as an emulative model. Orthodox Hindu widowhood was also a
position of extreme social marginality, and to embrace it willingly was a test
of Nivedita's character, supposedly enabling her to enter Hindu society from
her symbolic outcaste location. To be accepted into caste Hindu society, even
as a nun, was therefore possible only through a rigorous practice typical of
conservative Brahmin widowhood:

> You have to set yourself to Hinduise your thoughts, your needs, your
> conceptions, and your habits. Your life, internal and external, has to
> become all that an orthodox Hindu Brahmin Brahmacharini's ought
> to be. The method will come to you, if only you desire it sufficiently.
> But you have to forget your own past, and to cause it to be forgotten.
> You have to lose even its memory![106]

To be Hinduised was to entail the wilful loss of her former cultural memory.
All she was required to do was 'desire it sufficiently'; a performance that would

supposedly reconstitute her own subjectivity. Emulating an orthodox Hindu Brahmin *brahmacharini* was contingent on this forceful excision.

Vivekananda further warned her against eclectic socialising in Calcutta's reformist circles, especially with the Tagores, who represented a reformist lineage:

> [A]s long as you [Nivedita] go on mixing with that [Tagore] family Margot I must go on sounding this gong. Remember that that family has poured a flood of erotic venom over Bengal … and just you remember … my mission is not Ramakrishna's nor Vedanta's – nor anything but simply to bring MANHOOD to this people. 'I'll help you Swami' I said. 'I know it' he said – 'And so I beat the alarm.'[107]

Nivedita received the message to deliver 'Manhood' in capital. She did not intend to be confined to mere monasticism or women's education, a project that came to be characterised by many disruptions. To be able to deliver 'MANHOOD' to an emasculated nation, she needed to embody the powerful, 'pure' and chaste ideal of Celtic womanhood Vivekananda expected her to. Her increasing entanglements with revolutionary terrorism in India testify to the continuation of this pursuit: 'When will the Motherland rise again – the Gita on one hand, and the Sword in the Other?'[108] Vivekananda's death had extinguished in Nivedita for a brief while the possibility of personal attachment: 'Ever since He went, I have felt the utter impossibility of being personal in my love for anyone….'[109]

Yet her growing intimacy with men such as Swami Sadananda, Bose and Kakuzo Okakura, the leading Japanese artist and pan-Asian thinker, seemed to have concerned MacLeod. She alleged a 'physical awakening' in Nivedita, caused by her relationship with these men. Nivedita's terse replies evidence a moment of upheaval when her 'sexual purity' was questioned by her closest friend and confidante:

> I feel absurdly shocked and hurt at the warnings that you have just sent me … about massage and other matters. Are you referring to that sacred thing I told you about Sadananda after my illness? Oh Yum! I cannot think of anything else.

And are you warning me about entering people's bedrooms? I have never done such a thing except once in the middle of the night when Nigu [Okakura] was lying here ill and groaning so loudly … that I woke and dressed and came to him. But that was a matter for the doctors – it was so bad….

… You talk of a 'physical awakening', and I think you mean for me. I must be quite plain about this…. If I do wrong in these matters … the wrong will be a matter of failure of judgment, and never of temptation. You need not quote Swamiji's opinion on these points – because my own standards are far stricter and impose far more pain than ever His.

He [Bose] understands the idea that I represent, but his words of rapt worship half unconscious and involuntary showed me that I had not lowered it to him. And you know I have had no deceit any where … when I asked him if I had been a temptation, he said 'you made me natural, Dear, you made me a child of God'. [110]

These allegations must have stung Nivedita deeply. She flatly asked Bose if she had been a 'temptation'. Bose's reply, while phrased loftily, was evasive. Nivedita had always effusively referred to Bose as Bairn, Scottish for 'child' and cherished their relationship, the latter benefitting immensely from Nivedita's Western contacts. There might be some truth in the way idealised forms of relationship desperately attempted to contain the 'gender trouble' wrought by women's potent sexuality.

The letter only hinted at the nature of the 'massage' between Sadananda and Nivedita, or her care for Bose and Okakura in their of illness and wellness. Vivekananda had noted about Sadananda before: 'He loves you Margot, and wants to follow you about like a dog – and he was jealous!'[111] The limitations imposed by monastic celibacy on Sadananda meant that 'love' and 'jealousy' could only be expressed in other ways. Sadananda emerged as a devoted aide of Nivedita, always by her side during her travels and projects in the subsequent years. Personal infatuations for Nivedita were generally rendered in more acceptable terms – maternal, filial, cordial – by Sadananda, Okakura and Bose.

MacLeod's letter 'hurt and horrified' Nivedita. She alleged that MacLeod had not grasped their Master's idea of purity at all: 'Swami's saying that you were "as pure as purity itself" was NOT due to any of your puny definitions of purity'.[112] The invocation to purity did not fade away; it continued to determine their personal relationships, none of whom ever married or pursued any romantic relationships openly. The pursuit of purity remained a point of contention between Nivedita and MacLeod, the latter seemingly more Victorian in her emphasis on sexual purity even as she claimed a position of 'non-discipleship' and non-initiation. Nivedita, while acknowledging MacLeod's 'unerring, faultless', perfect renunciation, saw her abhorrence to sexual union as ultimately limiting:

> As to purity, dear Yum – do not we both torture ourselves too much trying to rush forward into definitions of wh[o]? We shall be intellectually capable only in some other life.

> You are wrong. We are hypnotising ourselves by this talk of pure and impure into looking at ourselves instead of at the One. The union of sexes is not impure – how could it be? … it is forgetting that all-is-One that constitutes impurity….[113]

Nivedita's impatience at MacLeod's failure to grasp the significance of 'purity' show the tensions that adhered to differing practices of discipleship. But her close relationships with other Indian and Asian men intensified Nivedita's love for India through new human attachments, particularly after Vivekananda's demise. She did not wish to propagandise in the West anymore, turning firmly instead towards India–Japan–Asia:

> I do not wish or expect to go West again…. Saradananda will do that. My place is here – possibly a visit to Japan, and certainly, if so, to China also, then, more India. Then the end.[114]

By 1903, the shift in her interiority and identification with India was more complete than any of Vivekananda's Western disciples:

> … you will understand that these festivals [Christmas and New Year] seem now scarcely to exist. In externals, I find I remain more steadily and even boldly European that I would have wished, but in heart, I think even Swamiji might be satisfied![115]

While Noble rose to great national prominence as the revered Sister Nivedita, Bull and MacLeod charted out distinct trajectories for themselves. They remained in constant touch with each other, Bull and MacLeod returning to the US and continuing to work mostly from abroad. The locus of their activities focused on developing the Vedantic movement in the West, though India remained a constant node of engagement. They did not renounce their Western privileges but wove in specific Hindu cultural practices in their everyday lives. Bull continued to manage, organise and host swamis for the Vedantic movement's work in the US. Both Bull and MacLeod became personal benefactors to Indians (such as the scientist J. C. Bose) seeking support for a range of causes, whose broad thrust was to expand Indian nationalism.

MacLeod refused to make herself 'subject to the discipline of renunciation and obedience' as others. She embraced Vedantism as an 'itinerant credo, a faith of nomadic pragmatism'.[116] To remain in one place became for her a sign of limitation. For her, Vedantism implied a logic of perpetual movement. Vivekananda became the source of inspiration for all her investments around India and beyond (Figure 4.7). Even as she vouched for her relationship with him as 'only a friend', her last letter, written only a few months before Vivekananda's death was a movingly intimate one-liner: 'I swim or sink with you'.[117] She never received a reply but was content that she had let Vivekananda know of her feelings for him. MacLeod regarded 29 January 1895 to be her real birthday, the day she first met Vivekananda. It was the greatest 'turning point' in her life: 'everything in her mind and heart ... revolved around him'.[118] An avid traveller, she fondly referred to her itinerant trips around the world as 'making lovers for Swamiji'.[119] She increasingly withdrew from a life of social indulgence, finding parties 'so worldly and vulgar':

> ... what was the sense in all that conversation? Why ask people to come to your house to eat? why not all sit on the floor and be simple?' after her ineffectual protests 'she would take to her bed and live on bread and milk and excerpts from the Bhagavat Gita'.[120]

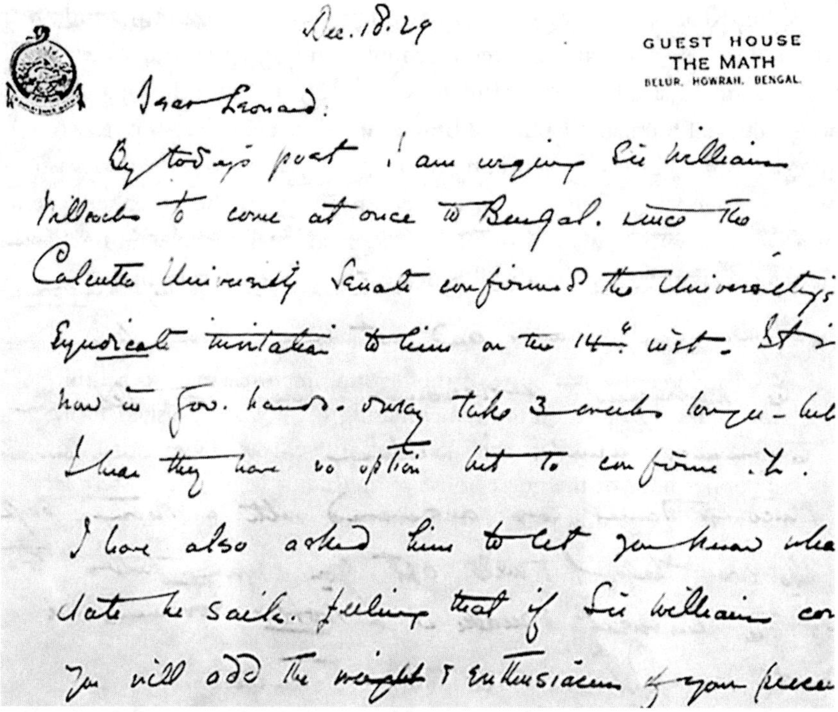
Dec. 18. 29

GUEST HOUSE
THE MATH
BELUR, HOWRAH, BENGAL.

Dear Leonard:

By today's post I am urging Sir William Willcocks to come at once to Bengal. since the Calcutta University Senate confirmed the University's Syndicate invitation to him on the 14th inst. It is now in Gov. hands. may take 3 months longer – but I hear they have no option but to confirm it.

I have also asked him to let you know when date he sails. feeling that if Sir William come you will add the weight & enthusiasm of your presen

Figure 4.7 Letter from Josephine MacLeod to Leonard K. Elmhirst, written on the Ramakrishna Mission's letterhead.
Source: Dartington Hall Trust.

Deep discipleship was naturalised through (cultural) practice. Sitting on the floor, surviving on bread and milk and reading the Gita were effects of this naturalisation. She lived frugally, travelled widely and had protégés everywhere 'to whom she wrote and who wrote back'.[121] Travelling in third-class carriages felt like an 'acme of comfort'. She lived on the milk from railway stations and carried

> in a small chamois bag tied by a string around her neck … the equivalent of at least a thousand dollars in rupees, sterling, lire, drachmas. She gave away freely what money she had to people who asked or needed it, often advising them to buy a second class ticket to India where, by the shores of the Ganges, emanated truth and wisdom.[122]

She mobilised resources for constructive work in various parts of rural and urban India: to build new irrigation systems, schools, sending a prize bull from the US to rejuvenate the strain of sacred Indian cows.[123] She brought the Japanese artist and intellectual Kakuzo Okakura to India, who pioneered ideas and networks of pan-Asianism in the early twentieth century.[124] Vivekananda's death devastated her; it changed her. She was no longer 'the devoted, heartbroken friend, but a woman with a mission – Tantine, Joyananda, Universal Aunt, Family Priestess'.[125] Fourteen years after his death, she returned to India:

> They like to have me at the monastery guest house, because I keep Vivekananda alive, as none of these young men has ever seen him. And I like to be in India, remembering once when I asked him, 'Swamiji, how can I best help you?' his answer was, 'Love India!' So the upper floor of the guest house at the [Belur Math] monastery is mine where I go and will probably go winters, until the end.[126]

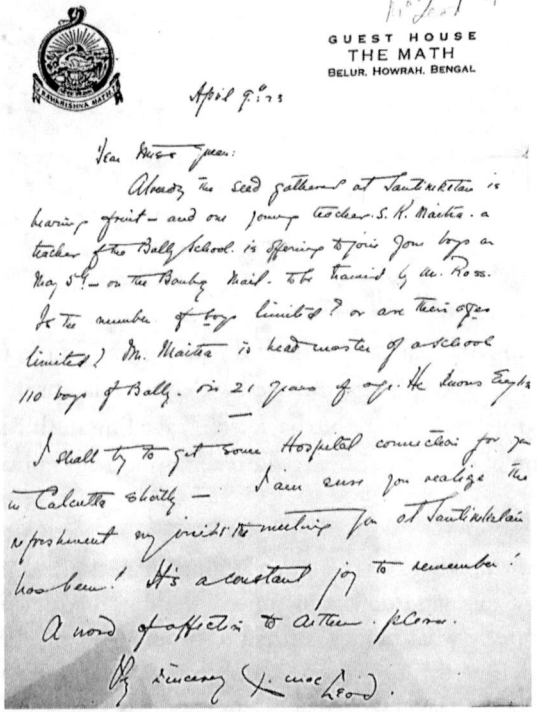

Figure 4.8   Letter from MacLeod to Elmhirst, offering a new recruit for Shantiniketan, April 1923.
Source: Dartington Hall Trust.

MacLeod remained involved in the Ramakrishna Mission's affairs, visiting almost every winter, starting a decade after Vivekananda's death. Her many letters to Leonard Elmhirst, a close disciple of Tagore, in the mid-1920s, indicate the frequency of her stay at Belur Math, the Mission's official headquarters (Figure 4.8).[127] MacLeod sustained a close interest in Tagore and 'the seeds gathered at Shantiniketan', fascinated by the poet and his work. She found in India the realisation of an imputed Vedantic unity: 'What India makes one know is that one is in Eternity! That gives space and time and serenity. It's such fun!'[128]

While MacLeod remained loyal to Vivekananda's broad vision of an inclusive Hinduism, Nivedita veered towards a more 'aggressive Hinduism'. MacLeod remained sharply critical of the conservative Hindu turn both Nivedita and the Mission took in the 1920s. She was

> scandalised by this degeneration of the ideal, and, strong with the authority conferred by her long intimacy with Vivekananda, she speaks harshly, from on high, to the monks. She is outraged that they plant shards of glass in the walls of their garden to prohibit Mahomedans from passing, or that they speak, in case of a disagreement, to go to the police. With a cold disdain, she thanks them for having given her bitterness over seeing the great teachings of Vivekananda denied. And they shut up, humiliated; they are ashamed.[129]

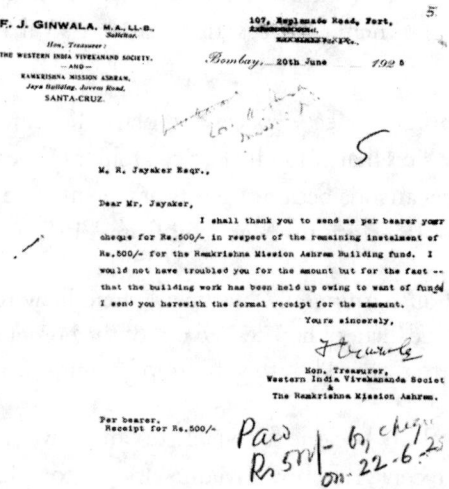

Figure 4.9   Letter to M. R. Jayakar, requesting funds to consolidate
Ramakrishna Mission's work in western India.
Source: Jayakar Papers, National Archives of India.

MacLeod invoked her direct intimacy with Vivekananda to impress her authority on a new generation of monks. Vivekananda's straitjacketing into a Hindu nationalist icon demonstrated the reach and success of the Hindu Mahasabha – already at work then – against which MacLeod's remonstrations were but feeble protests. Monks of the Ramakrishna Mission had been seeking the support of Hindu Mahasabha leaders, such as M. R. Jayakar, to expand their own activities (Figure 4.9) – particularly in western India – and these intersecting networks told on the practices of the Mission as it sought to align itself more closely to mainstream Hindu religiosity.[130] Nivedita was effusively invoked as an icon of this discourse, memorialised in the Hindu nationalist ideologue V. D. Savarkar's influential booklet in 1923: *Hindutva: Who Is a Hindu?*[131]

Vivekananda and Vedanta, therefore, spawned multiple trajectories, some of which will be taken up in the next chapter. Bull, Noble, Greenstidel and MacLeod remained attached to Vivekananda and the Vedantic cause throughout their lives, contributing greatly to the institutions and ideologies that grew around them.

Indophilia – constituted through a language of spiritual domesticity – became part of a larger imbrication. Love and longing for the mentor was intertwined with the spaces and places he lived through, congealed as an individual and collective experience. Deep discipleship produced subjective experiences that took them into 'realms of perception, imagination, fiction and fantasy', creating 'mental spaces and maps as so many mirages of the supposedly 'real' thing'.[132]

The material world of objects, spaces and places became traces of extended selves. They became sites that embodied a rich archive of meanings and feelings. Articles used by Vivekananda became objects of worship and affection. Nivedita scavenged a piece of the cloth for MacLeod from Vivekananda's funeral pyre:

> ... safe out of all burning and blackness, there blew to my feet the very two or three inches I had desired out of the border of the cloth. I took it as a Letter from Him to you, from beyond the grave.[133]

The 'border of the cloth' became for MacLeod an answer to her last letter, for which she had not received a reply. Nivedita also got for MacLeod the 'incense burner': 'I stole from the pillow – where it was used all through those last hours. I felt that it would bring you the one assurance for wh[ich] you w[ould] long – and it w[oul]d rightly do so.'[134] Bull pleaded with Sarada Devi for a photograph, so that she could take it back to America for worship. She hoped her photograph would remediate her presence, giving her strength and blessing.

Emerging as a medium in India in the 1850s, the novelty of the photographic mode redefined personal embodiment.[135] Sarada Devi cherished looking at Nivedita's photograph 'now and then' when the latter was away: '[a]nd it seems as if you are present with me'.[136] Swarupananda, another monk, longingly gazed at the photograph of MacLeod, uttering: 'My Mother!! How strange! When she was here I did not think so much about her!'[137] Nivedita often kissed MacLeod's photograph. A vibrant affective economy involving photographs connected women disciples to their guru and his wider social world. They constantly sought and exchanged pictures of Ramakrishna, Sarada Devi and Vivekananda, along with each other's, to feel the touch of distant or dead selves. Photographs reconstituted embodiment. They made possible a close visual conception of people in a way letters did not.

This did not however diminish the worth of letters. Letters from Sarada carried her love and blessings: 'May this letter carry all blessings! My dear love to you, Baby Daughter Nivedita…. You are a manifestation of the ever blissful Mother.'[138] Photographs, like letters, evidenced absent selves, by recreating their presence. It provided a material interface to convey embodiment. After Vivekananda's death, MacLeod followed in his footsteps in the US. She lived in the same places, inhabiting a form of intimate absence, that excess which makes even emptiness seem full. Practices of discipleship were replete with recursive traces of love, longing and loss.

Notes

1   Once again, the number of works on Ramakrishna and his influence is vast. Major representative works include but are not limited to Amiya P. Sen, *Hindu Revivalism in Bengal 1872–1905: Some Essays in Interpretation* (Delhi: Oxford University Press, 2006); see also Amiya P. Sen, *Three Essays on Sri Ramakrishna and His Times* (Shimla: IIAS, 2001); Gwilym Beckerlegge, *The Ramakrishna Mission: The Making of a Modern Hindu Movement* (Oxford: Oxford University Press, 2000); Sumit Sarkar, *An Exploration of the Ramakrishna Vivekananda Tradition* (Shimla: IIAS, 1993); also Sumit Sarkar, '"Kaliyuga", "Chakri" and

"Bhakti": Ramakrishna and His Times', *Economic and Political Weekly* 27, no. 29 (18 July 1992): 1543–1559, 1561–1566. Works that dismiss Ramakrishna's influence as purely propaganda include Narasingha P. Sil, 'Vivekānanda's Rāmakrsna: An Untold Story of Mythmaking and Propaganda', *Numen* 40, no. 1 (January 1993): 38–62.

2   There is a separate 'sister' organisation, Sri Sarada Math, that is run by and for women monastic members. It was founded in 1954, almost half a decade after the foundation of the Ramakrishna Math and Mission, to train 'brahmacharinis and sadhvis'.

3   Sarala Devi Chaudhuri, also Tagore's niece, came close to accepting his discipleship but it collapsed after opposition from his family, who were staunch Adi Brahmo Samaj supporters. See her autobiography *Jeebaner Jharapata* (Calcutta: Dey's, 1950), where she regrets not having joined Vivekananda due to her family's opposition (that included Tagore). She would come to play a major role in the cultural nationalist turn through the Swadeshi movement in Bengal during 1905–1910, contributing to the growth of physical culture and *akhadas*.

4   Several historians have problematised the politics of such interventions: see Kumari Jayawardene, *The White Woman's Other Burden: Western Women and South Asia during British Rule* (London: Routledge, 1995); Nupur Chaudhuri and Margaret Strobel, eds., *Western Women and Imperialism Complicity and Resistance* (Bloomington: Indiana University Press, 1992); Ware, *Beyond the Pale*.

5   Nivedita to Mrs Eric Hammond, 7 August [1898], *LSN*-I, 17. Though the Ramakrishna Mission did have one of its oldest ashram-cum-school centres in former Bihar (now Jharkhand).

6   Disciples of the same guru, in this instance Ramakrishna.

7   Christine Greenstidel quoted in *Reminiscences of Swami Vivekananda: His Eastern and Western Admirers* (Mayavati: Advaita Ashrama, 1983), 103.

8   13 May 1927, Josephine MacLeod's meeting with Rolland, *Inde*, 192.

9   Nikos Kazantzakis, *England: A Travel Journal* (London: Simon and Schuster, 1966). Kazantzakis is widely regarded as a major author in Modern Greek literature.

10   Sister Nivedita, *The Master as I Saw Him, Being Pages from the Life of the Swami Vivekananda* (London: Longmans Green, 1910), 11–12.

11   Reeve Calkins quoted in *Reminiscences of Swami Vivekananda*, 399.

12   Christine Greenstidel quoted in *Reminiscences of Swami Vivekananda*, 135.

13   Calve refused Bois's overtures, arguing that Vivekananda was a monk and 'she respected the God who was within him MacLeod'. In later life, she visited

Belur Math to pay her respects to Vivekananda and her guru Ramakrishna. The source of much of this gossip is Rolland, via MacLeod in Prabuddhaprana, *Tantine*, 215.

14 Swami Turiyananda quoted in *Reminiscences of Swami Vivekananda*, 341.

15 Nivedita, *The Master as I Saw Him*, 8.

16 Ibid., 11.

17 Linda Prugh, *Josephine MacLeod and Vivekananda's Mission* (Chennai: Sri Ramakrishna Math, 1999), 26.

18 Sister Christine quoted in *Reminiscences of Swami Vivekananda*, 105.

19 Noble to Mr and Mrs Hammond, 10 February 1898, *LSN*-I, 7.

20 Vivekananda to Shashi, March 1898, *LSV*, 377.

21 Noble to Macleod, January 1901, *LSN*-I, 167.

22 Cited from Beckerlegge, *The Ramakrishna Mission*, 171–174. Sturdy and Müller withdrew from the Vedanta Society work in England by 1899. New York also suffered as Abhedananda's relationship became strained with some longstanding disciples such as Francis Leggett. Swami Kripananda and Abhayananda, two of his American disciples, also defected. The personal financial support and underwriting of the cost of the society's activities suffered with these withdrawals (Beckerlegge, *The Ramakrishna Mission*, 169).

23 Mahendranath Dutta, *Londone Swami Vivekananda* (Calcutta: Mahendra Publishing Committee, 1931), 71 (author's translation).

24 Noble to MacLeod, [1 January 1899?], *LSN*-I, 32.

25 Pravrajika Prabuddhaprana, *Saint Sara: The Life of Sara Chapman Bull, The American Mother of Swami Vivekananda* (Calcutta: Sri Sarada Math, 2002), 104.

26 Vivekananda to Mary Hale, 1 February 1895, New York, *LSV*.

27 'Ole Bull Will Contest', *New York Times*, 13 February 1911; 'Spirits Urged $25,000 Gift, Said Mrs Bull', *Boston Herald*, 15 June 1911.

28 Christine quoted in *Reminiscences of Swami Vivekananda*, 134.

29 Gwilym Beckerlegge has dealt with the complex socio-economic organisation that shaped the multi-sited discourses of *seva* and *sadhana* in late nineteenth-century colonial Bengal in which the Ramakrishna Mission's legacy was rooted. See Gwilym Beckerlegge, *Swami Vivekananda's Legacy of Service: A Study of the Ramakrishna Math and Mission* (Oxford: Oxford University Press, 2006).

30 See Swami Gambhirananda, *History of the Ramakrishna Math and Mission* (Calcutta: Rupa, 1957), for a fairly extensive, if one-sided, account of the national and international growth of the organisation.

31 Prugh, *Josephine MacLeod*, 45.

32 Ibid.

33   A state of mind considered in Indian Yoga as the attainment of the highest
     state of consciousness, where the boundaries between the knower, the known
     and the act of knowing is dissolved.
34   Frances Leggett, *Late and Soon: The Story of a Transatlantic Marriage* (Boston:
     Houghton Mifflin, 1968), 278.
35   Frank to MacLeod, 6 January 1896, Leggett, *Late and Soon*, 102.
36   Josephine MacLeod quoted in *Reminiscences of Swami Vivekananda*, 160.
37   Leggett, *Late and Soon*, 115.
38   Frank Leggett to Betty, 17 July 1895, Prugh, *Josephine MacLeod*, 100
     (italics added).
39   The Blue Lotus is a symbol of enlightenment in Vedantic and Buddhist
     philosophy.
40   Leggett to Betty, 17 July 1895, Prugh, *Josephine MacLeod*, 106.
41   Christine quoted in *Reminiscences of Swami Vivekananda*, 112. The plan at
     Thousand Islands was to 'live as a community, without servants, each doing a
     share of the work'. It failed and an outsider had to be engaged for housekeeping
     with a couple of the more capable ones undertaking certain responsibilities
     (*Reminiscences of Swami Vivekananda*, 113).
42   Ibid., 112.
43   Vivekananda to Josephine MacLeod, 10 July 1897, Prugh, *Josephine Macleod*, 99.
44   Sara Bull to Olea Bull, Prabuddhaprana, *Saint Sara*, 262.
45   Sara to Olea, Prabuddhaprana, *Saint Sara*, 261.
46   On a plot that was purchased with Bull's money to build the headquarters
     of the Ramakrishna Mission. Josephine MacLeod quoted in *Reminiscences of
     Swami Vivekananda*, 157.
47   Vivekananda to Christina Greenstidel, *LSV*.
48   Rolland, *Inde*, 194.
49   Sister Nivedita, *Notes of Some Wanderings with Swami Vivekananda* (Calcutta:
     Udbodhan, 1913), 16.
50   Ibid.
51   MacLeod quoted in *Reminiscences of Swami Vivekananda*, 157.
52   Antoinette Burton's work on home-making shows how the materiality of the
     home, its constitutive structures and space, determine how attachments are
     formed. See Antoinette Burton, *Dwelling in the Archive: Women Writing House,
     Home, and History in Late Colonial India* (Oxford: Oxford University Press,
     2003), 15.
53   Ibid., 17.

54 Ibid.

55 Incidentally, Vivekananda was not Sarada's favourite 'son', it was his brother-disciples Yogen and Sarat, for whom she had extraordinary love and affection. Vivekananda might have been Ramakrishna's chosen one, but for Sarada, it were the other two who held her in the highest regard.

56 Nivedita to Mrs Eric Hammond, 22 May 1898, *LSN*-I, 10.

57 Ibid.

58 Prabuddhaprana, *Saint Sara*, 271.

59 Swami Asheshananda, *Glimpses of a Great Soul* (Chennai: Vedanta Press, 1982), 22.

60 Prabuddhaprana, *Saint Sara*, 271.

61 Rolland, *Inde*, 195.

62 Ibid., 195.

63 Cited from Max Müller, *The Life and Sayings of Ramakrishna* (Calcutta: Advaita Ashrama, 1951), 64–65, in Prabuddhaprana, *Saint Sara*, 273.

64 Nivedita, *The Master As I Saw Him*, 70.

65 Nivedita to Mrs Eric Hammond, 9 March 1899, *LSN*-I, 76.

66 Swami Tapasyananda, *Sri Sarada Devi: The Holy Mother, Her Life and Conversations* (Madras: Sri Ramakrishna Math, 1958), 315–316. She had also kept a decadent piece of Assam silk, or *endi*, that Nivedita had gifted to her, among other things such as her photo, as a token of Nivedita's love for her. After Noble had passed away in 1911, Sarada Devi tearfully recalled how she 'would prostrate herself before me and with great tenderness, take the dust off my feet with her handkerchief. I felt that she even hesitated to touch my feet' (Swami Gambhirananda, *Holy Mother Sarada Devi* [Madras: Ramakrishna Math, 1955], 391).

67 Jagadish Chandra Basu and Rabindranath Thakur, 'Bose to Tagore, 18 April 1900', in *Dui Bandhur Chithi: Parasparik o Paramparik, 1899–1936* (Calcutta: Manfakira, 2008), 23–24. Pal had commented on how casteism keeps down men of genius, including her own guru Vivekananda. She reacted with utter contempt, denouncing that Brahmos are 'neither Hindus nor Christians'.

68 Bull had offered 15,000 dollars to Vivekananda for the purchase of land for the Ramakrishna Math and helped him register the deed. Prugh, *Josephine MacLeod*, 153.

69 Prabuddhaprana, *Saint Sara*, 7. Bull was also funding Saradananda's brother's education.

70 Saradananda to Bull, Olea S. Kaland Collection, Prabuddhaprana, *Saint Sara*, 283.

71   'Saradananda Always Inquires for News', Sara to Olea, 24 May 1898, Prabuddhaprana, *Saint Sara*, 283.

72   Nivedita to Nell Hammond, 7 August 1898, *LSN*-I.

73   Saradananda to Sara, 13 September 1898, Prabuddhaprana, *Saint Sara*, 300.

74   A *naishtik* brahmachari vows to remain celibate till death.

75   Vivekananda to Nivedita, 26 March 1899, *LSN*-I, 93.

76   Henceforth I refer to Noble as Nivedita, as she largely identified and referred to herself in private and public using this name. MacLeod and Bull generally continued to use their Christian names, only occasionally, in private correspondence, using their Indian names.

77   Nivedita, *Notes of Some Wanderings*, 19.

78   Ibid., 23

79   Nivedita, *Notes of Some Wanderings*, 24.

80   Nivedita to Mrs Hammond, 5 June 1898, *LSN*-I.

81   Rolland, 16 May 1927, Rolland, *Inde*, 126. Based on MacLeod's recounting of these episodes to Rolland.

82   Nivedita, *The Master as I Saw Him*, 126.

83   Rolland, *Inde*, 127.

84   Nivedita, *Notes of Some Wanderings*, 32.

85   Ibid., 23–24.

86   Nivedita to Mrs Hammond, 5 June 1898, *LSN*-I.

87   Nivedita, *Notes of Some Wanderings*, 24.

88   Ibid., 28.

89   Nivedita, *The Master as I Saw Him*, 46.

90   Nivedita, *Notes of Some Wanderings*, 40–43.

91   Sara to Olea [undated, 1898], Prabuddhaprana, *Saint Sara*, 290.

92   Nivedita, *Notes of Some Wanderings*, 55.

93   Ibid., 72.

94   Nivedita to Mrs Eric Hammond, 7 August 1898, *LSN*-I.

95   Nivedita, *Notes of Some Wanderings*, 72.

96   N to [?], 13 October 1898, *LSN*-I, 24–25.

97   Sadhak Rāmprasād Sen was a Hindu Shakta poet and saint of eighteenth-century Bengal. His bhakti poems, known as Ramprasadi, are still popular in Bengal – they are usually addressed to the Hindu goddess Kali and written in Bengali.

98   Nivedita, *The Master as I Saw Him*, 62.

99   Bipin Chandra Pal, *Character Sketches* (Calcutta: Yugayatri, 1957), 97–98.

100 Boehmer, *Empire, the National, and the Postcolonial*, 59.

101 Vivekananda to Mary Hale, 1 February 1895, New York, *LSV.*

102 It is now institutionalised as a celebration in the Ramakrishna Mission as *kumari puja*, where a pre-pubescent virgin girl is worshipped as the divine form of Shakti.

103 Rolland, *Inde*, cited in Prabuddhaprana, *Tantine*, 217 (italics added).

104 Nivedita, *The Master as I Saw Him*, 76.

105 Ibid., 76.

106 Ibid., 146.

107 Nivedita to MacLeod, 12 March 1899, *LSN*-I, 82.

108 Nivedita to Alberta and Hollister, 28 January 1903, *LSN*-II, 537.

109 Nivedita to MacLeod, 24 July 1902 [?], *LSN*-II.

110 Nivedita to MacLeod, 23 October 1902, *LSN*-I, 517.

111 Nivedita to MacLeod, 27 August 1902, *LSN*-I, 497.

112 Nivedita to MacLeod, 23 October 1902, *LSN*-I, 519.

113 Nivedita to MacLeod, 11 October 1902, *LSN*-I, 513.

114 Nivedita to MacLeod, 23 October 1902, *LSN*-II, 518.

115 Nivedita to MacLeod, 28 January 1903, *LSN*-II, 537.

116 Leggett, *Late and Soon*, 239.

117 MacLeod quoted in *Reminiscences of Swami Vivekananda*, 163.

118 Leggett, *Late and Soon*, 11–12.

119 Ibid., 134.

120 Ibid., 112.

121 Ibid., 11–12.

122 Ibid., 241.

123 Ibid., 242.

124 Ibid., 134.

125 Ibid., 238.

126 MacLeod quoted in *Reminiscences of Swami Vivekananda*, 164.

127 The only ones still in public domain that has not been already claimed and locked away by the Ramakrishna Mission.

128 MacLeod to Elmhirst, 30 October 1924, Prabuddhaprana, *Tantine*. MacLeod, LKE/IN/13/B, Dartington Hall Trust Papers, Devon Heritage Centre, Exeter.

129 Rolland, *Inde*, 272. Rolland observantly notes that 'Nationalism is infiltrating into them'.

130 Swami Yatishwarananda to M. R. Jayakar, 21 October 1925, Roll_00024_File_No_233, PA_Microfilm, Digitized Private Papers, M. R. Jayakar, National Archives of India.

131 V. D. Savarkar, *Hindutva: Who Is a Hindu?* (Nagpur: V. V. Kalkar, 1923), 116.

132 Harvey, *Condition of Postmodernity*, 203.
133 Nivedita to MacLeod, 14 September 1902, *LSN*-I, 505.
134 Nivedita to MacLeod, 27 August 1902, *LSN*-I, 497
135 Nathaniel Gaskel and Diva Gujral, *Photography in India: A Visual History from the 1850s to the Present* (London: Prestel, 2019).
136 Sarada Devi to Nivedita, 13 May 1900. Translation made by Nivedita from the original Bengali, which is lost/unavailable. *LSN*-I, 412.
137 Nivedita to MacLeod, 9 January 1899, *LSN*-I, 42.
138 Ibid.

CHAPTER 5

Vedanta and Its Variables

The Politics of a 'World Religion', 1890–1910

In the wonderful disposition of Providence, it has been designed that truths revealed, perhaps for the first time to the sages of our country and treasured up by them in a monumental form, should cross oceans and mountains and spread among nations utterly foreign to us both in their past and present lives. The Kantian revolution in Western philosophy, the outpourings of the Upanishad-intoxicated Schopenhauer, ... the revival of Sanskrit Study, the Theosophic Movement, the conversion and activity of Mrs. Besant, the remarkable lectures of Max Müller, the Great Parliament of Religions and the timely appearance of Swami Vivekananda have all been unswervingly tending to the dissemination of those great truths, Kripananda, Abhayananda, Yogananda and a whole host of converts to Vedantism are springing up everywhere. Science itself has become a willing tool in the hands of our ancient philosophy. The word Vedanta is nearly as familiar on the shores of Lake Michigan as on the banks of the Ganges.

So declared the Tamil Brahmin editors in the first volume of *Prabuddha Bharata or Awakened India*, an English-language monthly journal started in 1896 to popularise Vivekananda's work in India and abroad. The introduction claimed that Vedanta – code for Hinduism – had been steadily making 'converts' in the West, its illustrious lineage stretching from Immanuel Kant and the 'Upanishad-intoxicated Schopenhauer' to the Theosophist Annie Besant and Orientalist Max Müller. Vivekananda represented the culmination in such a narrative, fulfilling the role Vedanta was destined to play on the world stage. Showcasing the conversion of Western men and women like Kripananda (Leon Landsberg) and Abhayananda (Mary Louise) to Vedantic Hinduism deepened that claim.

Every volume of the *Prabuddha Bharata* and *Brahmavadin*, the two English journals started by Vivekananda's Indian disciples with generous contributions from Western patrons, covered in detail the various exploits of their master and his interpretation of Vedanta. Disciples in Madras were as or even more active than their counterparts in Bengal, a point often underemphasised in situating either Vivekananda or Vedanta within India.[1] In the columns of *Prabuddha Bharata* and *Brahmavadin*, Vivekananda's 'conquest' of the West became a distinctive metaphor that entered Indian public discourse and spoke to forms of Hindu cultural nationalism that steadily grew in the twentieth century.

This chapter examines the strategies deployed in the remaking of Vedanta (an abstract and monist form of Hinduism) as a putative 'world religion', in the form of the Hindu monk Swami Vivekananda's voyages to the West, his reception in America, and the connections – material, financial, emotional – that he and his movement assiduously cultivated through Western networks.[2] By attending closely to practices and strategies of legitimation centred on the deployment of Vedantic networks, the chapter sheds new light on the consolidation of a Hindu identity through attempts to globalise Vedanta. It offers a close historical examination of the affective-activist networks which sustained this subtle form of Hindu supremacism, and the complex theological manoeuvres involved in accentuating both the universalism and nationalism of this new 'world religion'. It charts the way Vedanta was made congruent with an upper-caste Hindu idiom of respectable Indianness.[3] In this process, an expansive but also exclusionary idea of India was generated.

Vedanta and the World

This chapter locates Vedanta in the wider cultural context of late nineteenth-century India, America and Europe, examining its appeal as a category of liberal religion that drew Western disciples and interlocutors, and reconciled their disenchantments. Through Vivekananda and his cohort of fellow swamis, Vedanta became a master signifier of a Hindu civilisational and cultural form able to produce and sustain its claim to universality. As Vivekananda desired about Vedanta: 'Make it an [*sic*] universal property. It cannot remain in the hands of a few narrow-minded people [Brahmins]'.[4] Vivekananda and his Vedantic followers fought pitched rhetoric battles with Christian missionaries and Ramabai circles to consolidate fragile gains.[5] The appeal and desire for 'culture and learned audiences' – a tactic to testify Vedanta's (and thereby India's) own claim to high culture and learning – remained a recurrent trope.

The success of Vivekananda's interpretation of Vedanta lay in its deft discursive ambivalence, a strategy that helped gather a wide variety of audiences. Vivekananda and Vedanta's global career was intrinsically linked to this active network of disciples, collaborators and interlocutors in and from the West that continually reinforced their influence in India, if with different emphases. Western disciples' investments around Vedanta informed and reproduced the intimacy of their relationship with Vivekananda and his wider community. Unlike Tagore's and Gandhi's disciples, however, an archival lack characterises Vedanta and Vivekananda's followers.[6] This chapter offers an array of narratives contingent on the coming of Vedanta in the West, its uptake and 'worlding' in certain contexts and mobilisation for a wide variety of uses.

I use the term 'worlding' in the sense cultural geographers suggest: 'a mobile but more or less stable [or stabilising] ensemble of practices, involvements, relations, capacities, tendencies and affordances' that settled Vedanta as a discursive formation to these audiences.[7] There is a productive tension between Vedanta's claim to be a 'world' religion that takes the world as a macro-category and specific exercises in its 'worlding' that shaped the smaller scale of movements for its actors and networks.

Vedanta as a Modern Dialogic

The quest for a 'universal' religion to validate Indian cultural forms was an intellectual response to colonial modernity. Even as Vivekananda popularised Hindu universalism in the West, its genealogy is far more extensive.[8] A cursory glance at the intellectual history of modern Hinduism testifies to the continued fixation for a universalising narrative.[9] From Rammohun Roy, it stretched over a century to include the likes of Debendranath Tagore, Keshab Chandra Sen, Ramakrishna, Vivekananda, Dayananda Saraswati, Aurobindo, Tagore, Gandhi and Radhakrishnan, all of whom engaged in some form of Hindu universalist dialectics.

Attempts to move beyond the disciplining categories of liberal knowledge often relied on seeking to transcend those very categories. The dialectics around Vedanta's claim to universality demonstrated both the 'indispensability and inadequacy of European epistemic categories'.[10] Narrative regimes spawned by discourses on ethics, evolution, rationality and psychology became sites to evidence universalist claims.[11] These moves won new disciples and audiences in the West.

Vedanta was one of the six original schools in Hindu philosophy that developed out of the Vedic tradition in ancient India. It enjoyed a long and illustrious lineage in the Sanskrit commentarial tradition since the seventh century, continuing well into medieval and early modern times. A monist and abstract school of philosophy, the Vedantic/Upanishadic tradition is often regarded as a source for indigenous secularism or pluralism, in which different points of view are allowed to co-exist as part of a hierarchised but unified system in its approach to divinity.[12] The Advaita branch of Vedanta, espoused famously by the eighth-century Sanskrit scholar Shankara, posited a strictly non-dualist and monist view of the world, that of absolute identity between 'Man and Maker'.

Vedanta was resurrected as a modern dialogic by the early nineteenth-century social reformer Rammohun Roy (1772–1833). In Bengal itself, the seat of early British colonial state and the centre for Roy's own activities, the influence of Vedanta was quite minor, given the prevalence of the devotional Gaudiya Vaishnavite bhakti tradition or the more didactic Nyaya (Logic) school of philosophy. Between 1815 and 1820, Roy translated key texts of Vedanta, the *Brahmasutras*, into Bengali and English for wide circulation.[13] Its remarkably monist bearings were honed to great philosophical effect when rationalising Hinduism, a tradition that Vivekananda and his interlocutors continued when responding to missionary critics. Roy engaged extensively with Unitarian Christians in Britain and America on the possibilities of a reformed Hinduism. Contemporary Anglican missionaries thought of Vedanta as a new Hindu apologetic that precluded 'disillusioned Hindu' members from being drawn to Protestant Christianity.[14] Vedanta emerged as a modern dialogic that lent itself readily to the conceptual inflections of Enlightenment rationality.

For a newly mobile class of Bengali elites, Vedanta was not only an attempt to rationalise Hindu religiosity but also an effort to legitimate their material concerns. Vedanta emerged as a bhadralok cultural project – a bourgeoisie discourse for middle-class Hinduism that justified its members' material aspirations.[15] Though Vedanta sought to claim itself as more monotheistic than Christianity while making space for bourgeoisie aspirations, it was strongly disputed by major Hindu commentators. This included conservative pandits like Mrityunjay Tarkalankar of Calcutta (1762–1819), Sankara Sashtri of Madras or socio-religious commentators like Debendranath Tagore (1817–1905), Vidyasagar (1820–1891), Bankim Chattopadhyay (1838–1894) and Dayanand Saraswati (1824–1883).[16]

The early liberalism of the Bengali intelligentsia gradually gave way to strident cultural nationalist forms by the end of the nineteenth century. The late nineteenth century exposed the limits of liberalism, part of a wider crisis due to 'effects of industrialisation in Europe and in the non-European world, deindustrialisation'.[17] This marginalisation of Bengali capital from global capitalist networks led to an introverted response of its intelligentsia, who sought indigenist categories of thought not dominated or determined by the West. Crisis in capital and changing relations of property, land and enterprise, as Tanika Sarkar has argued, catalysed the 'abandonment of liberal reformism' and embracing of Hindu cultural nationalism.[18]

From the 1880s, there emerged a new cultural politics in Bengal that drew deeply from abstracted Hindu theological traditions.[19] Vedanta transformed, under these circumstances, from a liberal religious discourse (of the Roy variety) to embody a muscular Hindu project within India. It flourished as a 'world religion' in the West, drawing devotees from a wide cross-section of dissident religious cultures. Vedanta's ability to world itself in both 'universal' and 'nationalist' terms made it an extraordinarily powerful signifier. Western followers drawn to Vivekananda and Vedanta were increasingly involved in raising India's profile in the world – as a bearer of civilisation, learning and high culture. Within India itself, this authorising and mobilisation of Western networks formed a significant moment in the invocation of Hindu politics and publics.[20]

Vedanta in the West

Vedantic ideas had already entered American intellectual circles through Transcendentalists and Quakers in the mid-nineteenth century. It included the likes of Ralph Waldo Emerson, Jon Edwards, Henry Thoreau and Walt Whitman who engaged with texts and traditions such as the Bhagavad Gita, Vedas and Upanishads. However, ritual aspects of Hinduism played almost no part in them.[21] In the years immediately preceding 1893, the influence of

Theosophist networks and teachers such as Mohini Mohun Chatterjee in New England was important in drawing followers like Bull and MacLeod.

The expansion of modern scientific knowledge interlinked with historical criticism of Biblical scriptures had steadily produced a growing interest and awareness of religious pluralism outside of Christianity in *fin de siècle* Europe and North America. In the United States, specifically, evangelical pietism had transformed the dynamics of religious affiliation based on an individualised denominational culture by the mid-nineteenth century.[22] A logic of liberal universalism pervaded the World Parliament of Religions held in Chicago in 1893.[23] Its attempt to curate a variety of religious traditions and native experts from the non-West testified to the diverse secularisations at work in American public discourse. If the Parliament embodied this eclecticism to treat all varieties of thought equally (with the implicit premise of Protestant superiority), respective speakers often used it as an opportunity to present the superiority of their apologetics.

This heterodox fringe – in Europe and North America – saw the coming together of such diverse movements as vegetarianism, spiritualism, anti-colonialism and women's suffrage. Subcultural networks informed and sustained the interests of disciples like Noble, Bull, MacLeod and Sturdy and their avowals for Vivekananda and Vedanta. Sensitive to new 'waves of spiritual enthusiasms [that] periodically wash[ed] over American religious sensibilities',[24] they responded eagerly to Vivekananda's personality and teachings. Macleod and her sister Betty were part of the 'American women hungry for culture, for ever going to lectures, trying each new thing as it appeared on the limited horizon. It was the order of the day'.[25] In these circles, discussions on heterodox religions could blend fruitfully into limited critiques of race, class, gender and empire. The tensions between alternative religiosities and a dominant Protestant majority would continue to simmer in public discourse. Bull was claimed to have been driven insane by Vivekananda and his circle while Sarah Farmer, another American woman who had initially sought Vivekananda's discipleship but later submitted to Abdul Baha and the Persian Revelation, was 'incarcerated as a madwoman'.[26]

Vivekananda's audiences in the West comprised primarily of those disenchanted with institutional forms of Christianity – former Theosophists, spiritual seekers and suffragist women – whose personal religious and spiritual quests evinced a curious interest in Vedanta. They responded eagerly to intimations of alternative spirituality.[27] As an editorial comment of *Prabuddha Bharata* observed in its report on Tibetan mysticism in American New Thought: 'mysticism is growing like mushrooms in America. Her virgin soil seems to take anything'.[28]

Indian spirituality found fertile ground as it resonated with the spiritual despair felt by the 'old stock' American elite, settled primarily in the Northeast. As T. J. Jackson Lears has argued, by the 1880s, a cross-section of educated American bourgeoise sought escape from the transformations wrought by industrial capitalism. Their desire for spiritual solace led to deep engagements with 'Oriental' religions, traditions that were not yet as desacralised and demystified as Protestant Christianity. In these engagements, often profoundly antimodern, a class of Americans and Europeans sought therapeutic ways of aspiring beyond self and society.[29]

Vivekananda was, therefore, part of a wider import of gurus and teachers preaching forms of 'eastern' philosophy, medicine, faith-healing, mind-cure, religion and spirituality in the West. Vivekananda was quite aware of these circles within which Vedanta jostled for success (spiritualists, Theosophists, Christian Scientists), often in a state of ambiguous antagonism.[30] The Chicago Parliament itself had launched many international careers alongside his, including that of Jehangir Cola, the Parsi preacher from Bombay and Anagarika Dharmapala, the Theravada Buddhist preacher from Ceylon. Vivekananda's letters to his brother disciples reveal the extent of this contest for valuable resources and networks: '... the whole American nation loves and respects me, pays my expenses, and reveres me as a Guru ... Dharmapal is a nice boy. He has not much of learning, but is very gentle. He had a good deal of popularity in this country.'[31] Garnering Western disciples, networks and resources were extremely valuable for Vedanta's success.

To this heterodox array of individuals in the West, Vivekananda's success as an eloquent speaker on Hinduism in 1893 had generated considerable interest. Bull had been active in the 'Woman Suffrage' movement and the National Women's Temperance Union in the United States and was a generous donor to various progressive establishments. These included Tuskegee Institute, Booker T. Washington's first college for Black Americans, and Jane Addams' Hull House, an educational community for working female immigrants.[32] MacLeod was a regular in different non-conformist religious and cultural circles, travelling widely between America, Britain and Europe to cultivate her eclectic interests. Other important associates and patrons included Lewis Janes, President of the Brooklyn Ethical Society and Sarah Farmer, founder of the Greenacre conferences that showcased Transcendentalist thought. British followers included Margaret Noble, a schoolteacher who moved in feminist circles and reading clubs that characterised *fin de siècle* London; E. T. Sturdy and Henrietta Müller, former members of the Theosophical Society; and Captain James Sevier and his wife Charlotte, the former having served in the British Indian Army for five years before turning to spirituality. All of them drew on Vivekananda and Vedanta in different ways.

Many of these admirers and followers were already experimenting with heterodox spiritual practices, without openly disavowing Christianity. Bull was in touch with Mohini Mohan Chatterjee, a former Adept and member of the Theosophical Society, who introduced her to the Hindu text Bhagavad Gita. She was experimenting with vegetarianism when she encountered Vivekananda.[33] Sarah Farmer was a Transcendentalist, strongly attracted to the Occult movement as represented by the Theosophical Society.[34] Henrietta Müller and Edward Sturdy, Vivekananda's hosts in England, were formerly high-ranking members within the Theosophical Society. Both Sturdy and Müller later became disillusioned with Vivekananda, Müller in particular returning to Christian evangelism.

Consolidating Vedanta

Beneath the rhetoric of Vivekananda's success lay a tense recognition of the uncertainty of Vivekananda's own position. His Indian and Western networks proved crucial in Vedanta's early consolidation. The first few years after 1893 were characterised by continual aspersions on his authenticity and authority. An anguished Vivekananda chafed against the propaganda to malign him in the United States:

> … everything that is said by Christians in India is sedulously gathered by the missionaries and regularly published and they go from door to door to make my friends give me. They have succeeded only too well for there is not one word for me from India. Indian Hindu papers may laud me to skies, but not a word of that ever came to America, so that many people in this country think me a fraud. In the face of missionaries and with the jealousy of the Hindus here to back them

I have not a word to say.... I came here without credentials. How else to show that I am not a fraud in the face of the missionaries and Brahmo Samaj? ... I thought nothing would be so easy as to hold a meeting of some respectable persons in Madras and Calcutta and pass a resolution thanking me and the American people for being kind to me and sending it over officially, i.e, through the Secretary of the function, to America, for instance, sending one to Dr. Barrows [Chairman of the Chicago Parliament] and asking him to publish it in the papers and so on, to different papers of Boston, New York and Chicago. Now after all I found that it is too terrible a task for India to undertake. There has not been one voice for me in one year and every one against me....[35]

This longing for recognition of his authority delineated several absences. The Ramakrishna Mission had not been formalised yet as a sect (officially founded in 1897), and its uncertain location in the Hindu monastic hierarchy deprived Vivekananda of any immediate support within institutionalised Hindu structures. In India, his Brahmin followers in Madras were engaged in defending their guru's neo-Vedantic positions:

Such of his critics as call his views 'Neo-Hinduism.', 'Vedaless Vedantism', ... will be immensely benefitted by perusing these lectures [Lectures on Gnana Yoga, the newest of his published volumes], for they will soon learn that the Swami's views do not differ in any respect from the grand practical teachings of the Upanishads.[36]

That his interpretation of Vedanta differed significantly from canonical positions was acknowledged even by admirers:

His view of Vedanta was ... A great deal different from ... Traditional. His complaint appeared to be that Vedanta had been treated too much as the possession of a sect competing for the loyalty of the Hindu along with other sects, and not as a life-giving perennial source of inspiration that it really was.[37]

In various parts of India and outside, his Kayastha[38] caste status was cited as disqualifying his ambitions as a Hindu guru. Vaishnavite factions bitterly contested his claims to represent Hinduism in any capacity, as he was not Brahmin by caste. In response, Vivekananda emphatically traced his Kayastha lineage to Kshatriyas (warrior caste) that 'apart from the other services in the past, ruled half of India for centuries'.[39] The Kayasthas, claimed Vivekananda, were modern-day descendants of the Kshatriyas, who 'have equal right to be Sannyasins' and 'to the Vedas'.[40] Sarat Chandra Chakrabarti, a Bengali Brahmin disciple of Vivekananda, clarified in his many 'Letters to the Editor' of the *Indian Mirror* that Vivekananda's monastic credentials were beyond reproach. His knowledge of Vedic scriptures, he attested, was 'more authoritative than almost any Brahmin pundit could muster'.[41] His own brother-disciples in India, however, made light of the seriousness with which Vivekananda regarded his Vedantic mission:

> At Baranagore Math [near Calcutta] he would say that their names would be recorded in history. Yogananda and other brother disciples used to make fun of him for this. 'Swamiji retorted: "You will see if I am right or not! Vedanta is the only religion convincing to all. If you don't listen to me, I will go to the quarter of the untouchables and teach them Vedanta!"'[42]

They illustrate the challenges Vivekananda faced in the early years of his Vedantic work. Being in the West provided him with resources to consolidate his fledgling work but he still remained vulnerable to allegations levelled in India. Potential Western disciples and patrons were forever cautious in verifying his authenticity and frequently encountered allegations made against him. A frustrated Vivekananda wrote to his brother-disciples in Calcutta, of rumours circulating in the US of him being a cheat, 'committing every sin under the sun in America – especially 'unchastity' of the most degraded type!!!'[43] It revealed the reach of interlinked communication networks that facilitated the flow of such information between India, Britain and America through groups such as the Brahmo Samaj, Christian missionary networks and Ramabai circles. Julia Ward Howe, a poet, woman's rights activist and Ramabai Circle member told Vivekananda: if 'your gods are so good, let your women come to tell us of them'; to which he replied: 'our women do not travel'.[44] Christian missionaries picked up Hindu orthodox and reformist denunciations at home and publicised them widely through established evangelical circles in the US.

Western seekers whose help Vivekananda sought were aware of the slander made against him. Between 1893 and 1895, these potential patrons demanded attestations of his credibility, before investing in him or Vedanta more substantially. Pressed for proof, he and his followers discovered the system of 'credentials and character-certificates' on which accessibility to audiences was determined in the West, something that the Theosophical Society and the Brahmo Samaj possessed amply. Vivekananda pleaded with his disciples and high Indian contacts – mostly diwans and rajas of small Hindu princely states – to furnish him with such proofs, the burden of which rested almost solely on him. He and his disciples went to great lengths to vindicate his sannyasin status, without which his role as a teacher and interlocutor for Vedanta and Hinduism remained insecure. The fretting over credentials indicate how the Chicago Parliament was a key moment in the proliferation of popular spirituality mongers and gurus, along with interlocutors like Vivekananda and Dharmapala, whose mobilisations of Hinduism and Buddhism were tied to expanding scales of cultural nationalist politics.

Alasinga Perumal, a prominent Tamil disciple, assured Vivekananda that he had appealed to the Raja of Ramnad (near Madurai) to refute the deceitful smear peddled by missionaries and fellow Hindus.[45] Detractors sought to influence prospective patrons of Vivekananda and Vedanta. Lewis Janes, an organiser of the Cambridge Conferences that provided Vivekananda with a valuable platform to present his Vedanta work, noted with concern a letter sent by Pratap Chunder Mazoomdar, a prominent Brahmo Samaj leader (under the Keshab Sen faction) and scathing critic of Vivekananda. Janes forwarded it to Bull, his co-organiser and future patron of Vedanta:

> I should be glad to know how it impresses you, and whether you think it can be used to any advantage in certain quarters where the impression of Mr. Mozoomdar's antagonism to the Swami has prevailed.[46]

Early correspondence exchanged between Janes and Bull frequently referred to a string of allegations and misrepresentations rife in relevant American circles. Jeanne Sorabji, a Parsi woman who presented Zoroastrianism at the Chicago Parliament alleged that Vivekananda was a fake guru, with no authority to preach. Janes, increasingly more confident about Vivekananda's authenticity, comforted an anxious Bull and her coterie, that he received word from trusted sources in Detroit that the charges spread by Sorabji were utterly false:

> You can assure all that the Swami Vivekananda has made a deep
> and most favourable impression in Brooklyn.... For myself, I did
> not need this added assurance – but it is well to be able to say 'I
> know', and to give my authorities, if any of these slanders show their
> heads hereafter.[47]

Often these rumours and scandals emerged from former gurus and associates
of these Western patrons, suggesting the close-knit world they inhabited.
Janes took the lead, once again, in defusing Bull's former guru Mohini Mohan
Chatterjee's attempt to undercut Vivekananda's religious authority around
matters of caste:

> I return Mr. Sturdy's letter here ... I have had a talk with Miss Waldo
> about the Chattopadhyaya matter, and she read me a letter from
> Swami Saradananda that Mr. C falsely reputed in England that the
> Swami Vivekananda belonged to the Sudra caste (as reported by
> Mr Goodwin).[48]

The intricate system of checks was sustained by a diligent exchange of
letters and consultation since the 1890s between Western disciples and
interlocutors located in the US and England. Once established, this trust
in Vivekananda and Vedanta was continually adduced in affiliated journals
such as the *Prabuddha Bharata* and *Brahmavadin* by disciples located in
India. Letters and attestations from prominent Western interlocutors and
followers were sought, invoked and reproduced to underline Vivekananda's
authenticity and influence, which then entered Indian newspapers in
English (*Indian Mirror*) and vernacular languages (*Amrita Bazar Patrika*).
The *Indian Mirror* asserted Vivekananda's success as a story of spiritual
conquest: 'Truly, it may be said of Swami Vivekanand's work in America,
that he went, spoke and conquered.'[49]

Each issue of these journals reported in some detail the progress of
Vedantic work undertaken in Boston, New York and London, among other
places, and the various figures connected to them. They were curated to
showcase the 'tremendous influence which his teachings have obtained
over a large number of sincere and highly cultured men'. Audiences in the
West were always presumed to be 'sincere and highly cultured'. A letter
reproduced in the *Prabuddha Bharata* hailed Vivekananda as a 'living
example of Vedanta':

The students of the Vedanta Philosophy in London, under your remarkably able instruction, feel that they would be lacking in their duty and privilege if they failed to record their warm and heartfelt appreciation of the noble and unselfish work you have set yourself to do.[50]

Epistolarity was performed and repurposed for public legitimisation. Letters of appreciation and praise from Western followers were actively mobilised to consolidate work on the home front. They were regularly featured under the column 'News and Notes' in the *Prabuddha Bharata*, which also contained expositions of the Vedantic Hindu tradition. The following private letter to Vivekananda, signed by ten 'prominent American men and women' drawn to Vedanta through the Cambridge Conferences, buttressed this politics of transnational recognition:

As members of the Cambridge Conferences devoted to comparative study in Ethics, Philosophy and Religion, it gives us great pleasure to recognize the value of your able expositions of the Philosophy and Religion of Vedanta in America, and the interest created thereby among thinking people....[51]

The letter's appropriate referencing of learned societies, networks and individuals in the West made it a valuable testimonial for circulation and consumption within new Hindu cultural publics. Other letters seem to be specifically written to publicise this normalising task. A letter from the Brooklyn Ethical Society, signed by its office-bearers Janes and his colleague Z Sidney Sampson, evidenced the coming of learned Western audiences in the wake of Vivekananda and Vedanta. Addressed 'To our Indian Brethren of the Great Aryan Family', the letter offered a full endorsement and was published in the *Prabuddha Bharata*:

To testify to our high appreciation of the value of the work of the Swami Vivekananda in this country. His lectures before the Brooklyn Ethical Association opened up a new world of thought to many of his hearers, and renewed the interest of others.... We heartily endorse the words of the Venerable Dean of Harvard School: 'The Swami Vivekananda ... has been, in fact, a missionary from India to America. Everywhere he has made warm personal friends; and his expositions of Hindu philosophy have been listened to with delight....

> We thank you for sending him to us ... we earnestly hope that the
> new avenues of sympathy opened by his presence of himself and his
> brother Sannyasins will result in mutual benefits....[52]

The continuous soliciting of affirmative letters from generally white men
and women indexed the racialised nature of these attestations, often used
to counter opposition within India. Supporters in India eagerly vaunted
and reproduced these attestations to cite Vivekananda's authority as a
Hindu guru and his interpretation of Vedanta as canonical. They helped
produce perpetual refrain of conversion. 'Vivekananda has made a great
many converts of the Americans,' remarked an *Amrita Bazar Patrika*
editorial in 1895.[53] The *Indian Mirror* claimed: 'Hundreds of men and
women have enlisted themselves under the standard, which he unfolded
in America, and some of them have even taken to the bowl and the yellow
robes.'[54] Provoked, Christian missionary societies made angry rebuttals to
mass-conversion claims. Wilbert W. White, on behalf of the *Young Men's
Christian Association*, published an assorted volume of letters and media
reports from 'prominent Americans' that challenged claims like that of the
Indian Mirror.[55] Missionary attempts to play down his influence in India and
emphasise his incompetence only spoke to Vivekananda's growing renown.
The public impact of missionary bad press was not lost on Vivekananda:
'Vituperation by the low caste missionaries [evangelicals] made my cause
succeed better.'[56]

The prolific consolidation work, launched collaboratively by Western and
Indian disciples, successfully established Vivekananda as a Hindu guru. By
1899, Vivekananda was referred to as 'an unconverted Hindu' in the 'learned
circles' of Los Angeles, in contrast to 'Christianised Hindus' represented by
reformist Brahmo Samajis. As Alice Hansborough, a member of the New
Thought denomination that supported Vivekananda recounted:

> [O]n one occasion when Swamiji was going to speak at the Green
> Hotel, Professor Baumgardt was talking with some other gentlemen
> on the platform before the lecture began. One of them asked him,
> regarding Swamiji, 'He is a Christianized Hindu, I suppose?' And
> Professor Baumgardt replied, 'No, he is an unconverted Hindu. You
> will hear about Hinduism from a real Hindu.'[57]

Bernhardt Baumgardt, introduced to Vivekananda by Josephine MacLeod, was then secretary of the Southern California Academy of Science, and Chairman of the Math and Astronomy Sections. Being an 'unconverted real Hindu' was an important attribute for sustained access to Western networks.

A New Metaphor

In the years between 1893 and 1896, both Vivekananda and his Western followers presented Vedanta as a new metaphor that merged their personal and intellectual aspirations. It was part of the larger work undertaken to consolidate Vedanta as a category of 'world religion', in both India and America. The core of Vedanta's following in America and Britain generally came from its substantial heterodox fringe; seekers and interlocutors who had already been exposed to eclectic non-conformist traditions and new discourses that disputed the superiority of conservative Anglo-American Protestantism. Outside of this, Vivekananda and Vedanta made little progress in conservative Christian circles or the deep American South.

To this heterodox audience, seeking 'authentic' spiritual experience, Vedanta's appeal lay in presenting itself as an eclectic world-religion deriving from Hinduism. Vivekananda's own personal charisma exerted a definite charm on his audiences, aspects of which had been already highlighted in the previous chapter. Western admirers and followers, mostly women, repeatedly described the breathless experience of listening to his expositions: 'Time and space had vanished for us.'[58] Added to this personal charm was his mastery over hermeneutics. A report in August 1894 on 'The Reality of God' billed his eloquence: 'a defence of Mohamet by a Hindu to a Christian audience; the lesson that all prophets are to be revered and their teachings studied reverently'.[59]

Vivekananda's guru Ramakrishna was himself a master of eclectic religious practices. He pursued Muslim, Hindu, Parsi and Christian practices for brief periods of time to test their validity and declared them all to be true in realising God.[60] Alongside this, Vivekananda's ability to cite from a wide range of sources from different religious traditions and justify a comparable point was matchless. He was well-read, could move smoothly between a wide variety of traditions and texts, cited *Alice in Wonderland* to impress the Hindu idea of *maya*, or illusion, to his audiences. Fluency in different traditions made him an ideal interlocutor to present Vedanta and recruit potential disciples from his audiences.

Vedanta became the latest in a series of coveted cultural forms that spoke to ongoing Western discourses and desires for a universal religion that could be rationalised in modern scientific terms. Western collaborators representing the Ethical Culture Movement and New Thought eagerly appropriated Vedanta to expand their own personal and intellectual ambitions. Vedanta was folded within a wider project of religious pluralism. Even as most of his disciples came from within a non-conformist tradition, a broad understanding of Christianity continued to underpin heterodox dialectics. Vivekananda identified his audience in the following terms: 'In America one-third of the people are Christians, but the rest have no religion, that is they do not belong to any of the sects, but amongst them are to be found the most spiritual persons.'[61] Vedanta's appeal lay essentially within this 'spiritual but not sectarian' set of audiences. Through Vedanta, Vivekananda and his brother-disciples engaged with this broad idea of cultural Christianity.

Sarah Ellen Waldo, an early American disciple who served as his diligent transcriber, noted the careful attempt to harmonise Christianity with Vedanta:

> It must not be supposed that the teachings of the Vedanta are in any way antagonistic to Christianity. On the contrary, if we examine many of the sayings of Jesus by the light of its interpretation, we shall find how wonderfully they harmonize with this philosophy. For instance, in his teachings Jesus clearly recognizes and indicates the three stages of development into which the Vedanta divides its followers....
>
> It must always be remembered that Jesus was an Oriental and as such naturally used Oriental figures of speech.[62]

Vedanta was seen as enlightening Christianity to Christians, instead of taking away from their beliefs. Waldo was later initiated into brahmacharya as Sister Haridasi and was the first woman authorised by Vivekananda to teach Vedanta in the West.[63] Even as Vivekananda did not advocate 'conversion' as essential, a small but steady stream of conversions like Waldo's continued to happen throughout from among American and British followers. Prominent among these included Leon Landsberg, a young journalist (with Franco-Russian Jewish origins) on the staff of the *New York Tribune*, who became Kripananda and helped set up the Vedanta Society in New York and Mary Louise (a French immigrant). After being given monastic vows and the name Abhayananda, she dissociated herself from Vivekananda. Both Kripananda and Abhayananda fell out with Vivekananda's other disciples early in their careers and took up a mix of teaching yoga and other Hindu practices in the US. They constituted the first recorded group of 'white Hindus' operating in America. Those who remained faithful and came to embrace some form of Hinduism included the likes of J. J. Goodwin, Christine Greenstidel and Margaret Noble, all of whom became part of Vivekananda's Indian work. Greenstidel came to characterise Abhayananda and Kripananda as 'zealously fanatic[s]' and the former as 'unfit for discipleship, and useless as a worker in Swami Vivekananda's movement'.[64]

Given the sensationalism that surrounded the idea of conversion, a more preferred term was initiation, or *diksha*. Many long-term Western disciples were initiated in some form – ritually or more informally – by different swamis starting from Vivekananda. Initiating Western disciples on auspicious Christian holidays was commonplace, an attempt to shore up the concurrence between Christianity and Hinduism. News of initiations-as-conversions were proudly advertised in the columns of the organisation's journals. In 1899, news updates from New York informed readers of four new Western *brahmachari*s:

> On Easter Sunday when the great festival is observed, Swami Abhedananda initiated four Brahmacharins. It seemed peculiarly appropriate that Western disciples should take their vows on this greatest of our religious festivals.... After all the vows had been taken, the Swami gave to each Brahmachari a new name .... These meetings of the disciples are most helpful and serve to make us more devoted to Vedanta and to the teachings of Sri Ramakrishna.[65]

Initiation did the work of conversion with careful discretion. Alice Hanborough was 'baptised' by Vivekananda, along with her brother and sister Ralph and Dorothy.[66] At the Thousand Islands Park spiritual retreat:

> Every one of the students there, received initiation at the hands of the Swami [Vivekananda], thus becoming disciples, the Swami assuming towards them the position of guru, or spiritual father, as is done

in India, where the tie uniting guru and disciple is the closest one known, outranking that of parent and child, or even husband and wife. It was purely a coincidence that there were just twelve of us![67]

Receiving initiation from the guru tethered them to a new mode of discipleship, the cultural practice of which was almost completely new to those being initiated. The everyday worlding of Vedanta for Western disciples was juxtaposed with Christian celebrations:

> In the Vedanta Rooms on the Sunday morning before Christmas, a merry group of little children was gathered about a wonderful Christmas tree. Laughter and cries of delight were heard; they sang songs, played and recited and altogether had a glorious time. Swami Abhedananda was there, merry and happy as a child, and ... gave them a beautiful little talk touching the origin of Christmas.[68]

Christ was creatively co-opted within Vedanta and employed to validate the latter. Christmas and Janmashtami (the god Krishna's birth anniversary) were compared and emphasis laid on their similarity. Initiation – ritual or otherwise– did not negate or disrupt the personal relationships of Western disciples to Christ; Vedanta was portrayed as being able to harmonise them.

Nevertheless, Vedanta was chiefly promoted as a 'non-conversion' experience in the West. The identities and solidarities premised through such an ambivalent positioning might be fluid but often unsure. Waiving away conversion made Vedanta an attractive evangelical proposition for potential members, leaving the path open to become voluntary Hindus in a broader sense. Religious pluralism was actively used as a framework to prove the (subtle) superiority of Vedanta, and by implication, Hinduism. It was claimed to be a master paradigm that could fit all kinds of religions in the world:

> All of religion is contained in the Vedanta ... in the three stages of Vedanta philosophy, the Dvaita [Dualism], Vishistadvaita [Qualified Monism], and Advaita [Non-Dualism]; one comes after the other.... Each one is necessary.... The first stage, i.e. Dvaita, applied to the ideas of the ethnic groups of Europe, is Christianity; as applied to the Semitic groups, Mohammedanism. The Advaita applied in its Yoga-perception form is Buddhism, etc.[69]

Without suggesting any break from Christianity, Vedantic Hinduism could claim to be 'the Mother of all religions'[70] in a coherent hierarchy of world religions. Vedanta also appealed as a viable alternative to institutionalised Christianity whose limitations movements such as women's suffrage had drawn attention to.[71] The desire for a liberal spirituality had drawn women disciples like Bull, MacLeod and Noble. The *Brahmavadin* emphatically published in its columns the reconciling role Vedanta provided for disillusioned Westerners. Noble's account, for instance, framed Vedanta almost as a remedy for spiritual disquiet and despair in the West:

> Many of us had been conscious for years past of that growing uncertainty and despair with regard to Religion, which has beset the intellectual life of Europe for half a century. Belief in the dogmas of Christianity has become impossible to us, and we had no tool … by which to cut away from the kernel of Reality in our Faith. To these, the Vedanta has given intellectual confirmation and philosophical expression of their own mistrusted intuitions.[72]

Vedanta was portrayed as 'critical to the enlargement of western religious culture' and not in antagonism. For Bull, her

> first knowledge of Vedanta meant to me the vitalising of Christianity … I look to the Vedanta especially to meet the spirit of agnosticism towards Christianity rife among our students both men and women.[73]

Many saw Vedanta as as resolving their own struggles with faith. MacLeod averred to this conciliation:

> And he had such a place for us Westerners whom he called 'Living Vedantins'. He would say, 'When you believe a thing is true, you do it, you do not dream about it. That is your power.'[74]

The Anglo-American spirit was attributed as essentially embodying a living mode of Vedanta. Vedantic attributes, his disciples were told, were already present in Westerners; all they needed was the affirming touch of a true guru. The *Indian Mirror* fervently boasted about this imputed proximity and exhorted Hindus to migrate en masse to America:

The affinity between India and America is becoming clearer every day, and in the fact of the welcome that Hindu visitors obtain so readily on American soil, it is a matter of surprise that our Hindu countrymen do not repair to the so-called new continent in as large a number as they go to Europe.[75]

America was portrayed as a natural site for Vedanta to flourish and take root, and for Hindu Indian migration along with it. Awareness of the possibilities afforded by America as a Western and anti-imperial power, in that it gained freedom from the British, continued to increase further along the twentieth century, as Indian revolutionary and anti-colonial networks intensified.[76]

The claimed compatibility of Vedanta with Christianity meant that an acceptance of Vedanta need not spell a rejection of Christ. By partly stripping away the cultural specificities that bound Vedantic Hinduism and presenting it as a world-religion, Vivekananda exercised a wide theological latitude. Relativising other religious systems was a creative way of rationalising Hinduism through Vedanta, an approach that would increasingly gain wide currency after him.

Without denying the truth of their respective faiths, Vivekananda convinced important Western audiences of Vedanta's universality: 'to propound a philosophy which can serve as a basis to every possible religious system in the world ... my teaching is antagonistic to none'.[77] Testimonies from Western disciples that affirmed this universality of Vedanta continued to be printed and reproduced in its journals well throughout the early twentieth century. As 'A Western Disciple' attested: 'the aim of the *Advaita Vedantin* is to realise this substantial Unity'.[78]

While neutralising its overt Hindu moorings in the West, its uptake was projected within India as a decisive moment of Hindu pride. Vedanta became a deployment to contend Hinduism's claim to be the only true world religion:

> You hear of claims made by every one of the different religions as being the universal religion of the world. Let me tell you ... that perhaps there never will be such a thing, but if there is a religion which can lay that claim, it is only ours and none else, because every other religion depends on some person or persons. All the other religions have been built round the life of what they think a historical man, and what they think the strength of the religion is really the

weakness, for disprove the history of the man and the whole building tumbles to the ground.… Ours is the only religion … that does not depend on a person or persons; it is based upon principles.[79]

Vedanta, and more generally Hinduism, was presented as emanating out of an inspired divine tradition outside of history that made it superior to other religions.

Throughout the late 1890s, Indian disciples continued to conflate and publicise Western interest and the small number of initiations as 'conversion' to Vedanta, and by implication, Hinduism. The belief in Western conversion seemed to have snowballed rapidly, so much so that Janes had to clarify to Indian audiences that even as they had 'every high regard for Vivekananda and Vedanta', they 'may not be so near to actual conversion as some seem to believe'.[80] Nevertheless, the narrative of conversion-as-conquest seems to have only intensified:

> The tide of conversion seemed to have rolled back from the East to the West – the tables were completely turned – and the Hindu mission in the West was crowned with greater and more glorious success than what has ever been vouchsafed to Christian mission in the East.[81]

While described as conversion, there was however a recognition of its difference from more formal or explicit missionary conversion. Lay followers believed and asserted that the embracing of Vedanta did not mean their 'giving up the religion of our forefathers, nor the Christ', but rather an aid that helped them delve 'to the roots of all religions, leaving us free to worship in whatever form we choose'.[82] Hailed as superior for not creating any 'bitterness' unlike other missionary propaganda, this was attributed to the inherently 'universal' nature of his 'Religion':

> If the Swami Vivekananda's work here may be called a missionary effort, it may be contrasted with most of the other missionary efforts of the day by its not having given rise to a single instance of ill-feeling or sectarianism. The reason of this is simple, and great is its strength. The Swami is not a sectarian; he is the promoter of Religion, not of one religion only. The exponents of single points in the vast field of religion can find nothing in him to fight.[83]

Despite qualifications, the claim of hundreds and thousands converting to Hinduism persisted. In an 1896 report, the *Indian Mirror* claimed that in 'America, the Swami has converted nearly 4000 persons to Hinduism', a mysteriously precise figure that would not hold even if we considered initiations-as-conversion. Vivekananda's missionary work in the West was portrayed in this growing circle of Indian followers as a major moment in the public life of Hinduism. It flattened the nuances of the subtle work undertaken, but this flattening yielded a rhetoric that was fruitfully yoked to cultural nationalist discourse in late nineteenth-century India.

Occasionally there were bitter disillusionments, and a return to conservative Christianity, as with Henrietta Müller, a major British patron of Vivekananda. Noble notes:

> She [Müller] has thrown everything overboard, Shri R.K. [Ramakrishna] – Swami [Vivekananda] – Meditation – University of Religions – everything. She does not hesitate to say that Hinduism is Eroticism to the core, and that its truths have been 'kept from her'. By whom? 'Oh names are useless' she answers. All, meditation included, is dirty.
>
> She is now a Bible Christian of a virulent type, and tending towards millennialism.[84]

Inserted alongside public avowals of Vedanta and Vivekananda were also stories of withdrawal and dissociation. In its early years, Vivekananda grappled with sustaining the interest of his Western networks, without which his Indian work would have looked quite different. Even as Vedanta built on the institutional networks of the Theosophical Society, care was taken not to associate with the Theosophical Society, whose links with mysticism and occult were not endorsed by Vivekananda, though the Society claimed credit for his success. In 1894, the Society suffered a general loss of credibility owing to the Judge scandal that broke out in the US.[85] Sturdy, a former Theosophist and prominent British disciple of Vivekananda, warned:

> I hope your good work in America will not be spoiled by identification with the Theosophical Society there, as it is at the present time constituted ... I am too ardent a lover of pure Adwaita philosophy of India not to be jealous when I see it threatened in its interpretation by Western bias or Western charlatans.[86]

Figure 5.1   Vivekananda with Indian disciples and brother monks in Madras, 1897. Alasinga Perumal (with top-knot) is standing on the extreme left, top row.

Source: Wikimedia Commons, February 1897, https://commons.wikimedia.org/wiki/ File:Swami_Vivekananda_Chennai_1897.jpg (accessed on 15 December 2022).

Vivekananda assured Sturdy that 'Theosophy never had any place of respect in [his] soul.[87] Newspaper adverts often clarified that he belonged to 'no society'. Yet, many Indian supporters saw Vivekananda's success as made possible by the Theosophical Society's broader dissemination of eastern religions and philosophy in the West: 'It is due to the Theosophical Society to admit that its presentment of the higher doctrines of Hindu philosophy and religion has inspired the Americans with respect for the whole Hindu race.'[88] Vivekananda and Theosophists were placed in the same tradition, of introducing and representing Indian religions in the West. Vivekananda's denunciation of Theosophy were met with dismay and dissent by a section of the English-educated Hindu public, especially in Madras where it was headquartered (Figure 5.1). Several 'letters to the editor' pointed out that the 'Swami's utterances … have been purposefully ungenerous'.[89] Another quipped that Vivekananda should 'make up' with Annie Besant instead of fighting with her,[90] then President of the Theosophical Society based in Adyar (near Madras) and influential with members of the early Indian National Congress.

Exchanges such as these underline the value that prominent Western workers brought through their involvement in Indianist projects. Meanwhile, Madras-based journals supporting Vivekananda continued to advertise events related to the Theosophical Society, indicating an overlap in audiences.

Seeking Cultured Audiences

> Vedantism in America – We learn from the latest American cuttings that Mr Edward Day and Miss Mary Philips have an interesting programme before them for this season, the spreading of Vedanta in the higher circles of America.[91]

The desire for 'higher circles' continued to characterise Vedanta's uptake in the West. Vivekananda's American and European collaborators supplied and often embodied these circles. The rallying of respectable Americans to the Vedanta served to normalise a form of Hinduism as also its bearers as distinct from the less desirable Indian labour immigrating to the US. From the late nineteenth century, there emerged and grew within the US a consistent anti-immigrant rhetoric specific to Asian presence. Overall Asian migration, as Nayan Shah has noted, was considered an 'invasion, subversion and unwelcome amalgamation that threatened to contaminate the superiority of European culture and civilisation'.[92] Immigrant Indian labour, employed in the expansion of railways and mills, was seen as part of the same 'undesirable' narrative. South Asian migrants came to work in the timber extraction industry and processing plants of British Columbia, Washington and Oregon. They were broadly labelled 'Hindu', a referent for a largely Sikh but also smaller numbers of Muslim and Hindu populations from the subcontinent. Indian labour immigrants largely settled on the west coast of the US and Canada.[93] Their collective numbers were far smaller than Indian migrations to different parts of the British Empire. Yet, the presence of Indian immigrants in America became a national concern, spurring anti-Indian immigration campaigns and prohibitive legal interventions by the Federal State. From the 1880s to 1910s, a series of 'anti-Asiatic' legislations were introduced first to control – then prohibit – all Asian immigration into the US. Indians, like other Asians (predominantly Chinese), were subjected to severe anti-miscegenation, anti-naturalisation and property laws.[94]

It culminated in the Immigration Act of 1917, prohibiting immigration from the entire region stretching from the Middle East to Southeast Asia. India featured on the list of 'barred zones'.[95]

Indian presence was seen as deeply threatening to 'white' national purity and ways of life.[96] The avowed celibacy practised by Vivekananda and monks of the Ramakrishna Mission may have helped contain the fear of sexual threat, but it also cast them in a rarefied halo, seen as distinct from the bulk of (male) Indians migrating to America.[97] For monastic gurus, the impossibility of sexual desire and its perpetual refusal made them alluring objects to a largely female community of disciples. Even as Vivekananda and other Asian gurus became famous at the 1893 World Fair, there continued a steady rhetoric and rise in the practice of exclusion against Indians. Saradananda, a brother-monk of Vivekananda and a Vedantic preacher, felt in New York that his 'sealskin cap ... makes him look like a coloured driver'.[98] Vivekananda regarded the company of white women as protection against street assaults: 'people hurling abuses and throwing stones'.[99] The high regard for Indian religious forms in heterodox circles contrasted sharply with everyday experiences of exclusion, lay or monastic. The company of distinguished white men and women brought a fragile sense of inclusion.

The anxious quest for 'higher circles' was an endeavour to rescue India and Indians from their 'uncivilised' and colonised narratives. In this, Indophile investments around Vivekananda and Vedanta acted comparably to Indian emigrants and indenture. Most of Vivekananda's prominent supporters, patrons and disciples were upper- to middle-class white men and women, and part of influential international networks. The occasional entry of working-class disciples such as Alice Hansborough in Western Vedantic deployments and their claim on Vivekananda provided a sharp contrast vis-à-vis disciples like McLeod:

> Miss MacLeod set aside her superior airs when she was with us. It was principally with people who affected the same airs that she put them on. And she never made the mistake of putting on airs with Swamiji. He often told her 'where to get off' when she had a tendency to be too high-toned. But the only time I ever heard him speak sharply to her was before class in the ballroom of the Green Hotel. She was expressing an opinion as to what should be done about some phase of Swamiji's work, and he suddenly turned on her. 'Keep quiet about what should be done!' he said.[100]

Not possessing the clout either Bull or MacLeod had in terms of money or reach, they nevertheless provided valuable help tending to Vivekananda. Hansborough personally cooked and cleaned for him while her brother waited on him and shined his shoes.[101] Differences in class between played out in disciples' claims-making on Vivekananda. They zealously asserted a stake in Vivekananda and his work.

Yet, even as there was a degree of diversity within white disciples, Black followers remained absent in this narrative. Educated Indian immigrants resented being mistaken as Black, leading them to cultivate greater distance with such communities.[102] To settle Vedanta as well as Hindu Indians as 'respectable' examples of Indian high culture and civilisation, Vivekananda helped produce an enduring image of the tolerant, 'mild Hindu' for Western consumption: 'I suppose a Hindu could never persecute. He never yet has done so; he is the most tolerant of all the races of men.... In India, the Muhammadans were the first who ever took the sword.'[103]

Hindu tolerance was paired with a belief in Aryan civilisational superiority. A 1900 address of Vivekananda set up caste and race favourably for his American audience:

> There is something in caste, so far as it means blood; such a thing as heredity there is certainly.... If you mix up with Negroes and American Indians, surely this [Western] civilization will fall down. But hundreds ... [of] years after, out of this mixture will come a gigantic race once more, stronger than ever; but, for the time being, you have to suffer. The Hindus believe..., and I do not know, I have nothing to say to the contrary, I have not found anything to the contrary ... there was only one civilized race: the Aryan.... The Aryan gives his blood to a race, and then it becomes civilized ... would you give your blood to the Negro race? Then he would get higher culture.[104]

Vivekananda was not uncritical of racial disparity in the US or caste inequality in India. Despite his strange reading of racial and caste intermixing, the address is almost an endorsement of miscegenation as the only panacea in the long run. But the moving power lay firmly with the 'higher' race or caste, and without their civilising touch, the 'Negro' or 'Untouchable' would remain in darkness.

Built on the putative claim of an Aryan family that unified Europeans and Indians, this shared narrative placed Aryans as givers of high culture, to which those lower in the hierarchy must be beholden. The desire for respectability reproduced overtly and covertly the very logic for anti-Blackness.[105] Shared visions of a pan-Aryan racial identification were, however, foiled when the US Supreme Court unanimously decided that Bhagat Singh Thind, who self-identified as a 'high caste Aryan', was deemed racially ineligible for naturalised citizenship in 1923.[106]

A coterie of 'affirmative Orientalists' – comprising white men and women– was instrumental in verifying Hindu greatness.[107] Vedanta was carefully calibrated to make it commensurable to Western epistemes of liberal religion and rationality. The political value of soliciting white collaborators through Vedanta was not lost on Vivekananda, who explained to his Indian disciples their role in building a consensus against imperial rule:

> If you could send and maintain for a few years a dozen well educated strong men, to preach in Europe and America, you would do immense service to India, both morally and politically. Every man who morally sympathises with India becomes a political friend.[108]

Western scholarly interest in Vedantic tradition was greatly coveted, as for instance that of Orientalists Max Müller (Oxford) and P. Deussen (Germany), and later Romain Rolland (France).[109] Abhedananda, a brother-monk of Vivekananda, enthusiastically reported from London that

> he met two of the greatest European Vedantins, Prof. Max Müller and Prof Deussen, and had an interesting conversation with the latter in Sanskrit. He is now working with Swami Vivekananda, who is holding classes on Vedanta, at Wimbledon, which a large number of influential ladies and gentlemen eagerly attend.[110]

The portrayal of prominent Orientalist scholars as 'European Vedantins' generated useful scholarly support for Vivekananda's work in India and abroad. 'Higher circles' or 'cultured audiences' in the West were habitually white spaces, some of which intersected with liberal activist circles.

Vedanta societies, founded from 1894 onwards in the Northeastern region, represented the start of organisational consolidation in the US. First established in New York, Waldo recounted its hopeful beginnings in a humble part of Brooklyn: 'Earnest people flocked to … hear the constant lessons of the Swami on a world-wide, universal religious toleration'.[111] Apart from the New York and Boston Vedanta Societies in the first decade, major efforts included work undertaken by the Brooklyn Ethical Association in New York, and the Greenacre and Cambridge Conferences in Maine and Massachusetts. Together, they were at the forefront of presenting Vedanta and Vivekananda to American audiences seeking new forms of faith and philosophy. Several followers and interlocutors provided valuable introductions for Vivekananda's work to grow in America. Referred to as the 'refined and educated' of the West in Hindu Indian press, they spread 'Universal thought and Wisdom' under the tutelage of various Hindu swamis led by Vivekananda.[112] Vedanta was placed and presented in these spaces as an intellectual-cum-spiritual project.

Greenacre–Cambridge–New York–Harvard

Vedanta fitted well with liberal projects of religious universalism. Led mostly by followers and interlocutors, the early years saw Vivekananda and Vedanta being appropriated for different agendas:

> My idea is for autonomic independent groups in different places. Let them work on their own account and do whatever they like. I do not want to entangle myself in any organisation.[113]

Accepting the limited say he might have over his Western work, his plans for India seemed more decisive. Along with plans to build a monastery in Bengal, he advised Alasinga to create societies for the study of Vedas and Upanishads in Madras. Categorically spelt out in a letter to Alasinga in 1895:

> We must have a college in Madras to teach comparative religions, Sanskrit, the different schools of Vedanta and some European languages; we must have a press, and papers printed in English and in the Vernaculars. When this is done, then I shall know you have accomplished something.[114]

Vivekananda's aim was to collect as many funds as possible to realise his Indian work. For this, he depended on the goodwill and generosity of his Western patrons. The trade-off between spirituality and money was tense but acknowledged: 'I have come to America, to earn money myself.... I give them spirituality and they give me money.'[115] This eventually came, but only through a larger entanglement with Western individuals and investments.

Influenced by the liberal ethos of the Chicago Parliament, Sara Bull had instituted the Cambridge Conference series in 1895 to forward the aim of religious harmony. Bull had come to know of Vivekananda through her collaborator Sarah Farmer at Greenacre (Maine), where Vivekananda found an opportunity to follow up on his Chicago success. Co-organised by Farmer and Bull in 1894, Greenacre was envisaged as a centre for spiritual discourse in the manner of the Chicago Parliament. Farmer wanted the Greenacre Congress to be an open-ended summer retreat – perfect for inviting multiple speakers to discuss a wide variety of eclectic themes and ideas.[116] Vivekananda gave three formal lectures and daily classes on the Upanishads, Bhagavad Gita and Shankaracharya. Bull wrote of his effect on the audience:

> The interest awakened has been very unusual and the effect is to be deep and permanent with many. We have urged him always to give the positive side of his Vedanta philosophy whatever topic was given him; for he can always lead up to that.[117]

Other speakers included the suffrage activist Lady Henry Somerset who spoke on 'Woman Suffrage' and Ernest Fellonosa, a Harvard philosophy professor, who talked on 'Art as Related to Religion'. Participants included William James, the noted American psychologist of religion; Lewis Janes, President of the Brooklyn Ethical Society (Figure 5.2); and Edward Henry Carpenter, prominent British socialist and homosexual activist.[118] Greenacre drew big names among speakers and audiences. Several poets, scientists, transcendentalists, suffragists, artists, scholars and preachers were in attendance.

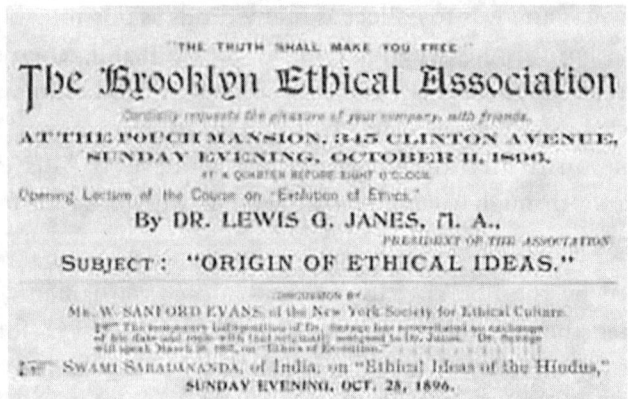

Figure 5.2 'Origin of Ethical Ideas', lecture by Lewis Janes.
Source: Bull Curtis Papers, Cambridge Historical Society, MA.

Vedanta's scholarly-intellectual placing continued with the Cambridge Conferences in December 1895 (Figures 5.3–5.6). Bull roped in Janes, a scholar of ethics and political science and member of the Free Religious Association as co-organiser. Janes found Bull's 'conception of the scope and purpose of our proposed work in entire harmony with [his] own'.[119] At the outset of this initiative, Janes reiterated his belief in the grand narrative of Evolution: 'the *constructive* side of scientific and evolutionary thought seems to me very great ... which ought not to be left out of our discussions.'[120] Vivekananda's endorsement of Evolution appealed greatly to Janes' social Darwinist beliefs. Vivekananda was placed as an important constituent in Bull and Janes' meticulously planned line-up. Between the two, they solicited scholarly interest with sufficient means to subscribe and attend these programmes. Both agreed on the need to make the Cambridge Conferences a public movement and 'have the Vedanta represented by a competent native teacher.' A native teacher was the most desirable for reasons of authenticity; he also had to be sufficiently well versed in Sanskrit and English. [121]

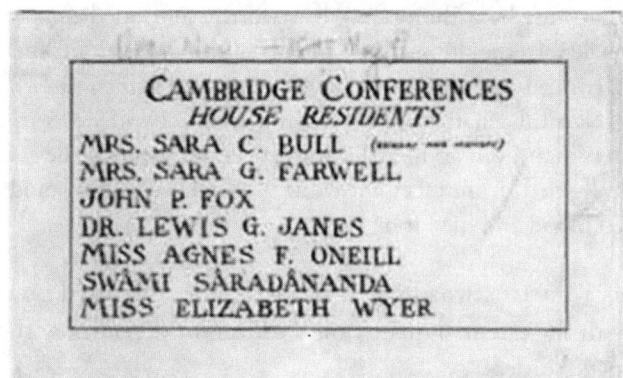

Figure 5.3   Cambridge Conference: List of House Residents.
Source: Bull Curtis Papers, Cambridge Historical Society, MA.

Vivekananda spoke twice at the inaugural session in December 1895 – first on 'The Vedanta Philosophy' and later, the 'The Rajpoot Women and Ideals of Motherhood in India'. Both were statements on Hindu greatness – the first on Hindu philosophy and the second on producing and preserving an unbroken tradition of Hindu masculinity. His lecture was part of a larger showcase on social and cultural ideas: 'Woman Suffrage', 'Orderly Thought and Personal Culture', 'Art as Related to Religion', etc.[122] This would become common practice, folding Vedanta along with other liberal pursuits of ethics, religion or politics. When Vivekananda left to travel and lecture outside of the US – particularly Britain and India – his brother-disciples were enlisted to carry on in his stead. The need for good 'native' teachers – well versed in Sanskrit and English, and approved by Vivekananda – remained a recurrent concern in sustaining the American work.

Saradananda was instructed by Vivekananda to take up the London work, but he was initially reluctant, fearing hardship. Anxieties over shortage of suitable swamis continued to haunt Vivekananda and his Western associates:

> … I have sent for a Sannyasin from Calcutta, to leave him in London. I want one more for America. *I want my own man.* Can't you send a strong fellow from Madras? Of course I will pay everything. He must know both English and Sanskrit pretty well – English more.…

Again he must be a thoroughly trustworthy and obedient man ...
Gurubhakti is the foundation of all spiritual development. You
cannot come I am afraid, leaving your paper [*Brahmavadin*]. Can
G. G. [Narsimhachariar] come? I want to have two fellows in these
2 centres, then I can go to India and send fresh men to relieve them.
I am really tired from incessant work. Any other Hindu would have
vomited blood and died if he had to work as hard as I have.[123]

The emphasis on trustworthiness, Sanskrit and English knowledge was
conjoined with the essential quality of devotion for the guru, without which,
all was deemed fruitless.

Cambridge *Conferences*

168 BRATTLE ST.
CAMBRIDGE, - - MASS.

November 6th, 1898, to May 7th, 1899

LEWIS G. JANES
DIRECTOR

THE work of the *Conferences* will be continued for
a third season, by the courtesy of Mrs. OLE BULL,
in the Studio House, 168 Brattle Street, Cambridge,
which is also the residence of the Director.
The leading idea of the *Conferences*, as heretofore, will be to
afford opportunity for the comparative study of *Ethics*, *Philosophy*, *Sociology* and *Religion*. The following program, somewhat more varied in scope than those of previous years, has
been arranged for the Sunday *Conferences*, in co-operation with
the University of Vermont. A number of the Lectures will
be repeated on alternate Monday Evenings, in Burlington.

1898.   *Sundays,* 4 *P. M.*

November 6. *Opening Meeting.*	Professor Franklin H. Giddings, Ph.D., of Columbia University. The Popular Instruction Most Necessary in a Democracy.
November 13.	Mr. Thomas Davidson, Author of " Education of the Greek People," etc. The Task of the Twentieth Century.
November 20.	Professor Lester F. Ward, LL.D., of the Smithsonian Institution, Washington, D. C. Nature and Nurture, or Heredity and Opportunity.

Figure 5.4   Cambridge Conferences Brochure, 1898.

Source: Bull Curtis Papers, Cambridge Historical Society, MA.

Consequently, Saradananda Abhedananda, took up Vivekananda's American obligations, lecturing at New York, Greenacre and Cambridge. The demand for 'authentic' Indian swamis became a source of bitter rife and rivalry within various Vedanta Societies. New York disciples threatened to hire an Indian Theosophist to teach Vedanta should Saradananda not join their activities.[124] Overworked, Saradananda continued to participate and present Vedanta and Hinduism in the broad eclectic programme at Cambridge from 1896 onwards. His lectures satisfied Janes: 'I like the Swami's lecture very much. It will be an admirable contribution to our series and I am sure will be appreciated both in Brooklyn and in Cambridge.'[125] Janes, following his interest in 'Ethical Ideas', promptly drafted Saradananada to speak at Brooklyn on the 'Ethical Ideas of Hindus'. Vedanta was presented as part of a wider 'evolution of Ethics' programme at Brooklyn. Speakers were billed for talks on the philosophy of Parsis, Buddhists, 'Chinese sages', 'Epicurean Philosophers', Greek Philosophers, Hebrews, Christian Ethics, Utilitarian Ethics and 'Ethics of Evolution'. Saradananda's brief was to cover: 'the earlier Vedic period. Influence of Pantheistic religious conceptions on the moral development of the Indian races. The Vedanta and its ethical teachings….'[126] Speakers at Brooklyn were generally invited to speak at Cambridge and Greenacre. Indian and Asian religions were often in focus, represented by their proponents. Featured recurrently on this list along with Vivekananda and Saradananda were Dharmapala, Virchand Gandhi (Jainism) and Jehangir Cola (Zoroastrianism). Disciples and interlocutors appropriated Vedanta and its Hindu monastic teachers to fit universalist projects of pan-religious unity and ethics.

In December 1896 of the same year, Jane and Bull listed Saradananda as a 'House Resident' for the Cambridge Conferences. The near-complete financial dependence of these monastic gurus on their patrons often meant little choice in their lecture schedules. Janes instructed Bull to ensure that Saradananda perform the scripted spectacle of a native Hindu guru during his presentations: 'Kindly tell the Swami also that our Brooklyn audience will expect to see him in the orange robe and turban.'[127] These claims – made on Indian monks – continued in tandem with their growing proximity to female figures. Saradananda effusively invoked the maternal role of Bull: 'Keep in your mind the position which you have taken yourself namely that of a grand-mother, not only of myself but of all the world.'[128]

Meanwhile, claims-making in India continued on the strength of these connections. The *Prabuddha Bharata* and *Indian Mirror* picked on reports from American and British newspapers on their activities and reprinted them:

> A writer in the Boston Evening Script under date July 14, says, 'The Swami Saradananda of India continues his study classes under the pines.... This evening the Swami will form and instruct a class in Raja Yoga practice; and if the secret of his serene and beautiful calmness of gaze and manner can be taught to the restless West, it will be a lesson well worth the learning. [129]

As well as letters from Western disciples:

> [Saradananda] has fulfilled all the high words you spoke of him, and has been a great inspiration to us.... As it was with you, the Vedanta philosophy seemed to meet all needs. The Swami Saradananda seemed ready to meet questions of all kinds and his patience knew no bounds. As he gained confidence, and understood our people better, he became quite fluent in speech. [130]

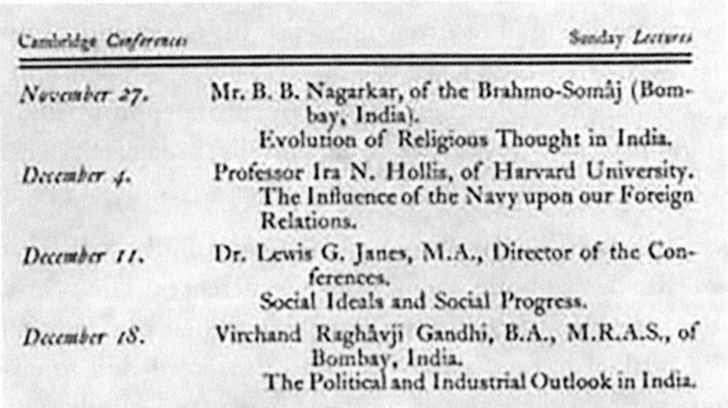

Cambridge Conferences	Sunday Lectures
November 27.	Mr. B. B. Nagarkar, of the Brahmo-Somâj (Bombay, India). Evolution of Religious Thought in India.
December 4.	Professor Ira N. Hollis, of Harvard University. The Influence of the Navy upon our Foreign Relations.
December 11.	Dr. Lewis G. Janes, M.A., Director of the Conferences. Social Ideals and Social Progress.
December 18.	Virchand Raghâvji Gandhi, B.A., M.R.A.S., of Bombay, India. The Political and Industrial Outlook in India.
December 25.	(*HOLIDAY INTERMISSION.*)

Figure 5.5   Brahmo Samaj, Zorastrianism and Evolution lectures.
Source: Bull Curtis Papers, Cambridge Historical Society, MA.

Vedanta was folded carefully in such presentations as part of a wider eclectic engagement, though afforded more space and time than the others. Saradananda (and Dharmapala, whose reputation was growing in global pan-Buddhist discourse) was scheduled to give ten lectures at the Monslavat School of Comparative Religion at Greenacre, compared to less than half by Virchand and others. He was joined by Abhedananda and Turiyananda from 1898 to 1899. Janes wrote to Bull with evident satisfaction: 'I am glad of your good report from the Swami, and in regard to the Swami Turiyananda whom I hope to meet. It would be pleasant to have them all here when Abhedananda speaks on Ramakrishna.'[131]

Abhedananda was promptly drafted to deliver a series of class lectures on 'The Vedanta Philosophy and Religions of India' at Cambridge, Massachusetts. Each season sought to curate a range of non-Western speakers discoursing on their respective religions, philosophies and ethics. The Cambridge Conference of 1898–1899 boasted several big names, including that of Nagarkar, a Brahmo Samaji from Bombay with whom Vivekananda was on rival terms. The mutual bitterness and contestation between rival organisations seemed to have been briefly subverted through liberal projects abroad. Initiatives such as Greenacre, Cambridge and Brooklyn were able to script seemingly irreconcilable narratives as part of a more unified pantheon on 'universal religion'. In London, Vivekananda was received enthusiastically to speak on Vedantic morality at Moncure Conway's Ethical Society at the South Place chapel in Finsbury, well known as a bastion of freethinkers, agnostics, secularists, mystics and non-conformists. Conway had earlier welcomed several non-Christian religionists to address from his pulpit, including the Brahmo leaders Keshab Sen and Protap Mazumdar. Vivekananda was the latest addition to this illustrious repertoire.[132]

The 'Right Kind of People'

Vedanta's networks continued to grow thanks to his Western disciples and their influential intellectual connections. Vivekananda seems to have tacitly accepted early the arrangement that his American work would be guided by his patrons:

> [Y]ou may do anything you please with my affairs, I will not even
> murmur; – I will be only too glad to take Miss Farmer's advice, in
> spite of ghosts and spooks.... Even I will allow Landsberg to 'monkey'
> with my affairs from time to time; but here I put a full stop. Help
> from any other persons besides these frightens me.... I regard you
> as my mother and will always abide by any advice you may have for
> me – but only personally.[133]

Vivekananda had to step carefully around the foibles of individual patrons.
Yet, tensions emerged early. They manifested in attempts to settle Vedanta
with the 'right kind of people', usually wealthy, white and respectable circuits.
While the Boston work undertaken by Bull and Jane preferred to place Vedanta
within 'an international co-operation of scholars', the New York-based Vedanta
Society sought a more lay-oriented tactic. New York members, led by Waldo
and Mary Phillips, resented the elitist undertakings of Bull and her Boston
centre. New York and Boston embodied tensions around class that underlay
Vivekananda's community of disciples. Bull's attempts to control Vivekananda's
conduct caused him to chafe:

> You are mistaken if you think I have a work as Mrs Bull thinks – I
> have no work under or beyond the sun.... I will neither Hinduise my
> message, not Christianise it, nor make it any 'ise' in the world. I will
> only my-ise it and that is all.[134]

Anticipating the limits money would place on his freedom, he refused a
donation of 5,000 dollars from Bull. Unlike the hefty subscriptions paid by
audiences in Boston to listen to Vivekananda, in New York

> [t]he Swami gave his services free as air. The rent was paid by
> voluntary subscriptions, and when these were found insufficient,
> Swami hired a hall and gave secular lectures on India and devoted
> the proceeds to the maintenance of the classes. He said that Hindu
> teachers, of religion felt it to be their duty to support their classes and
> the students too, if they were unable to care for themselves; and the
> teachers would willingly make any sacrifice they possibly could to
> assist a needy disciple.[135]

The audience included the 'old and young, rich and poor, wise and foolish,
stingy ones who dropped a button in the collection basket, and more generous

ones, who gave a dollar bill or even two'.[136] He found greater freedom in the impoverished settings of New York, if not necessarily the required resources. Living with Leon Landsberg in humble settings, he found truer affinity with his monastic creed:

> I am very happy now. Between Mr Landsberg and me, we cook some rice and lentils or barley and quietly eat it, and write something or read or receive visits from poor people who want to learn something, and this I feel I am more a Sannyasin now than I ever was in America.[137]

The affiliation he felt with 'poor people' vindicated his own feeling of *sannyasa*, though only temporarily. The poor, however, faded away soon after. For a brief period, he continued to refuse the comfort of financial security from wealthy patrons, fearing the obligations this would make him subservient to:

> Every one of my friends thought it would end in nothing, this my living and preaching in poor quarters all by myself, and that no ladies will ever come here. Miss Hamlin especially thought that 'she' or 'her right sort of people' were way up from such things as to go and listen to a man who lives by himself in a poor lodging. But the 'right kind' came for all that, day and night, and she too.[138]

Vivekananda's refusal to distinguish between the 'right kind' and 'wrong' amounted to a limited critique of class, if framed in abstract terms: 'Shiva! Shiva! Where is the right kind? And where is the bad? It is all *He* [God]!!'[139] Pecuniary support imposed greater strings on the freedom of work but also brought on the realisation of its necessity. Within two decades, his American work would spread even more widely. The prominent Indian nationalist leader, Lala Lajpat Rai, while visiting America in 1916, attested to this proliferation:

> Vedanta centres of [the Vivekananda Mission] ... are to be found in all the most important cities of the United States. He has personal knowledge of those at New York, Boston, Washington, Chicago and San Francisco and except that at New York, he found all the centres financially flourishing.[140]

Cambridge Conferences	Sunday Lectures
March 12.	Professor Samuel S. Curry, Ph.D., of the Boston School of Expression. Ethical Value of Art.
March 19.	Rev. William Norman Guthrie, of Cincinnati, Ohio. William Blake, Mystic, Poet and Painter. (*Illustrated.*)
March 26.	Professor William James, Ph.D., of Harvard University. (*Topic to be announced.*)
April 2.	Frank Russell, Ph.D., of the Peabody Museum, Cambridge. Religious Ideas of the Athabascan Indians.
April 9.	Professor Crawford Howell Toy, LL.D., of Harvard University. Religion of the Polynesian Peoples.
April 16.	Rev. Charles Gordon Ames, D.D., of Boston. Religious Symbolism and Myth-Making.
April 23.	Professor Nathaniel Schmidt, of Cornell University. Religious Life in Arabia before Mohammed.
April 30.	The Swâmi Abhedânanda, of India. Religious Ideas in Ancient India.
May 7.	(It is hoped that Mrs. Ole Bull will speak concerning the impressions of her visit in India.)

Figure 5.6   Cambridge Conference Brochure advertising Abhedananda's lecture.
Source: Bull Curtis Papers, Cambridge Historical Society, MA.

A widening network of European Orientalists, American interlocutors and wealthy patron-disciples were part of this prolific expansion work. The anxiety for learned audiences found a new moment of fulfilment on Vivekananda's invitation to speak at Harvard University. Bull was able to secure an invite for Vivekananda through her contact John Fox, an alumna of the Harvard Divinity School, in March 1896.[141]

Fox assured that he would be speaking at the coveted Graduate Philosophical Club instead of the Harvard Religious Union, 'the most philosophical organisation at Harvard – so that the audience will be the best the University can afford'.[142] Vivekananda eagerly vaunted the Harvard lecture: 'I will be only too glad to come to Boston for the Harvard lecture specially.'[143] It was touted to be one of the most 'learned' audiences he would address in years since Chicago. Among the audience were John Wright,

Professor of Greek Studies, who introduced him to the Chairman of the Managing Committee of the Parliament of Religions in Chicago, and William James, the distinguished psychologist of religion.

Vivekananda's lecture, entitled 'The Vedanta Philosophy', explained concisely the 'origin, development, and meaning of Vedanta' in its various phases'.[144] The lecture restated Vedanta's claim to be 'world religion' through the usual epistemic gestures: its grand inclusive schema, its ability to reconcile modern science with religion and the universality of its tenets. His emphasis on self-abnegation while explaining Advaita, or the convergence of self with an absolute entity had resonance with Christian ideas of self-sacrifice and Unitarianism.[145] He declared:

> ... you are a born Vedantist, each one of you. Every time that your heart goes out towards the world, you are a true Vedantist, only you do not know it.[146]

Cambridge Conferences — *Sunday Lectures*

"The Relation of Science to Religious Thought," on successive Wednesday afternoons in January and February.
The Swâmi Abhedânanda, of India, will give a series of class lectures on "The Vedanta Philosophy and Religions of India" during the month of April, on dates to be subsequently announced.
Terms and conditions for the above courses will be given in special circulars. Other Classes and Conferences may be announced from time to time during the season.

Conference *Extension*

THE Director will be pleased to communicate with Lecture Committees, Educational Institutions, or the Managers of Lecture Courses, in all parts of the country, with a view to the extension of the work of the *Conferences* wherever it can be of service. Arrangements may be made for individual Lectures, or for courses on different topics. The successful inauguration of co-operative work in Brooklyn, N. Y., and Burlington, Vt., leads us to hope for further appreciation of systematic educational work in lecture courses like those offered by the *Conferences*.

Figure 5.7 Cambridge Conference Programme
Source: Bull Curtis Papers, Cambridge Historical Society, MA.

The allure of a 'hidden self' waiting to be realised attracted the interest of William James on whom Vedanta made a favourable impression.[147] Vedanta was carefully presented as a liberal hermeneutic. That it was part of the Hindu tradition seemed to be incidental: 'It is quite possible for me to be a dualist, and for my wife to be a monist, and so on. One of my sons may worship Christ or Buddha or Mohammed.'[148]

The Harvard lecture gained for Vivekananda lasting relationships and resources. Within weeks, Bull commissioned its publication as a pamphlet.[149] He secured two important allies, the comparative religionist Charles Everett of the Harvard Divinity School, and William James, a pioneering authority on the psychology of religion. In these exchanges, Vedanta was offered as a potent hypothesis within wider metaphysical discourses of eclecticism that ranged from ethics to ether.[150]

Bull spelt out what she expected of Vedanta:

> Indian customs, titles or degrees may be helpful to individuals but the universal phase of the Vedanta, assimilated by and adapted to our life here, is what I would personally like to see incorporated more consciously by the general mind.[151]

Her distinction between the universal and narrow cultural specificities hints at the kind of denaturalisation she sought from Vedanta. This was a bind that non-Western cultural forms entering the West from a variety of colonial contexts and a claim to 'universal' usually felt.

The validity of Vedantic Hinduism was acknowledged as central by both sides. The need for teachers who could defend Hinduism from allegations was directly linked to the sustenance of its appeal to American audiences. Bull and Janes worried that Saradananda was 'too mild mannered for the American audience' and not combative enough to fend off virulent attacks on India and Hinduism as Vivekananda.[152] Nonetheless, Saradananda and Abhedananda (Figure 5.7), among others, continued to perform the double act of propagating a 'world-religion' and representing the 'Hindu Mission in America'.[153] Abhedananda's book *India and Her People* based on the lectures given at the Brooklyn Institute of Art and Sciences was published in 1906 during the Swadeshi movement in Bengal. Promptly proscribed by the Indian government, James Campbell Ker, in his confidential report on the proliferation of anti-British activities on foreign soil, noted the nationalist tendencies of the Society under Abhedananda. He further observed that the convicted revolutionary nationalist Bhupendranath Dutta was Vivekananda's brother, who had fled to New York in 1908.[154]

Epilogue: Made in the West

As the historian of religion Tomoko Masuzawa remarks, the language of 'world religions', popularised after 1893, became a category to rationalise the relationship of Christianity to non-Christian religions. Masuzawa argues that it preserved the claim to European superiority in a carefully articulated language of pluralism.[155] Vivekananda's Vedantic dialectics, however, show an intimate subversion of that same framework. Without displacing the category itself, he was able to fold Hinduism's subtle claim to superiority within it.

Popular Orientalist stereotypes in early nineteenth-century America portrayed India as an ancient (now colonised) land of idolatry, godmen, levitation tricks and the Occult. This was an image that Vivekananda and his followers wished to challenge sharply, even as they built on its essential binary of a spiritual East versus a material West. What differed was an emphasis on the kind of spirituality that could be rationalised, modernised and polemicised to great effect. In comparison to the 'low-brow' popular Hinduism that was in widespread vogue in America, Vivekananda and his collaborators focused on a high literary Sanskritic tradition, curated specifically for the heterodox cultural elite. 'I must touch the brain of America and stir it up if I can', Vivekananda had asserted in 1894, soon after his Chicago success.[156] By the close of the century, Harvard, New York, Boston and other learned networks represented a coming together of this 'brain of America'. Assembled through the close personal and ideological energies of Western followers, their participation made Vedanta go 'global'. It also marked the growing recognition of America as an alternative site to counterpose Britain's influence. Historians such as Ross Bassett have shown that the increasing technological superiority of the US and Germany over Britain greatly appealed to nationalist opinion in India.[157] The *Mahratta*, a journal founded by the Hindu nationalist leader Bal Gangadhar Tilak, prophesied that Chicago will soon supersede London.[158] Columns in the *Prabuddha Bharata* prominently featured world events pertaining to the US and Japan.

The significance of the American 'West' in manufacturing a world legacy for Vivekananda and Vedanta was recognised in his lifetime. *The Indian Mirror* asserted: 'It is doubtful whether Swami Vivekananda would have become so widely known, if he had not visited America.'[159] Vivekananda upheld this claim when he exclaimed in 1894 that 'America is the best field in the world to carry on any idea, so I do not think of leaving America soon.'[160] The importance of the West as an ideal 'field of [missionary] work' was repeatedly stressed. Vivekananda's long exposure to liberal thought had made him particularly keen on the possibilities wrought by an emergent global liberal order facilitated through imperial networks. He exhibited a critical awareness of this global order and the benefits to be reaped:

> From ocean to ocean run the roads of England. Every part of the world has been linked to every other part.... Under all these circumstances we find again India reviving and ready to give her own quota to the progress and civilisation of the world ... that I have been forced, as it were, ... to go over to America and preach to England is the result.... everything looks propitious, and Indian thought, philosophical and spiritual, must once more go over and conquer the world ... it is not only that we must revive our own country – that is a small matter; ... but my idea is the conquest of the whole world by the Hindu race.[161]

Vivekananda was prescient in his conviction that networks of global capital would be harnessed to export Indian spirituality abroad. He understood the value of the US not being an imperial power (the Monroe Doctrine still being operative; Philippine wars did not happen until 1898) but an 'exceptional' land of opportunity. Vivekananda almost echoed the principle of American exceptionalism: 'I love the Yankee land ... In America is the place, the people, the opportunity for everything'.[162] It was a different kind of West, but an increasingly important West. His success demonstrated that Hindu universalist claims need no longer be legitimised through the British metropole but could form their own axes of interlocution. The increasing role of America in shaping the cultural politics and trajectories of discourses such as Vedantic Hinduism or Theravada Buddhism attests to this expanding scale. This fracturing of the West, while not displacing existing Orientalist typologies, created possibilities for cultural encounters that could be different from Britain or other imperial European countries. The US became part of an extended West, whose racial privileges and presumptions of 'whiteness' remained intact, but more open to 'eastern' forms of knowledge that spoke to its considerable non-conformist fringe. In later years, these circles would support a variety of anti-imperial imperatives including that of India's.

The decades 1890s–1900s represented a gradual culmination of Vedanta's intellectualisation project. The movement to make Hinduism respectable occurred against the backdrop of increasing anti-Asian immigration measures in North America. As a prescient communique from a Canadian labour minister to British leaders revealed: 'the native of India is not suited to this country'.[163] In spite of their avowed discipleship or claims on Vivekananda, no major American disciple ever took up or identified with the cause of Indian labour immigrants. Their investments generally remained fixed on a spiritual interest in Hinduism, reproducing an idea of India tethered to the high cultural imaginaries of an upper caste Hindu nationalist elite (but rendered in casteless terms). Vedanta became formative in influencing their efforts to realise an idealised India, in science, religion, agriculture, education and national freedom. It informed their investments outside of the strictly spiritual, as with MacLeod who saw Vivekananda as making her free: 'I've freedom. Freedom to see and help India to grow – that's my job and how I love it…. It's so curious to feel free, not needed any more in the West, but all my characteristics – in India.'[164] MacLeod, like Bull, contributed to projects that would 'make India great again'. Her efforts to involve William Willcocks (the irrigation engineer who built the Aswan Dam) in 'the restoration of the Ancient Irrigation of Bengal or the agricultural scientist Boshi Sen for his 'Vivekananda Laboratory' in Almora (on the Himalayan foothills) exemplified such investments.[165] Elsewhere, Nivedita and Bull provided personal and material support to Jagadish Bose, in the belief that his scientific work on the unity of 'response in living and non-living' would realise the premise of Advaita Vedanta. Science remained an important site to stake out claims for Vedanta.

This symbolic coming together of the 'world' to vindicate Vedanta–Vivekananda–Hinduism was significant. They might be numerically small, but their cumulative discursive effect in India was amplified. Western recognition for Indians like Vivekananda came to be coveted as a victory over the West, notwithstanding its limited bearings. As Vivekananda believed: 'These white faces will have more influence in India than Hindus.' It sustained powerful claims-making around aggressive forms of cultural nationalism,[166] speaking to Hindu narratives of deficit masculinity in colonial India, particularly the desire to 'manufacture men' out of an India 'only inhabited by women and eunuchs'.[167] Nivedita embodied the very project as well as its lack, bringing masculinity to an emasculated nation: 'I seem to be realising everyone of Swamiji's opinions over again, and feel myself able to make the 10000 Vivekanandas of whom He was always talking.'[168] Vedanta continued to perform the dual task of raising India's profile in the West and bringing masculinity to its own people – moves that converged in projecting and producing a respectable India for consumption at home and abroad.

'The value of foreign appreciation is in rousing India up', argued Vivekananda.[169] Western Indophile investments around Vedanta revolved around producing a Hindu India that was moral, high-cultured and representative of its stature. As the flow of Hindu godmen and spiritual forms intensified over the twentieth century to the West along with increasing skilled migration of upper caste and middle-class Indians, transnational Hinduism became embroiled in the contest for an elusive respectability around migrating Indians. Vivekananda and his Western disciples' deployments around Vedanta represent an early, if major, episode of that history.

Notes

1   The volume of serious historical publications on Vivekananda's influence in Bengal is massive, compared to the rather cursory attention given to Madras as an ancillary site. Major works such as William Radice, ed., *Swami Vivekananda and the Modernisation of Hinduism* (London: Sri Sarada Math, 1999); Amiya Sen, *Swami Vivekananda* (Oxford: Oxford University Press, 2000) do not dwell the Madras connection. This scholarship tends to locate Vivekananda within a largely colonial Bengali setting that does not adequately explain the remarkable number of lay and princely patrons and disciples Vivekananda had already gathered in Madras even before his Chicago success. This chapter acknowledges this problem but unfortunately does not fill that lack, partly due to constraints of language.

2   Vedanta was one of the six original schools of Hindu philosophy that developed in ancient India. The Advaita branch of Vedanta posited a strictly non-dualist view of the world, with absolute identity between man and maker.

3   Caste is the central institution that defines Indian social hierarchy. The Hindu
    caste system has four major *varna*s, or professional classes, which in descending
    order of ritual superiority are: Brahmins or priests, Kshatriyas or warriors,
    Vaishyas or merchants, Shudras or menials. Those outside of the caste system
    are called Untouchables; Adivasis or aboriginal communities too were outside
    of the four-fold caste system. Upper castes refer to people who belonged to
    the first three varnas. Each of these varnas have huge internal stratifications.
4   Dutta, *Londone Swami Vivekananda*, 150.
5   Pandita Ramabai (1858–1922): Indian social reformer and pioneering women's
    educationist. Scathing critic of Hindu Brahminical orthodoxy (she was herself
    a Brahmin), she converted to Christianity in 1883. She was the first Indian
    woman to have received a medical degree. See Uma Chakravarti, *Rewriting
    History: The Life and Times of Pandita Ramabai* (New Delhi: Zubaan, 2013),
    2–4. Ramabai's wide campaigns in support of Hindu widows in Britain and
    America led to the formation of Ramabai Circles, many of them supported
    by well-known suffragists. Vivekananda's attempt to preach the greatness of
    Hinduism often ran counter to the members of these circles.
6   Historical sources to connect their trajectories are only available to us in
    fragments, given the restrictive ownership the Ramakrishna Math and Mission
    asserts over the personal papers of their founding figures.
7   Anderson and Harrison, *Taking-Place*, 8. A more deviant and distinctively
    queer trajectory is traced by Karl Scoonover and Rosalind Galt, whose work
    on 'Queer Cinema in the World' argues for a 'queer worldliness', that disrupt
    normative ways of cultural being and belonging in the world. See Karl
    Schoonover and Rosalind Galt, *Queer Cinema in the World* (Durham: Duke
    University Press, 2016).
8   Ruth Harris, 'Introduction', in *Guru to the World: The Life and Legacy of
    Vivekananda* (Cambridge, MA: Harvard University Press, 2022).
9   See Arvind Sharma for a detailed discussion of the precepts and texts of these
    thinkers for a dialectic of universal religion that drew from various traditions
    of Hinduism deeply. Arvind Sharma, *The Concept of Universal Religion in
    Modern Hindu Thought* (Basingstoke: Palgrave Macmillan, 1998).
10 Dipesh Chakrabarty, *Provincializing Europe: Postcolonial Thought and Historical
    Difference* (Princeton: Princeton University Press, 2007), 22.
11 Several historians have dwelt on the rationalising of Vedanta modern science
    and Vedanta. See Dermot H. Killingley, 'Yoga-sūtra IV, 2–3 and Vivekānanda's
    Interpretation of Evolution', *Journal of Indian Philosophy* 18, no. 2 (June 1990):
    151–179. Historians of science Dhruv Raina and Irfan Habib place it within a

wider context of bhadralok engagements with modern science: Dhruv Raina and S. Irfan Habib, 'The Moral Legitimation of Modern Science: Bhadralok Reflections on Theories of Evolution', *Social Studies of Science* 26, no. 1 (February, 1996): 9–42.

12   Christopher Minkowski, 'Advaita Vedanta in Early Modern History', *South Asian History and Culture* 2, no. 2 (April 2011): 205–231.

13   Dermot H. Killingley, 'Vedanta and Modernity', in *India: Society and the Beginnings of Modernisation, c. 1830–1850*, ed. C. H. Philips and Mary Doreen Wainwright (London, 1976), 133–134.

14   Indeed, attempts to grapple with the challenge of Vedanta was evident in contemporary advertisements that awarded monetary prizes (up to 300 pounds) for essays that could prove its fallibility to learned Hindus. Proposal for a Prize of £300, for the Best Essay in Refutation of the Errors of Hindu Philosophy according to the Vedanta, Nyaya and Sankhya systems, 1 April 1853, *The Times of India*, accessed through Pro-Quest.

15   Brian A. Hatcher, 'Bourgeois Vedanta: The Colonial Roots of Middle-Class Hinduism', *Journal of the American Academy of Religion* 75, no. 2 (June 2007): 306.

16   Killingley, 'Vedanta and Modernity', 137. A handful of Brahmo Samaj members, however, continued on Roy's line: Anandachandra Vedantavagis translated Shankara's commentary on the Brahmasutra into Bengali and Chandrasekhar Basu wrote a Bengali 'Introduction to Vedanta'.

17   C. A. Bayly, 'South Asian Liberalism under Strain c. 1900–1914', https://www.qub.ac.uk/schools/happ/Events/annual-lectures/wiles-lecture-series/Secure-access/Filetoupload,967433,en.pdf (accessed on 9 January 2023).

18   Tanika Sarkar, *Hindu Wife, Hindu Nation* (Delhi: Permanent Black, 2001), 1–2.

19   Sartori, *Bengal in Global Concept History*, 136–142.

20   Sophie-Jung H. Kim draws out aspects of this in her essay, 'An International Event and Its Multiple Global Publics: The Parliament of the World's Religions (Chicago, 1893) and Vivekananda', in *Global Publics: Its Power and Its Limits*, ed. Valeska Huber and Jürgen Osterhammel (Oxford: Oxford University Press, 2020), 177–201.

21   Travis D. Webster, 'Secularization and Cosmopolitan Gurus', *Asian Ethnology* 75, no. 2 (2016): 332.

22   Ibid., 330. It is interesting, though, that only one representative of Islam attended the World Parliament.

23   Ibid., 49. It is interesting how the Chicago Parliament – aimed at celebrating
      the eclectic religious diversity in the world and seeking to 'condemn
      sectarianism, fanaticism and bigotry' – ended up empowering such narratives in
      specific nationalist discourses, particularly Vivekananda in Hindu nationalism
      and Anagarika Dharmapala in Sinhalese nationalism.

24   Harris, 'Vivekananda, Sarah Farmer, and Global Spiritual Transformations', 179.

25   Leggett, *Late and Soon*, 95–96.

26   The Ole Bull will gave away most of her wealth to various Indians or India-
      centred activities: Margaret Noble/Sister Nivedita, prominent British Hindu
      disciple of Vivekananda; Jagadish Bose, eminent scientist; Swami Saradananda,
      President of the Ramakrishna Mission; and Mohini Mohun Chatterji, a lapsed
      Theosophist. The will was contested by her daughter Olea Vaughan Bull, who
      challenged her Hindu bequests, and eventually won the trial, though she died
      hours after the victory. 'Ole Bull Will Contest', *New York Times,* 13 February
      1911; 'Spirits Urged $25,000 Gift, Said Mrs. Bull', *Boston Herald,* 15 June
      1911. Ruth Harris elaborates on this in her essay 'Vivekananda, Sarah Farmer,
      and Global Spiritual Transformations'.

27   See Gandhi, *Affective Communities*; also Dipesh Chakrabarty, 'From
      Civilization to Globalization: The "West" as a Shifting Signifier in Indian
      Modernity', *Inter-Asia Cultural Studies* 13, no. 1 (2012), of how Asian
      religiosities influences various eclectic movement in late nineteenth-century
      metropolitan British culture.

28   *Prabuddha Bharata,* June 1902, 110. All copies of the *Prabuddha Bharata* have
      been accessed via Archive.org, https://archive.org/details/PrabuddhaBharata-
      July1896-Dec2001/page/n16 (accessed on 16 February 2022).

29   T. J. Jackson Lears, *No Place of Grace: Antimodernism and the Transformation
      of American Culture, 1880–1920* (London: University of Chicago Press, 1994),
      xii–xix.

30   Vivekananda to Brother Disciples, 25 September 1894, *LSV,* 139–140.
      Vivekananda compares them to the Kartabhaja sect in India. It was founded
      by Aulchand and became popular in eighteenth-century Bengal, preaching
      literalist practices of worshipping the Master.

31   Vivekananda to Brahmananda, 19 March 1894, Chicago, *LSV,* 96.
      Dharmapala's gentleness would, however, give way to a muscular pan-Buddhist
      propaganda over the control of Bodh Gaya in the later 1900s. In 1904, Sister
      Nivedita became actively aligned with the Hindu side in this contest. See
      Nivedita to Gokhale, 24 September, 1904, *LSN*-II, 682.

32 Prabuddhaprana, *Saint Sara*, 2–3.

33 Bull to Chatterjee, 15 August 1893, Prabuddhaprana, *Saint Sara*, 86–87.

34 Stefanie Syman, *The Subtle Body: The Story of Yoga in America,* (New York: Farrar, Straus & Giroux Inc., 2010), 51–52.

35 Vivekananda to Madras Disciple, 28 June 1894, *LSV,* 121–122.

36 *Prabuddha Bharata* 1, no. 4 (October 1896): 3.

37 G. S. Bhate quoted in *Reminiscences of Swami Vivekananda*, 61.

38 A dominant caste of indeterminate varna location. The Kayasthas emerged and rose to prominence as a scribal/bureaucratic class under Mughal patronage in various parts of north India. Influential strands of conservative Brahminical opinion viewed Kayasthas as having Shudra (Untouchable) origin.

39 Swami Vivekananda, 'My Plan of Campaign', Madras, *Lectures from Colombo to Almora* (Madras: Vyjyanti Press, 1897), 123.

40 Ibid.

41 Sarat C. Chakrabarti, 'Letter to the Editor', *Indian Mirror,* 24 April 1901, in *Vivekananda in Indian Newspapers* [henceforth *VIN*], ed. Shankari Prasad Bose (Calcutta: Modern Book Agency, 1960).

42 Swami Turiyananda quoted in *Reminiscences of Swami Vivekananda*, 340.

43 Brother Disciples to Vivekananda, March 1894, Burke, *Swami Vivekananda in the West,* vol. 2, 90. This was attributed to P. C. Mazoomdar of the Brahmo Samaj, who also spoke at the Chicago Parliament along with Vivekananda.

44 *Hampton-Columbian* magazine, October 1911, 405–406.

45 Alasinga Perumal to Vivekananda, 28 March 1895, Cambridge Conferences papers, Bull-Curtis Papers, Cambridge Historical Society, Boston. Henceforth MSS/BC/F/CC.

46 Janes to Bull, 5 September 1895, MSS/BC/F/CC.

47 Janes to Bull, [undated] 1895, MSS/BC/F/CC.

48 Janes to Bull, 9 October 1896, MSS/BC/F/CC.

49 'The Great Hindu in America', 8 August 1894, *Indian Mirror, VIN*, 31.

50 News and Notes, *Prabuddha Bharata* 1, no. 8 (February 1897): 2.

51 *Prabuddha Bharata*, March 1897, 96.

52 *Prabuddha Bharata*, 31 December 1896 (emphasis added).

53 'Purushtwam Rao Telang', Editorial, 29 January 1895, *Amrita Bazar Patrika, VIN*, 308.

54 'Swami Vivekenanda in Ceylon', 21 January 1897, *Indian Mirror, VIN*, 124.

55 The Christian Literature Society for India, *Swami Vivekananda and his Guru; with Letters from Prominent Americans on the Alleged Progress of Vedantism in the U.S.* (London; Madras, 1897). Another pamphlet, entitled *The World's First*

Parliament of Religions: Its Christian Spirit, Historic Greatness and Manifold Results (Chicago: American Theological Library Association Historical Monographs, 1895), denied wholesale the narrative of Asian conquest pf American minds, cited in Kim, 'An International Event and its Multiple Global Publics', 200.

56 'The Missionary Work of the First Hindu Sannyasin to the West and His Plan of Regeneration of India', 7 February 1897, *Madras Times*, *VIN*, 131.

57 Mrs Alice Hansborough quoted *Reminiscences of Swami Vivekananda*, 312.

58 Sister Christine, recounting her experience of listening to Vivekananda at the Thousand Island Park and other places. See *Reminiscences of Swami Vivekananda*, 106.

59 *Boston Evening Transcript*, 11 August 1894, 11. Accessed through ProQuest Historical Papers.

60 Sumit Sarkar has analysed the contradictions of Ramakrishna's rustic appeal to a group of urban bhadraloks, framed by the disciplining regime of 'chakri' or clerical service. See Sarkar, '"Kaliyuga", "Chakri" and "Bhakti"'.

61 7 February 1897, *Indian Mirror, VIN*, 131.

62 'News and Notes', *Prabuddha Bharata* 1, no. 7 (January 1897): 3.

63 Amrita M. Salm and Judy Howe Hayes, *The Inspired Life of Sarah Ellen Waldo* (Mayavati: Advaita Ashrama, 2019).

64 Sister Christine quoted in *Reminiscences of Swami Vivekananda*, 109.

65 'Our New York Letter', *Prabuddha Bharata* 34 (May 1899): 79.

66 Alice Hansborough quoted in *Reminiscences of Swami Vivekananda*, 326.

67 Sister Christine quoted in *Reminiscences of Swami Vivekananda*, 81.

68 'News and Notes', Prabuddha Bharata 4, no. 58 (May 1901): 77.

69 Vivekananda to Alasinga Perumal, 6 May 1895, *LSV*, 222.

70 Vivekananda to Alasinga Perumal, 29 September 1894, *LSV*, 149.

71 Kali, for instance, could fit the quest for a 'Divine Feminine', as Divine Mother. Joy Dixon discusses the spiritual membership of Madame Blavatsky and other women followers in movements like Theosophy; see Dixon, *Divine Feminine*.

72 Margaret Noble, 'Report on Vedanta Missionary Work, Wimbledon (London)', *Brahmavadin*, 15 September 1897, *Complete Works of Sister Nivedita*, vol. 2 (Calcutta: Advaita Ashrama, 1967), 399.

73 Bull to Macleod, 17 September 1896, Prabuddhaprana, *Saint Sara*, 228.

74 MacLeod quoted in *Reminiscences of Swami Vivekananda*, 158.

75 'The Great Hindu in America', 8 August 1894, *Indian Mirror, VIN*, 31.

76   Such as the Ghadr movement, and the American League for India's Freedom. Harald Fischer-Tiné notes these intersections in his essay: Fischer-Tiné, 'Indian Nationalism and the "World Forces"', 325–344.

77   'An Indian Yogi in London', *Westminster Gazette*, 23 October 1895, in Vivekananda, *The Complete Works of Swami Vivekananda*, vol. 5 (Calcutta: Sri Ramakrishna Math, 1973), 184–186.

78   A Western disciple, 'Chasing the Shadows', *Prabuddha Bharata* 14, no. 150 (January 1900): 8.

79   Swami Vivekananda, 'The Work before Us', *Lectures from Colombo to Almora*, 195.

80   Janes and Z. Sidney Sampson, 'Letter to "Our Indian Brethren of the Great Aryan Family"', 31 December 1896, 'News and Notes', *Prabuddha Bharata* 1, no. 9 (March 1897): 98.

81   'Swami Vivekananda in Action', Editorial, 21 January 1897, *Indian Mirror*, *VIN*, 125.

82   'Hindu Ideas Gain in America', 3 July 1896, *Indian Mirror*, *VIN*, 103.

83   'Swami Vivekananda's Departure from London', 14 December 1896, printed on 7 January 1897, *Indian Mirror*, *VIN*, 121.

84   Nivedita to MacLeod, 7 December 1898, *LSN*-I, 27.

85   The public scrutiny faced by the society over the forged letters purportedly sent by secret Tibetan Mahatmas to Judge authorizing him for the post of the President led to its widespread loss of appeal and membership. Disillusioned, both Müller and Sturdy, among many others, resigned from their primary memberships to the society. Things 'Oriental' and mystical linked even remotely to Indian spiritual/religious traditions were completely discredited in British and American intellectual circles for a while and any individual/ institution propagating the same regarded as highly suspect. Dixon, *Divine Feminine*, 55.

86   E. T. Sturdy to Vivekananda, 30 March 1895, *Swami Vivekananda in the West*, vol. 3, 218.

87   V to Sturdy, 24 April 1895, *Swami Vivekananda in the West*, vol. 3, 219.

88   'The Great Hindu in America', 8 August 1894, *Indian Mirror*, *VIN*, 31.

89   A. Krishnamachari, Letter to the Editor, 'Swami Vivekananda and Theosophy', 2 March 1897, *Indian Mirror*, *VIN*, 166.

90   Letter to the Editor, 'Swami Vivekananda and the Theosophical Society', 20 February 1897, *Indian Mirror*, *VIN*, 145.

91   *Prabuddha Bharata* 1, no. 5 (November 1896): 3 (emphasis in original).

92   Nayan Shah, 'Adjudicating Intimacies on U.S. Frontiers', in *Haunted by Empire*, ed. Stoler, 119.

93   Slate, *Coloured Cosmopolitanism*, 27.

94   The first census that counted South Asians was in 1910. The US Census declared that pure-blood Hindus belong ethnically to the Caucasian or white race, and to be deemed so in naturalisation proceedings, suggests how far the typology of caste had already interpenetrated American state discourse. Slate, *Coloured Cosmopolitanism*, 29.

95   Slate, *Coloured Cosmopolitanism*, 27. Indians often played their 'Caucasian connection' card to claim legal whiteness.

96   Seema Sohi, *Echoes of Mutiny: Race, Surveillance, and Indian Anticolonialism in North America* (New York: Oxford University Press, 2014), 8.

97   Shah discusses the multiple usages of Hinduism around two separate legal contests in the early twentieth century that questioned and advocated the sanctity of Hindu marriage. See Shah, 'Adjudicating Intimacies on U.S. Frontiers', 130.

98   Janes to Bull, 16 December 1896, Bull Curtis Papers, Cambridge Historical Society, Boston, MA.

99   G. S. Bhate quoted in *Reminiscences of Swami Vivekananda*, 314.

100   Hansborough quoted in *Reminiscences of Swami Vivekananda*, 316.

101   Ibid., 325 and 328.

102   Rajani Kanta Das's report *Hindustani Workers on the Pacific Coast* offers an early and insightful account of the Indian diaspora in America. Rajani Kanta Das, 'Principal Problems', in *Hindustani Workers on the Pacific Coast* (Berlin: W. de Gruyter & Co., 1923), 109–110.

103   'Swami Vivekananda in London', an interview in London, *Prabuddha Bharata* 1, no. 3 (September 1896): 2.

104   Swami Vivekananda, 'Buddhistic India', in *The Complete Works of Swami Vivekananda*, vol. 3 (Calcutta: Advaita Ashrama, 2002), 535–536.

105   Vijay Prashad notes that it reflects a trend in Indian diasporic politics that would continue to grow in the twentieth century: the predominant drive in South Asian immigrants and figures in an extended West (including settler colonies) to pursue their affiliations within a frame of liberal white respectability instead of identifying with strains of Black cultural politics. See Vijay Prashad, *The Karma of Brown Folk* (London: University of Minnesota, 2001).

106   The Supreme Court clarified that Thind was not 'Caucasian in the popular sense', as against an 'ethnological sense'. 'Constitutional Law: Naturalization – Hindu Excluded from Citizenship', *Yale Law Journal* 32, no. 6 (April, 1923): 625.

107   I borrow this term from Richard G. Fox, 'East of Said', in *Edward Said*, 152.

108   V to Alasinga, 6 May 1895, *LSV*, 221.

109 Several scholars have noted the importance of Orientalist scholars in the making of modern Hinduism as a syndicated system. See Richard King, 'Orientalism and the Modern Myth of "Hinduism"', *Numen* 46, no. 2 (1999): 146–185. For its effects beyond India and particularly in Europe, see Sheldon Pollock, 'Deep Orientalism? Notes on Sanskrit and Power beyond the Raj', in *Orientalism and the Postcolonial Predicament*, ed. Breckenridge and Veer, 76–13. German Orientalism was used to create the myth of a pure Aryan race, cited in King, 'Orientalism and the Modern Myth of "Hinduism"', 149.

110 'Swami Avedananda in London', *Prabuddha Bharata* 1, no. 5 (November 1896): 3.

111 Waldo quoted in *Reminiscences of Swami Vivekananda*, 79.

112 *Indian Mirror*, 7 January 1897, *VIN*, 121.

113 Vivekananda to Bull, [undated, 1895?], Prabuddhaprana, *Saint Sara*, 171.

114 Vivekananda to Alasinga, 12 January 1895, *LSV*.

115 Vivekananda to Brahmananda, 19 March 1894, *LSV*.

116 Farmer later drifted from Vedanta to the Baha'i faith after her encounter with Abdul Baha in 1900.

117 Bull to Jane, *Swami Vivekananda in the West*, vol. 2, 230.

118 Prabuddhaprana, *Saint Sara*, 108–109. There is a studied silence on Carpenter in almost all of Vivekananda hagiographers (and even more academic biographers), hinting at the deep-seated discomfort the tradition has had in dealing with homosexuality. This is also reflected in the Vedanta Society's strained relationship with Christopher Isherwood, who was a Vedanta Society member and went on to write a popular biography of Ramakrishna, allegedly pruned of its homosexual interpretations when published by monastic editors. Sheila Rowbotham's magisterial biography of Carpenter indexes the many radical movements he was involved in, a reflection of the intersections facilitated by *fin de siècle* utopianism. See Sheila Rowbotham, *Edward Carpenter: A Life of Liberty and Love* (London: Verso, 2008). More recently, the historian Alison Twells has argued that Carpenter's 'comradely love', fired by a deeply anti-bourgeois commitment, unified disparate interests such as his anthropological curiosity in Vedantic mysticism, male friendships in India and Ceylon and his romantic pursuits with Northern English working-class men. See Alison Twells, '"Eros the Great Leveller": Edward Carpenter, Sexual Cosmotopianism and the Northern Working Man', *Journal of Colonialism and Colonial History* 22, no 3 (Winter 2021): 2.

119 Janes to Bull, 4 June 1896, MSS/BC/F/CC.

120 Janes to Bull, 14 June 1895, MSS/BC/F/CC (emphasis added).

121 Janes to Bull, 4 June 1896, MSS/BC/F/CC.

122 Printed brochure of Cambridge Conferences, December 1895, Prabuddhaprana, *Saint Sara*, 112.

123 Vivekananda to Alasinga, 18 November 1895, Burke, *Swami Vivekananda in the West*, vol. 3, 302.

124 Prabuddhaprana, *Saint Sara*, 215.

125 Janes to Goodwin, 3 October 1896, MSS/BC/F/CC.

126 Brooklyn Ethical Association's 'Evolution of Ethics' Programme, 1896, MSS/BC/F/CC.

127 Janes to Bull, 9 October 1896, MSS/BC/F/CC.

128 Saradananda to Bull, 27 October 1896, MSS/BC/F/CC.

129 'News and Notes', *Prabuddha Bharata* 1, no. 4 (October 1896): 3.

130 Excerpt from Sara Farmer's letter to Vivekananda, 'News and Notes', *Prabuddha Bharata* 1, no 6 (December 1896).

131 Janes to Bull, 19 October 1899, MSS/BC/F/CC.

132 Burke, *Swami Vivekananda in the West*, vol. 3, 264–267.

133 Vivekananda to Bull, 25 April 1895, *LSV.*

134 Vivekananda to Mary Hale, 1 February 1895, *LSV.*

135 Laura Glen, later Sister Devamata, *Prabudhha Bharata*, Mayavati, April 1932, 132.

136 Glen, *Prabudhha Bharata*, April 1932, 132.

137 Vivekananda to Bull, 11 February 1895, *LSV.*

138 Vivekananda to Bull, 11 April 1895, *LSV.*

139 Sister Christine quoted in *Reminiscences of Swami Vivekananda*, 110.

140 *Times of India* (1861–current); Bombay, 18 May 1916, 6, ProQuest Historical Newspapers: TOI.

141 Mary Louise Burke, Vivekananda's biographer, contends that Fox was nowhere as influential in 1896 to be able to invite Vivekananda. Fox had graduated from Harvard in 1894, and in the first half of 1896 was employed in his brother's real estate business. She surmises he may have been a corresponding secretary for the Graduate Philosophical Club, though there is no record to evidence this. See Burke, *Swami Vivekananda in the West*, vol. 4, 90. Nonetheless, he did play an important part in brokering Vivekananda's invitation, though to what extent, is unclear.

142 Fox to Bull, 15 January 1896, cited in Prabuddhaprana, *Saint Sara*, 175.

143 Vivekananda to Bull, January 1896, Burke, *Swami Vivekananda in the West*, vol. 4, 91.

144 Ibid., 92.

145 Swami Vivekananda, *The Vedanta Philosophy: An Address before The Graduate Philosophical Society of Harvard University, 25 March 1896* (New York: Vedanta Society, 1901), 14.

146 Vivekananda, *The Vedanta Philosophy*, 24.

147 William James, *The Varieties of Religious Experience* (New York: Longmans, Green, and Co., 1917), 504–505.

148 Vivekananda, *The Vedanta Philosophy*, 20.

149 Ibid.

150 Vivekananda perfected the method of scientism in his analogies, grafting latest theories of evolution and thermodynamics to explain yogic practice. For a critical take on Vivekananda's use of science, see Mira Nanda, 'Yoga Scientized: How Vivekananda Rewrote Patanjali's Yoga Sutra', in *Science in Saffron: Skeptical Essays on History of Science* (New Delhi: Three Essays Collective, 2016), 132.

151 Bull to Mary Louise, August[?] 1895, Prabuddhaprana, *Saint Sara*, 150.

152 Prabuddhaprana, *Saint Sara*, 195.

153 Saradananda delivered a lecture entitled 'Hindu Mission in America' on 23 April 1898. Audiences included Bull, Bose, (probably) Macleod, Nivedita and Mohini Chatterjee; see Debanjan Sengupta, ed., *Nivedita o Jagadish Chandra: Ek Achena Samparker Sandhan* (Kolkata: Gangchil, 2010), 18.

154 Ker, *Political Trouble in India*, 218.

155 Masuzawa, *The Invention of World Religions*.

156 Swami Vivekananda, quoted in Burke, *Swami Vivekananda in America*, 161.

157 Bassett, *The Technological Indian*, 15.

158 Ibid., 19.

159 *Indian Mirror*, 21 January 1897, *VIN*, 124.

160 Vivekananda to a Madrasi Disciple, 29 June 1894, *LSV*, 118.

161 Vivekananda, *Lectures from Colombo*, 191.

162 Burke, *Swami Vivekananda in the West*, vol. 4, 312.

163 Cited in Prashad, *The Karma of Brown Folk*, 43.

164 Greenstidel quoted in *Reminiscences of Swami Vivekananda*, 164.

165 See Letters from 1928 to 1930 between Macleod to Leonard Elmhirst, an English disciple-cum-collaborator of Tagore, Tantine MacLeod, LKE/IN/13/B, Dartington Hall Records, Devon Heritage Centre, Exeter

166 Vivekananda himself is, of course, a far more complicated figure than his current straitjacketing as a Hindutva icon.

167 Vivekananda to Alasinga, 1 July 1895, *LSV*, 242.

168 Nivedita to MacLeod [1902], *LSN*-II, 535.

169 Vivekananda to Alasinga, 29 September 1894, *LSV*.

Epilogue

What Settles After

The 'Ole Bull Will Contest'

February 1911 saw a curious contest in the religio-legal history of the United States, over the will of 'one Mrs Sara Bull' who died on 18 January 1911. A prominent American philanthropist, she was also the widow of the famous Norwegian violinist Ole Bull. Her last will and testament reportedly gave away the greater part of her estate worth 500,000 dollars to four Indian or India-based individuals and institutions: Margaret Noble/Sister Nivedita (50,000 dollars), prominent British Hindu disciple of Vivekananda; Jagadish Bose, eminent Indian biophysicist; Swami Saradananda, President of the Ramakrishna Mission; and Mohini Mohan Chatterjee, a lapsed Theosophist.[1] Her daughter Olea Bull Vaughan challenged these 'Hindu bequests', blaming her circle of Hindu swamis and friends for a psychic plot that caused her death. Olea's lawyer Sherman L. Whipple declared: '[T]he late Mrs Bull was the subject of a "psychic conspiracy" for some time prior to her death' (Figure E.1)[2] The trial itself was sensational and well covered by dailies like the *New York Times* and *Boston Herald*, sometimes making front page.[3]

SAYS PSYCHIC PLOT
SWAYED MRS. BULL

Counsel Seeking to Break Will of Violinist's Widow Tells of "Mystic Meditation Ring."

MEMBERS HINDU CONVERTS

Participation in Their Mysterious Rites Drove Mrs. Bull and Others Insane, Lawyer Declares.

Special to The New York Times.

Figure E.1   'Psychic Plot Swayed Mrs Bull', *New York Times*, 23 May 1911.
Source: ProQuest.

The deposing lawyer accused the late Vivekananda of leading an Indian cult behind this psychic conspiracy. Both his monastic and non-monastic disciples were held guilty of spreading occult beliefs and practices that drove Bull mad.[4] Vivekananda's death was blamed on his excessive dabbling in occult exercises. Whipple frontally charged Sister Nivedita for Bull's death:

> Miss Margaret Noble, an Englishwoman converted to the Hindu religion and now living in Calcutta, was, in his estimation, the chief factor in this conspiracy…. He also produced a letter in which one of the members of the 'Mystic meditation ring' had written to another member, alluding to Mrs Bull as the subject of a psychic conspiracy.[5]

On cross-examination, Siri Swanander, Bull's Norwegian caretaker, confirmed that Nivedita was 'a priestess of the Hindu cult', who attended to Bull during her last days, administering unknown 'Indian medicine'.[6] Other witnesses said that the medicines were corrosive in their impact.[7] Mention was made of a 'little black pill' which gave off a 'strange odor'[8]: 'Mrs Bull "would lie with her mouth partly open and her eyes partly closed"'.[9] An 'East Indian Doctor' supposedly fed her 'pumpkin seed milk, Bread Made of Walnuts, Pepper and

Wheat' (weirdly anticipating vegan/new lifestyle experiments undertaken much later).[10] Mention was made of 'one Yum' (Josephine MacLeod), a close friend of Bull and Nivedita, frequent visitor to her household and part of the 'mystic meditation circle'.[11] The case must have ruffled some serious official feathers in the British Foreign Office. A relieved confidential despatch ensued from the Indian Criminal Intelligence Office to the British Consul General at Boston via the London Foreign Office:

> With reference to your Letter ... dated the 28th April 1911 regarding Miss M.E. Noble, better known as Sister Nivedita, I write to let you know that this lady died at Darjeeling on the 13th instant.
>
> Perhaps this information would be of use to the H.B.M.'s Consul General at Boston.[12]

This is one of the rare times Nivedita's name figures in criminal intelligence papers.[13] She managed to evade official censure despite her suspected involvement in revolutionary terrorist activities against the colonial government.[14] Nivedita may have been 'wanted by the Police in India', though this was not formally confirmed. However, it was acknowledged that she had 'slipped quietly away from New York on March 1st' after Bull's death and financial bequests were revealed.[15] On the margins of the communique, Herbert Risley (of the First Census Commission of India fame), then Permanent Secretary of the India Office, had scribbled: 'I have always been sceptical as to Miss Noble's motives[?]'.[16] Decades later, Rolland, recounting this episode in his diary, was scandalised at the allegation of Nivedita's involvement in manipulating Bull's bequests: 'The wife of Caesar – the great disciple of Vivekananda – must not be suspected. Vivekananda would never have allowed it.'[17]

Despite opposing 'occult' and 'esoteric' practices throughout his lifetime, Vivekananda was portrayed as the yogic leader of a mysterious cult: 'Swami Vivekananda ... died from excessive participation in the mysteries of the chamber of meditation'.[18] Bull, Nivedita, MacLeod and many Western followers had, however, persisted in their indulgences in 'alternative medicine' that included magnetic healing. There was some truth in the allegations that Noble provided Indian treatments for her American friends: 'Tell Mrs Walden if there is any Indian drug or oil that she thinks she would like, I would be so happy to obtain it for her.'[19] Mrs Walden [or Mrs Melton] was a magnetic healer based in California who treated Bull, MacLeod and her sister Betty, even Vivekananda. Though Olea eventually won the case, she died mere hours before the final settlement hearing on the same day, a point whose irony is still noted by commentators within the Ramakrishna–Vivekananda tradition.[20]

The 'Ole Bull Will Contest' revealed what Stephen Prothero has termed 'Hinduphobia' and 'Hinduphilia' in American popular culture.[21] The controversy illustrated anxieties around race, religion and border-making at a time of America's rapid rise on the global stage. The scare of non-white minority cultures overwhelming America was enough to exhort journalistic, popular and legal opinion to converge against any kind of symbolic power. 'White Hindu' converts were chastised, but the ultimate blame was laid on Asian gurus and swamis for taking advantage of 'rich and gullible' Western women. The controversy exemplified the scope, limits and movements of transnational Hinduism, tied around larger anxieties about India's place in the world. Travelling gurus, since Vivekananda, increasingly became key agents in the globalising of Hinduism, as well as its commercialisation in the world marketplace.[22]

Anxieties of Representation

This book has shown how networks of Western Indophiles were mobilised around specific projects led by prominent Indian figures that took India as their point of cultural reference. This India is not solely about Indians rooted in subcontinental politics and culture but wherever Indians migrated for social, economic or cultural prospects. The image of the impoverished labourer or colonised heathen militated against the upwardly mobile aspirations of the (upper-caste) educated immigrant.[23] India's emergence as a chief labour supplier in the British imperial economy (and beyond) contributed to its common stereotype as a land of coolies and impoverished labour. In post-slavery British political discourse, indenture was actively propagated as beneficial for civilising Indian primitive labour.[24] Throughout the latter half of the nineteenth and early twentieth centuries, especially around wartime and inter-war periods, India came to occupy a central role in the global labour market.

Scientific racism was joined with the rhetoric of free trade that argued for indenture as a form of 'free labour'.[25] Millions of labourers migrated to the sugar plantations of Mauritius, Fiji and the Caribbean, to the railways, mines and agricultural plantations of South and East Africa and increasingly to different parts of North and South America. Added to this was also a significant community of mercantile Indians, doctors and lawyers that represented more middle-class aspirations in the lands they settled, an aspiration that was predominantly yoked to Indian nationalist politics.[26] Western Indophiles verbalised this connection, arguing that the struggle for India's freedom was dispersed but not decentred:

> The struggle for freedom and independence in India cannot be separated for a moment from the struggle that is always going on in the most distant colony where Indians are domiciled. A victory over there is a victory for India itself. A defeat ... humiliation.[27]

Indian nationalist aspirations to be a 'respectable' community of immigrants made possible space for Indophile politics to be useful. Vivekananda, Gandhi and Tagore's disciples and their institutional networks remained invested in settling India and Indians as globally respectable. Tagore's literary recognition, Gandhi's political renown and Vivekananda's universal religion spoke to that transnational politics of respectability. Immigrant mobilities sought respectable embourgeoisement but their deep entrenchment as colonial subjects frustrated that desire. Indophile deployments proved useful in legitimising claims to civilisational greatness and high culture.[28]

Indophile association with projects around Hindu high culture marked its arrival and (unsteady) consolidation as 'universal'. Grasping this transnational move is important, for it also elucidates the larger effects of Indophile actors within India and other world geographies. Many scholars have highlighted what a transnational scale brings to our understanding of history and politics. Inderpal Grewal and Goldie Osuri, for instance, see transnational as a way of transcending the 'fixity and boundedness of national space' in their study of Indian diasporic politics.[29] Vivekananda's Vedantic dialectics demonstrated how colonial cultural politics could form a different kind of interlocution through extra-imperial circuits such as the US. This difference was limited but real and subject to strict anti-Asian immigration regimes within the American state and society.[30]

Transnationalism unsettles the nation but also re-territorialises something after. More importantly for this work, transnational moves also reified the nation. They tethered extraterritorial Indian communities to notions of glory and greatness that align them in a position of discursive superiority, particularly in contexts of minimal political empowerment. As the chapters on indenture and Vedanta evince, Western Indophile actors were enormously influential in producing – and territorialising – a certain idea of India consumed eagerly within upper-caste nationalist publics. In this, their own Indophilia found fulfilment. Essentially inspired by a (white) liberal understanding of equality, Western Indophiles helped sustain a 'politics of respectability' in global contexts. Black feminist scholars have written enduringly on the gatekeeping tendencies of 'uplift politics' in African-American history, which generally take the middle-class white self as its emulative ideal and through which marginalised communities seek to improve themselves.[31]

Conclusion

Affective politics produced an anxiety of excess. In Indophile subjects such as Mira, Nivedita, Pearson and Andrews, this becomes almost cathartic in their attempts to embody ideal discipleship. Yet, this moment of absolute transformation into some utopian Indianised self never really arrives. Andrews, despite being beaten up and assaulted (by white supremacists) for representing Indian immigrants, was regularly accused of being a British spy; Pearson and Mira felt outsider-ly in the very ashrams they wanted to be part of; Nivedita found herself sidelined from the monastic community Vivekananda helped found. Nevertheless, it is this peculiarity of 'not quite but still' that opens up Indophile investments to a series of continual appropriations. In their deaths, they become part of a memorial politics used to consolidate their gurus' institutions. After Pearson's death, Tagore issued an appeal for a 'Pearson Memorial Fund', used to build a hospital (Figure E.2). Andrews assured Tagore:

> I have shown Mahatmaji your appeal on behalf of the Pearson Memorial, and he was very deeply impressed by it. He and I will now be practically responsible for the amount and I am quite certain that we shall raise it. I do not think that you need now have any anxiety whatever about it. Indeed I hope that the amount needed will be exceeded by the donations. We ought to begin to build at once.[32]

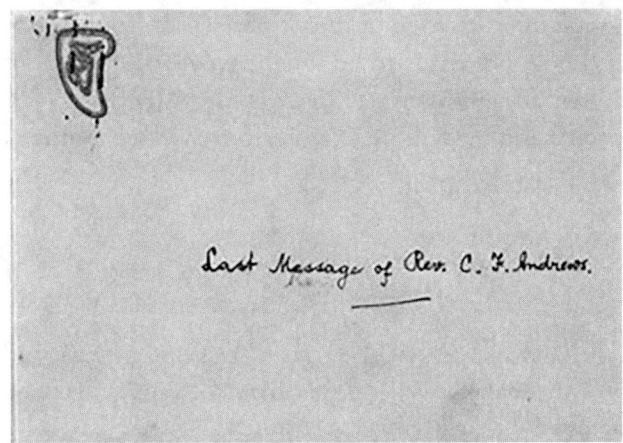

Figure E.2   Last Message of C. F. Andrews, in Tagore's hand, 1940.
Source: Rabindra Bhavan.

A similar exercise followed Andrews' death, wherein Gandhi raised 5 lakh rupees to aid Shantiniketan, whose finances were always precarious. Intimacies created narratives of embodiment that were not beyond material use. Indeed, Indophile recognition and the success of their claim to Indian-ness could be measured by the amount of public memorialisation they attracted. Andrews and Nivedita's popularity in Indian nationalist circles was beyond reproach. Indophile whiteness allowed them to inhabit both universal and particular modes. Andrews and Pearson could slip into a dhoti and kurta, Mira into a *khadi* skirt and Nivedita into a white (later saffron) *brahmacharini* garb, assumptions that raised their estimation in Indian eyes.

Participating in transnational projects, these disciples became central figures in the story of Western Indophilia, intersecting with major currents in Indian nationalism and global idealism. Between 1890 and 1940, they became involved in multiple projects to represent Indians at home and abroad that required the active deployment of their racial privilege for access to valuable networks and audiences. In postcolonial decades, the political landscape changed and hence an earlier notion of Western Indophilia, divested of its anticolonial significance. As Indian immigration to the West increased in the decades after independence, many of these networks were instrumental in producing new forms of Indophilia, such as the growth of transnational Hinduism around the Indian Emergency in 1979 and after.[33] Yet this Indophilia is rarely innocent.

They were regularly invoked to insinuate projects of 'aggressive Hinduism' or Aryan pasts, whose present is to be sought only in culture-bearing Indians; an act that often delegitimised and disavowed contemporary labour or anti-caste movements and made little attempt to move beyond the narrow logics of 'East–West' union.

Notes

1   'Ole Bull Will Contest', *New York Times*, 13 February 1911, 1; 'Spirits Urged $25,000 Gift, Said Mrs Bull', *Boston Herald*, 15 June 1911, 1. All newspaper items accessed through ProQuest Historical Newspapers.

2   'Says Psychic Plot Sways Mrs Bull', *New York Times*, 23 May 1911, 1.

3   'Mrs Bull's Indian Tonics', *New York Times*, 27 June 1911, 5; 'Bull's Cook Tells of Indian Drugs', *New York Times*, 17 June 1911, 5.

4   'Says Psychic Plot', 1.

5   Ibid.

6   'Mrs Bull Objected to Indian Medicine', *New York Times*, 3 June 1911, 3.

7   'Mrs Bull's Indian Tonics', 5.

8   Could be *bhang gola*/hemp tablets, used to induce a feeling of spiritual transcendence, and commonly used by a range of religious wanderers in India.

9   'Mrs Bull Objected to Indian Medicine', *New York Times*, 3 June 1911.

10   Ibid.

11   'Says Psychic Plot'.

12   Criminal Intelligence Office, Shimla to M. C. Seton, Assistant Secretary, Judicial and Public Dept, India Office, London, 25 October 1911, IOR/l/PJ/6/1124, British Library, London.

13   The other Western disciple who figured in Criminal Intelligence files was Christine Greenstidel. She was denied entry into India in later life as she was branded a potential revolutionary by the Intelligence Branch in India, cited in Kim, 'An International Event and Its Multiple Global Publics', 199.

14   Aurobindo attributed this to her high official contacts within the British administration.

15   Seton to H. H. Risley, 30 March 1911, IOR/l/PJ/6/1124.

16   Ibid.

17   Rolland, *Inde*.

18   'Says Psychic Plot', 1.

19   Nivedita to MacLeod, 7 February 1906, *LSN*-II.

20   'Bull Fortune Won, She Dies', *New York Times*, 2.
21   Stephen Prothero, 'Hinduphobia and Hinduphilia in U.S. Culture', in *The Stranger's Religion*, ed. Ann Lannestrom (Notre Dame: University of Notre Dame Press, 2004), 13–27.
22   Jacob Copeman and Aya Ikegame, drawing on C. J. Fuller and John Harris, shed important insights on this move, 'The Multifarious Guru: An Introduction', in *The Guru in South Asia: New Interdisciplinary Perspectives*, ed. Jacob Copeman and Aya Ikegame (London: Routledge, 2012), 11.
23   Hugh Tinker, *The Banyan Tree: Overseas Emigrants from India, Pakistan, and Bangladesh* (Oxford: Oxford University Press, 1977), 8.
24   Connolly, 'Indentured Labour Migration and the Meaning of Emancipation', 89.
25   Ibid., 113–114. Though the association of 'indenture' as free labour would dissipate by the 1920s.
26   Anti-Indian immigration laws were passed in the postcolonial decades in several east African nations that ousted significant communities of Indian settlers. 'Africa for Africans' became a sign to mobilise anyone complicit in an exploitative relationship with native Africans. Indians had long acted as sub-imperialists for British or other colonial powers in opening up inner African markets. In the mid-1920s, after Germany lost its African colonies, Indian groups in East Africa, through the local Indian Congress demanded a colony for themselves, carved out of that. C. F. Andrews advised them that they should abandon this plan:

> [T]he more I think over Sir Theodore Morison's idea of a specially 'Indian' German East Africa the less I like it. I am afraid I shall have difficulty in persuading the British East African Indian Associations to share my view. I am quite certain it would be used as a lever everywhere to take away Indian rights in territory where Indians are already settled and domiciled.

See Andrews to Gandhi, 29 November 1919, Folder 21, Letters from CFA to Gandhi (1914–1933), CFA Papers; File 1–26, 28 (ii), RBVB-018. Pursuing such a line of superior difference with regard to native Africans in effect made them similar to the British in India. This sub-imperialist role came to haunt Indians with vengeance in instances such as Idi Amin in Uganda who expelled Europeans and Indians and took control of their business in the 1970s.
27   C. F. Andrews, *India and the Pacific* (London: Allen and Unwin, 1937), 214.
28   Prashad, *The Karma of Brown Folk*, 118.
29   Goldie Osuri, 'Transnational Bio/Necropolitics: Hindutva and its Avatars (Australia/India)', *Somatechnics* 1, no. 1 (2011): 138.

30   Kunal M. Parker, *Making Foreigners Immigration and Citizenship Law in America, 1600–2000* (New York: Cambridge University Press, 2015), 153. Indians entering the US were classed as members of the Caucasian race, an identification that only strengthened Indian immigrant desire for an elusive desire to whiteness. The US Supreme Court was however, quick to assert the difference: 'It may be true that the blond Scandinavian and the brown Hindu have a common ancestor..., but the average man knows perfectly well that there are unmistakable and profound differences between them to-day.' United States v. Bhagat Singh Thind, 261 US 204, 209 (1923), cited in Parker, *Making Foreigners Immigration*, 153.

31   The foundational text for African-American respectability politics is Evelyn Brooks Higginbotham, *Righteous Discontent: The Women's Movement in the Black Baptist Church, 1880–1920* (Harvard: Harvard University Press, 1994).

32   Andrews to Tagore, 6 April 1924, C. F. Andrews-I, LKE/IN/2/E, Dartington Hall Trust.

33   Edward Anderson and Patrick Clibbens, '"Smugglers of Truth": The Indian Diaspora, Hindu Nationalism, and the Emergency (1975–77)', *Modern Asian Studies* 52, no. 5 (2018): 1729–1773, DOI: 10.1017/S0026749X17000750.

Bibliography

Archival and Manuscript Sources

National Archives of India, Delhi
B. D. Chaturvedi Papers.
M. R. Jayakar Papers.

Nehru Memorial Museum and Library, New Delhi
Mira Behn Papers.
Papers relating to Indian Struggle in South Africa, Servants of India Society.
All India Congress Committee Papers.

Rabindra Bhavan, Shantiniketan
C. F. Andrews Papers.
William Winstanley Pearson Papers.
Edward J. Thompson Letters.

Sabarmati Ashram, Ahmedabad
Mira Behn Papers.
C. F. Andrews Papers.

British Library, London

Indians Overseas, India Office Records.
C. F. Andrews Papers, European Manuscripts.
Criminal Intelligence Records.

Bodleian Library, University of Oxford

E. J. Thompson Papers.

Devon Heritage Centre, Exeter

Leonard K. Elmhirst Papers, Dartington Hall Records.

University of Edinburgh, Edinburgh

Fraser–Tagore Collection.

University of Pennsylvania, Philadelphia

Richard Bartlett Gregg Papers, Manuscripts, Kislak Center for Special Collections.

Cambridge Historical Society, Boston, MA

Bull Curtis Papers.

Newspapers and Journals

ProQuest

New York Times.
Boston Herald.
Times of India.

Archive.org

Modern Review.
Indian Mirror.

Published Primary Sources

Andrews, Charles F. *India and the Pacific*. London: Allen and Unwin, 1937.

———, ed. *Mahatma Gandhi at Work: His Own Story Continued*. London: George Allen and Unwin, 1931.

———. 'Mr Gandhi and the Commission'. *Modern Review*, July 1914, 97.

———. 'Railway Journey: Indian Settlers in Africa'. *Modern Review* 1, June 1920.

———. *Sandhya Meditations at the Christukula Ashram*. Madras: Natesan, 1940.

———. *The Indian Question in East Africa*. Nairobi: Swift Press, 1921.

———. *The Relation of Christianity to the Conflict between Capital and Labour*. London: Methuen, 1896.

Andrews, Charles F., and W. W. Pearson. *Report on Indentured Labour in Fiji: An Independent Enquiry*. Calcutta: Star Printing Works, 1916.

Asheshananda, Swami. *Glimpses of a Great Soul: The Life of Swami Saradananda*. Chennai: Vedanta Press, 1982.

Basu, Jagadish Chandra, and Rabindranath Thakur. *Dui Bandhur Chithi: Parasparik o Paramparik, 1899–1936*. Calcutta: Manfakira, 2008.

Behn, Mira. *The Spirit's Pilgrimage*. London; New York: Great Ocean Publishers, 1960.

Bhattacharya, Sabyasachi, ed. *The Mahatma and the Poet*. Delhi: NBT, 1997.

Bishi, Pramathanath. *Rabindranath o Shantiniketan*. Calcutta: Visvabharati, 1944.

Bose, Shankari Prasad, ed. *Vivekananda in Indian Newspapers*. Calcutta: Modern Book Agency, 1960.

Burke, Marie Louise. *Swami Vivekananda in the West: New Discoveries*. Vols. 1–4. Calcutta: Advaita Ashrama, 1984.

Chaturvedi, Banarsidas. *Fiji Dwip Mein Mere Ikkis Varsh*. Agra: Rajput Anglo-Oriental Press, 1914.

Chaturvedi, Benarsidas, and Marjorie Sykes. *C. F. Andrews: A Narrative*. London: George, Allen and Unwin, 1949.

Chaudhuri, Sarala Devi. *Jeebaner Jharapata*. Calcutta: Dey's, 1950.

Das, Rajani Kanta. 'Principal Problems'. In *Hindustani Workers on the Pacific Coast*, 109–110. Berlin: W. de Gruyter & Co., 1923.

Das, Sudhiranjan. *Amader Shantiniketan*. Calcutta: Visvabharati, 1959.

Dasgupta, Uma, ed. *A Difficult Friendship: Letters of Edward Thompson and Rabindranath Tagore, 1913–1940*. New Delhi: Oxford University Press, 2003.

———. *Friendships of 'Largeness and Freedom': Andrews, Tagore, and Gandhi; An Epistolary Account, 1912–1940*. Oxford: Oxford University Press, 2018.

———, ed. *The Oxford India Tagore: Selected Writings on Education and Nationalism*. Oxford; Delhi: Oxford University Press, 2009.

Dutta, Mahendranath. *Londone Swami Vivekananda*. Calcutta: Mahendra Publishing Committee, 1931.

Edib, Halide. *Inside India*. London: Oxford University Press, 1937.

Elmhirst, Leonard. *Poet and Plowman*. Calcutta: Visvabharati, 1975.

Gandhi, Gopalkrishna, ed. *My Dear Bapu: Letters from C. Rajagopalachari to Mohandas Karamchand Gandhi, Devadas Gandhi and Gopalkrishna Gandhi*. Delhi: Viking, 2012.

Gandhi, M. K. *An Autobiography, or the Story of My Experiments with Truth*. Ahmedabad: Navajivan Publishing House, 1927.

———. *Ashram Observances in Action*. Translated by Valji Govindji Desai. Ahmedabad: Navajivan Publishing House, 1955.

———. *Collected Works of Mahatma Gandhi*. Vols. 12–77. www.gandhiashramsevagram.com. Accessed on 20 October 2021.

Gokhale, Gopal K. *Speeches and Writings of Gokhale*. Vol. 2, *Political*. London: Asia Publishing House, 1966.

Gupta, Krishna M. *Mira Behn: Gandhiji's Daughter Disciple Birth Centenary Volume*. New Delhi: Himalaya Seva Sangh, 1992.

Kazantzakis, Nikos. *England: A Travel Journal*. London: Simon and Schuster, 1966.

Ker, James Campbell. *Political Trouble in India, 1907–1911*. Calcutta: Editions India, 1917.

Lago, Mary, ed. *Imperfect Encounter: Letters of William Rothenstein and Rabindranath Tagore, 1911–1941*. Cambridge, MA: Harvard University Press, 1972.

Leggett, Frances. *Late and Soon: The Story of a Transatlantic Marriage*. Boston: Houghton Mifflin, 1968.

McNeill, James, Indian Civil Service, and Mr Chimman Lal, India. *East India (Indentured Labour) Report to the Government of India on the Conditions of Indian Immigrants in Four British Colonies and Surinam*. London: H. M. Stationery Off., 1915. Printed in India.

Müller, Max. *The Life and Sayings of Ramakrishna*. Calcutta: Advaita Ashrama, 1951.

Nivedita, Sister. *Complete Works of Sister Nivedita*. Vol. 2. Calcutta: Advaita Ashrama, 1967.

———. *Notes of Some Wanderings with Swami Vivekananda*. Calcutta: Udbodhan, 1913.

———. *The Master as I Saw Him, Being Pages from the Life of the Swami Vivekananda*. London: Longmans Green, 1910.

O'Connor, Daniel. *The Testimony of C. F. Andrews*. Madras: Christian Literature Society, 1974.

Pal, Bipin Chandra. *Character Sketches*. Calcutta: Yugayatri, 1957.

Pearson, W. W. *For India*. Tokyo: Asiatic Society of Japan, 1917.

———. *Shantiniketan: The Bolpur School of Rabindranath Tagore*. New York: MacMillan, 2007.

Polak, Henry. *The Indians of South Africa: Helots within the Empire and How They Are Treated*. Madras: Natesan, 1909.

Reminiscences of Swami Vivekananda: His Eastern and Western Admirers. Mayavati: Advaita Ashrama, 1983.

Rolland, Romain. *Inde: Journal, 1915–1943.* Paris: Albin Michel, 1960.

———. *Mahatma Gandhi: The Man Who Became One with the Universal Being.* Translated by Caroline D. Growth. London: The Swarthmore Press, 1924.

Rolland, Romain, and Mahatma Gandhi. *Romain Rolland and Gandhi Correspondences.* Delhi: Publications Division, Government of India, 1976.

Savarkar, Vinayak D. *Hindutva: Who Is a Hindu?* Nagpur: V. V. Kalkar, 1923.

Shivani. *Amader Shantiniketan.* Delhi: Rajkamal, 2007; Delhi: Radha Krishna Prakashan, 2016.

Suhrud, Tridip, and Thomas Weber, eds. *Beloved Bapu: The Gandhi–Mirabehn Correspondence.* New Delhi: Orient Blackswan, 2014.

Tagore, Rabindranath. *Towards Universal Man.* London: Asia Publishing House, 1961.

Tagore, Rathindranath. *On the Edges of Time.* Calcutta: Orient Longman, 1958.

Tapasyananda, Swami. *Sri Sarada Devi: The Holy Mother, Her Life and Conversations.* Madras: Sri Ramakrishna Math, 1958.

The Christian Literature Society for India. *Swami Vivekananda and his Guru; with Letters from Prominent Americans on the Alleged Progress of Vedantism in the U.S.* London; Madras, 1897.

Thompson, Edward J. *Rabindranath Tagore: His Life and Work.* London: Association Press (YMCA), 1921.

Vivekananda, Swami. *Lectures from Colombo to Almora.* Madras: Vyjyanti Press, 1897.

———. *The Complete Works of Swami Vivekananda.* Vols. 1–8. Calcutta: Sri Ramakrishna Math, 1973; Calcutta: Advaita Ashram, 2002.

———. *The Vedanta Philosophy: An Address before The Graduate Philosophical Society of Harvard University.* New York: Vedanta Society, 1901.

Published Secondary Sources

Ahmed, Sara. 'Collective Feelings, or The Impressions Left by Others'. *Theory, Culture and Society* 21, no. 2 (2004): 25–42.

Aiyar, Sana. 'Empire, Race, and the Indians in Colonial Kenya's Contested Public Political Sphere, 1919–1923'. *Africa: Journal of the International African Institute* 81, no. 1 (2011): 132–154.

———. *Indians in Kenya: The Politics of Diaspora.* Cambridge, MA: Harvard University Press, 2015.

Alston, Charlotte. *Tolstoy and His Disciples: The History of a Radical International Movement.* London: Palgrave Macmillan, 2014.

Altman, Janet Gurkin. *Epistolarity: Approaches to a Form.* Columbus: Ohio State University Press, 1982.

Amin, Shahid. 'Gandhi as Mahatma'. In *Selected Subaltern Studies,* edited by Ranajit Guha and Gayatri Spivak, 282–342. Delhi: Oxford University Press, 1989.

Amrith, Sunil S. *Crossing the Bay of Bengal: The Furies of Nature and the Fortunes of Migrants.* Cambridge, MA: Harvard University Press, 2013.

Anderson, Ben, and Paul Harrison, eds. *Taking-Place: Non-representational Theories and Geography.* Farnham: Ashgate, 2010.

Anderson, Benedict. *Imagined Communities: Reflections on the Origin and Spread of Nationalism.* London: Verso, 1983.

Anderson, Edward, and Patrick Clibbens. '"Smugglers of Truth": The Indian Diaspora, Hindu Nationalism, and the Emergency (1975–77)'. *Modern Asian Studies* 52, no. 5 (2018): 1729–1773.

Arondekar, Anjali. *For the Record: On Sexuality and the Colonial Archive in India.* Durham: Duke University Press, 2009.

Bannet, Eve Tavor. *Empire of Letters: Letter Manuals and Transatlantic Correspondence, 1688–1820.* Cambridge: Cambridge University Press, 2005.

Bassett, Ross. *The Technological Indian.* Cambridge, MA: Harvard University Press, 2016.

Bayly, Christopher A. *Recovering Liberties: Indian Thought in the Age of Liberalism and Empire.* Cambridge: Cambridge University Press, 2012.

Beckerlegge, Gwilym. *Swami Vivekananda's Legacy of Service: A Study of the Ramakrishna Math and Mission.* Oxford: Oxford University Press, 2006.

———. *The Ramakrishna Mission: The Making of a Modern Hindu Movement.* Oxford: Oxford University Press, 2000.

Bellenoit, Hayden J. A. 'Missionary Education, Religion and Knowledge in India, c.1880–1915'. *Modern Asian Studies* 41, no. 2 (2007): 369–394.

Berg, Maxine, ed. *Writing the History of the Global Challenges for the 21st Century.* Oxford: British Academy, 2013.

Bhabha, Homi. *The Location of Culture.* Routledge Classics Series. New York: Routledge, 1994.

Bhattacharya, Sabyasachi. *Talking Back: The Idea of Civilization in the Indian Nationalist Discourse.* Delhi: Oxford University Press, 2012.

Biswas, Somak. 'Approaching Migration in World History: How to Use Primary Sources'. *Research Methods Primary Sources,* Adam Matthew Digital, Marlborough, 2021.

Bloembergen, Marieke. 'The Politics of "Greater India", a Moral Geography: Moveable Antiquities and Charmed Knowledge Networks between Indonesia, India, and the West'. *Comparative Studies in Society and History* 63, no. 1 (2021): 170–211.

Boehmer, Elleke. *Empire, the National, and the Postcolonial: Resistance in Interaction, 1890–1920.* Oxford: Oxford University Press, 2005.

Bose, Sugata, and Kris Manjapra, eds. *Cosmopolitan Thought Zones: South Asia and the Global Circulation of Ideas.* London: Palgrave Macmillan, 2010.

Breckenridge, Carol A., and Peter van der Veer, eds. *Orientalism and the Postcolonial Predicament: Perspectives on South Asia*. South Asia Seminar. Philadelphia: University of Pennsylvania Press, 1993.

Brown, Judith, and Anthony Parel, eds. *The Cambridge Companion to Gandhi*. Cambridge: Cambridge University Press, 2011.

Brown, Judith, and M. Prozesky, ed. *Gandhi and South Africa: Principles and Politics*. Pietermaritzburg: University of Natal Press, 1996.

Burton, Antoinette. *Dwelling in the Archive: Women Writing House, Home, and History in Late Colonial India*. Oxford: Oxford University Press, 2003.

Butler, Judith. *Senses of the Subject*. New York: Fordham, 2015.

Carter, Marina. *Voices from Indenture: Experiences of Indian Migrants in the British Empire*. London: Leicester University Press, 1996.

Carter, Marina, and Khal Torabully. *Coolitude: An Anthology of the Indian Labour Diaspora*. London: Anthem Press, 2002.

Certeau, Michel de. *The Writing of History*. Translated by Tom Conley. New York: Columbia University Press, 1988.

Chakrabarty, Dipesh. 'From Civilization to Globalization: The "West" as a Shifting Signifier in Indian Modernity'. *Inter-Asia Cultural Studies* 13, no. 1 (2012): 138–152.

———. *Provincializing Europe: Postcolonial Thought and Historical Difference*. Princeton: Princeton University Press, 2007.

Chakravarti, Uma. *Rewriting History: The Life and Times of Pandita Ramabai*. New Delhi: Zubaan, 2013.

Chatterjee, Elizabeth, Megan Robb and Sneha Krishnan. 'Feeling Modern: The History of Emotions in Urban South Asia'. *Journal of the Royal Asiatic Society* 27, no. 4 (2017): 539–557.

Chaudhuri, Nupur, and Margaret Strobel, eds. *Western Women and Imperialism Complicity and Resistance*. Bloomington: Indiana University Press, 1992.

Connolly, Jonathan. 'Indentured Labour Migration and the Meaning of Emancipation: Free Trade, Race and Labour in the British Public Debate, 1838–1860'. *Past and Present* 238 (February 2018): 85–119.

Cooper, Fred, and Ann Stoler. *Tensions of Empire: Colonial Cultures in a Bourgeois World*. Berkeley: University of California Press, 1997.

Copeman, Jacob. 'Violence, Non-Violence, and Blood Donation in India'. *Journal of the Royal Anthropological Institute* 14, no. 2 (June 2008): 278–296.

Copeman, Jacob, and Aya Ikegame, eds. *The Guru in South Asia: New Interdisciplinary Perspectives*. London: Routledge, 2012.

Cossart, Brice. '"Global Lives": Writing Global History with a Biographical Approach'. *Entremons, UPF Journal of World History*, no. 5 (June 2013): 1–14.

Dalrymple, William. *White Mughals: Love and Betrayal in Eighteenth-Century India*. Delhi: Harper Perennial, 2002.

Das, Santanu. *Touch and Intimacy in the First World War*. Cambridge: Cambridge University Press, 2006.

Dasgupta, Uma. *A History of Sriniketan: Rabindranath Tagore's Pioneering Work in Rural Reconstruction*. New Delhi: Niyogi Books, 2022.

———. 'In Pursuit of a Different Freedom: Tagore's World University at Santiniketan'. *India International Centre Quarterly* 29, nos. 3/4 (Winter 2002–Spring 2003): 34–35.

———. *Rabindranath Tagore: An Illustrated Life*. Delhi: Oxford University Press, 2013.

Desai, Ashwin, and Goolam Vahed. *The South African Gandhi: Stretcher-Bearer of Empire*. Delhi: Navayana, 2020.

Devji, Faisal. 'Gandhi's Racism'. *Asia Dialogue,* 2 October 2019.

———. *The Impossible Indian: Gandhi and the Temptation of Violence*. London: Hurst and Co., 2012.

Dixon, Joy. *Divine Feminine: Theosophy and Feminism in England*. London: Johns Hopkins University Press, 2001.

Dube, Saurabh, ed. *Enchantments of Modernity: Empire, Nation, Globalization*. London: Routledge, 2009.

Earle, Rebecca, ed. *Epistolary Selves, Letters and Letter Writers, 1600–1945*. Aldershot: Ashgate, 1999.

Fedorowich, Kent. 'Restocking the British World: Empire, Migration and Anglo-Canadian Relations, 1919–30'. *Britain and the World* 9, no. 2 (2016): 236–269.

Fielder, Leslie A. *Come Back to the Raft Ag'in, Huck Honey, An End to Innocence: Essays on Culture and Politics*. New York: Beacon Press, 1972.

Fischer-Tiné, Harald. 'Indian Nationalism and the "World Forces": Transnational and Diasporic Dimensions of the Indian Freedom Movement on the Eve of the First World War'. *Journal of Global History* 2, no. 3 (2007): 325–344.

Foucault, Michel. *The History of Sexuality*. Vol. 1. New York: Random House, 1978.

———. *Discipline and Punish*. London: Vintage Books, 1977.

Fox, Richard G. 'East of Said'. In *Edward Said: A Critical Reader*, edited by Michael Sprinker, 144–156. Oxford: Blackwell Publishing, 1992.

Foxe, Barbara. *Long Journey Home: A Biography of Margaret Noble (Nivedita)*. London: Rider, 1975.

Frost, Mark R. 'Pandora's Post Box: Empire and Information in India, 1854–1914'. *English Historical Review* 131, no. 552 (2016): 1043–1073.

Gabbacia, Donna R., and Dirk Hoerder, eds. *Connecting Seas and Connected Ocean Rims*. Boston: Brill, 2011.

Gambhirananda, Swami. *History of the Ramakrishna Math and Mission*. Calcutta: Rupa, 1957.

———. *Holy Mother Sarada Devi*. Madras: Ramakrishna Math, 1955.

Gandhi, Leela. *Affective Communities: Anticolonial Thought and the Politics of Friendship*. New Delhi: Duke University Press, 2006.

Gandhi, Rajmohan. *Mohandas: A True Story of a Man, His People, and an Empire*. Delhi: Penguin Books, 2006.

Gangopadhyay, Sunil. *Rānu o Bhānu*. Kolkata: Ananda Publishers, 2001.

Ganguly, Debjani, and John Docker, eds. *Rethinking Gandhi and Nonviolent Relationality*. New York: Routledge, 2008.

Gaskel, Nathaniel, and Diva Gujral. *Photography in India: A Visual History from the 1850s to the Present*. London: Prestel, 2019.

Gerritsen, Anne, and Giorgio Riello, eds. *Writing Material Culture History*. London: Bloomsbury, 2014.

Gopal, Priyamvada. *Insurgent Empire: Anticolonial Resistance and British Dissent*. London: Verso, 2019.

Goyal, Yogita. 'On Transnational Analogy: Thinking Race and Caste with W. E. B. Du Bois and Rabindranath Tagore'. *Atlantic Studies* 16, no. 1 (2019): 54–71. DOI: 10.1080/14788810.2018.1477653.

Guha, Ramachandra. *Gandhi before India*. London: Allen Lane, 2013.

Gupta, Charu. '"Innocent" Victims/"Guilty" Migrants: Hindi Public Sphere, Caste and Indentured Women in Colonial North India'. *Modern Asian Studies* 49, no. 5 (2015): 1345–1377.

Halberstam, Jack. *The Queer Art of Failure*. Duke: Duke University Press, 2011.

Harris, Jonathan G. *The First Firangis: Remarkable Stories of Heroes, Healers, Charlatans, Courtesans and Other Foreigners Who Became Indian*. Delhi: Aleph Book Company, 2014.

Harris, Paisley Jane. 'Gatekeeping and Remaking: The Politics of Respectability in African American Women's History and Black Feminism'. *Journal of Women's History* 15, no. 1 (2003): 212–220.

Harris, Ruth. *Guru to the World: The Life and Legacy of Vivekananda*. Cambridge, MA: Harvard University Press, 2022.

———. 'Rolland, Gandhi and Madeleine Slade: Spiritual Politics, France and the Wider World'. *French History* 27, no. 4 (2013): 579–599.

———. 'Vivekananda, Sarah Farmer, and Global Spiritual Transformations in the Fin de Siècle'. *Journal of Global History* 14, no. 2 (2019): 179–198.

Harvey, David. *The Condition of Postmodernity: An Enquiry into the Origins of Cultural Change*. Oxford: Blackwell, 1990.

Hatcher, Brian A. 'Bourgeois Vedanta: The Colonial Roots of Middle-Class Hinduism'. *Journal of the American Academy of Religion* 75, no. 2 (June 2007): 298–323.

Higginbotham, Evelyn Brooks. *Righteous Discontent: The Women's Movement in the Black Baptist Church, 1880–1920*. Harvard: Harvard University Press, 1994.

Hofmeyr, Isabel Gaskel. *Gandhi's Printing Press*. Harvard: Harvard University Press, 2013.

Howe, Stephen, ed. *The New Imperial Histories Reader*. New York: Routledge, 2010.

James, William. *The Varieties of Religious Experience*. New York: Longmans, Green, and Co., 1917.

Jayawardene, Kumari. *The White Woman's Other Burden: Western Women and South Asia during British Rule*. London: Routledge, 1995.

Kakar, Sudhir. *Intimate Relations: Exploring Indian Sexuality*. Gurugram: Penguin, 1990.

———. *Mira and the Mahatma*. Delhi: Penguin, 2005.

Kapila, Shruti, ed. *An Intellectual History for India*. Cambridge, MA: Foundation Books, 2010.

Kaviraj, Sudipta. *The Invention of Private Life, Literature and Ideas*. New York: Columbia University Press, 2015.

Kay, Saunders, ed. *Indentured Labour in the British Empire, 1834–1920*. London: Croom Helm, 1984.

Kelly, John, and Martha Kaplan. 'Diaspora and Swaraj, Swaraj and Diaspora'. In *From the Colonial to the Postcolonial: India and Pakistan in Transition*, edited by Dipesh Chakrabarty, Rochona Majumdar and Andrew Satori, 311–331. New Delhi: Oxford University Press, 2007.

Killingley, Dermot H. 'Vedanta and Modernity'. In *India: Society and the Beginnings of Modernisation, c. 1830–1850*, edited by C. H. Philips and Mary Doreen Wainwright, 133–134. London: School of Oriental & African Studies, University of London, 1976.

———. 'Yoga-sūtra IV, 2–3 and Vivekānanda's Interpretation of Evolution'. *Journal of Indian Philosophy* 18, no. 2 (June 1990): 151–179.

Kim, Sophie-Jung H. 'An International Event and Its Multiple Global Publics: The Parliament of the World's Religions (Chicago, 1893) and Vivekananda'. In *Global Publics: Its Power and Its Limits*, edited by Valeska Huber and Jürgen Osterhammel, 177–201. Oxford: Oxford University Press, 2020.

King, Richard. 'Orientalism and the Modern Myth of "Hinduism"'. *Numen* 46, no. 2 (1999): 146–185.

Kripal, Jeffery. *Kali's Child: The Mystical and the Erotic in the Life and Teachings of Ramakrishna*. Chicago: University of Chicago Press, 1995.

Kumar, Arun. 'Letters of the Labouring Poor: The Art of Letter Writing in Colonial India'. *Past and Present* 246, no.1 (February 2020): 149–190.

Kumar, Ashutosh. *Coolies of the Empire: Indentured Indians in the Sugar Colonies, 1830–1920*. Cambridge: Cambridge University Press, 2017.

Kumar, Udaya, *Writing the First Person: Literature, History, and Autobiography in Modern Kerala*. Ranikhet; Shimla: Permanent Black and Indian Institute of Advanced Studies, 2016.

Lannestrom, Ann, ed. *The Stranger's Religion*. Notre Dame: University of Notre Dame Press, 2004.

Lambert, David, and Alan Lester, eds. *Colonial Lives across the British Empire: Imperial Careering in the Long Nineteenth Century*. Cambridge: Cambridge University Press, 2006.

Lears, T. J. Jackson. *No Place of Grace: Antimodernism and the Transformation of American Culture, 1880–1920*. London: University of Chicago Press, 1994.

Legg, Stephen. 'Transnationalism and the Scalar Politics of Imperialism'. *New Global Studies* 4, no. 1, Article 4 (2010): 1–7.

Macnicol, Nicol. *C. F. Andrews: Friend of India*. London: J. Clarke, 1944.

Maddipati, Venugopal. 'Architecture as Weak Thought: Gandhi Inhabits Nothingness'. *Marg* 71, no. 2 (December 2019): 44–51.

Magee, Gary B., and Andrew S. Thompson. *Empire and Globalisation: Networks of People, Goods and Capital in the British World, c. 1850–1914*. Cambridge: Cambridge University Press, 2010.

Manjapra, Kris. *Age of Entanglements: German and Indian Intellectuals across Empire*. Harvard: Harvard University Press, 2014.

Manning, Patrick, and Daniel Rood, eds. *Global Scientific Practice in an Age of Revolutions, 1750–1850*. Pittsburgh: University of Pittsburgh Press, 2016.

Mantena, Karuna. *Alibis of Empire: Henry Maine and the Ends of Liberal Imperialism*. New Delhi: Princeton University Press, 2010.

Marashi, Afshin. 'Imagining Hāfez: Rabindranath Tagore in Iran, 1932'. *Journal of Persianate Studies* 3, no. 1 (2010): 46–77.

Massumi, Brian. *Parables of the Virtual*. Durham; London: Duke University Press, 2002.

Masuzawa, Tomoko. *The Invention of World Religions, or How European Universalism Was Preserved in the Language of Pluralism*. Chicago: University of Chicago Press, 2005.

McKeown, Adam. 'Global Migration, 1846–1940'. *Journal of World History* 15, no. 2 (June 2004): 173–174.

———. 'Integration and Segregation in Global Migration'. In *Connecting Seas and Connected Ocean Rims: Indian, Atlantic, and Pacific Oceans and China Seas Migrations from the 1830s to the 1930s*, edited by Donna R. Gabbacia and Dirk Hoerder, 42–64. Leiden: Brill, 2011.

Metcalf, Thomas. *Ideologies of the Raj*. Delhi: Cambridge University Press, 1994.

Minkowski, Christopher. 'Advaita Vedanta in Early Modern History'. *South Asian History and Culture* 2, no. 2 (April 2011): 205–231.

Mishra, Amit Kumar. 'Global Histories of Migration'. In *Global History, Globally: Research and Practice around the World*, edited by Sven Beckert and Dominic Sachsenmaier, 195–214. London: Bloomsbury, 2019.

Mongia, Radhika. *Indian Migration and Empire: A Colonial Genealogy of the Modern State*. Durham: Duke University Press, 2018.

Nanda, Mira. *Science in Saffron: Skeptical Essays on History of Science*. New Delhi: Three Essays Collective, 2016.

Nandy, Ashis. *The Intimate Enemy: Loss and Recovery of Self Under Colonialism*. New Delhi: Oxford University Press, 1983.

Nandy, Ashis. *Traditions, Tyrannies and Utopias: Essays in the Politics of Awareness.* Delhi: Oxford University Press, 1987.

Neima, Anna. *Practical Utopia: The Many Lives of Dartington Hall.* Cambridge: Cambridge University Press, 2022.

———. *The Utopians: Six Attempts to Build the Perfect Society.* London: Picador, 2021.

Nieuwenhuis, Marijn, and Aya Nassar. 'Dust: Perfect Circularity'. *Cultural Geographies* 25, no. 3 (2017): 501–507.

Northrup, David. *Indentured Labor in the Age of Imperialism, 1834–1922.* Cambridge, MA: Cambridge University Press, 1995.

O'Connor, Daniel. *A Clear Star: C. F. Andrews and India, 1904–1914.* Delhi: Orient Blackswan, 2015.

Oddvar, Hollup. 'The Disintegration of Caste and Changing Concepts of Indian Ethnic Identity in Mauritius'. *Ethnology* 33, no. 4 (Autumn 1994): 297–316.

Orsini, Francesca, ed. *Love in South Asia: A Cultural History.* Cambridge: Cambridge University Press, 2006.

Osuri, Goldie. 'Transnational Bio/Necropolitics: Hindutva and its Avatars (Australia/India)'. *Somatechnics* 1, no. 1 (2011): 138–160.

Pal, Prashanta. *Rabijibani.* Vol. 4. Calcutta: Ananda Publishers, 2012–2013.

Parker, Kunal M. *Making Foreigners Immigration and Citizenship Law in America, 1600–2000.* New York: Cambridge University Press, 2015.

Pernau, Margrit. 'Feeling Communities: Introduction'. *Indian Economic and Social History Review* 54, no. 1 (2017): 1–20.

Pernau, Margrit, Helge Jordheim, Orit Bashkin, Christian Bailey, Oleg Benesch, Jan Ifversen, Mana Kia, et al., eds. *Civilizing Emotions: Concepts in Nineteenth Century Asia and Europe.* Oxford: Oxford University Press, 2015.

Philips, C. H., and Mary Doreen Wainwright, eds. *India: Society and the Beginnings of Modernisation, c. 1830–1850.* London: School of Oriental and African Studies, 1976.

Pitcan, Mikaela, Alice E. Marwick and Danah Boyd. 'Performing a Vanilla Self: Respectability Politics, Social Class, and the Digital World'. *Journal of Computer-Mediated Communication* 23, no. 3 (May 2018): 163–179.

Poskett, James. *Materials of the Mind: Phrenology, Race, and the Global History of Science, 1815–1920.* Chicago: University of Chicago Press, 2019.

Poustie, Sarah. 'Re-Theorising Letters and "Letterness"'. Olive Schreiner Letters Project, Working Papers on Letters, Letterness and Epistolary Networks, no. 1, 2010.

Prabuddhaprana, Pravrajika. *Saint Sara: The Life of Sara Chapman Bull, The American Mother of Swami Vivekananda.* Calcutta: Sri Sarada Math, 2002.

———. *Tantine: The Life of Josephine MacLeod, Friend of Swami Vivekananda.* Calcutta: Sri Sarada Math, 1990.

Prashad, Vijay. *The Karma of Brown Folk.* London: University of Minnesota, 2001.

Prugh, Linda. *Josephine MacLeod and Vivekananda's Mission*. Chennai: Sri Ramakrishna Math, 1999.

Radice, William, ed. *Swami Vivekananda and the Modernisation of Hinduism*. London: Sri Sarada Math, 1999.

Raina, Dhruv, and S. Irfan Habib. 'The Moral Legitimation of Modern Science: Bhadralok Reflections on Theories of Evolution'. *Social Studies of Science* 26, no.1 (February 1996): 9–42.

Ralston, Helen. 'The Construction of Authority in the Christian Ashram Movement'. *Archives de sciences sociales des religions* 67, no. 1 (January–March 1989): 53–75.

Ramagundam, Rahul. *Gandhi's Khadi: A History of Contention and Conciliation*. Delhi: Orient Blackswan, 2008.

Raza, Ali, Franziska Roy and Benjamin Zachariah, eds. *The Internationalist Moment: South Asia, Worlds, and World Views, 1917–39*. New Delhi: SAGE Publications, 2015.

Reddy, William M. 'Sentimentalism and Its Erasure: The Role of Emotions in the Era of the French Revolution'. *Journal of Modern History* 72, no. 1 (2000): 109–152.

Reymond, Lizelle. *The Dedicated: A Biography of Nivedita*. New York: The John Day Company, 1953.

Robinson, Andrew, and Krishna Dutta. *Rabindranath Tagore: The Myriad Minded Man*. London: Bloomsbury, 2009.

Rosenwein, Barbara H. *Emotional Communities in the Early Middle Ages*. Cornell: Cornell University Press, 2006.

Rowbotham, Sheila. *Edward Carpenter: A Life of Liberty and Love*. London: Verso, 2008.

Said, Edward. *Orientalism: Western Conceptions of the Orient*. New York: Pantheon Books, 1978.

Salm, Amrita M., and Judy H. Hayes. *The Inspired Life of Sarah Ellen Waldo*. Mayavati: Advaita Ashrama, 2019.

Sarkar, Sumit. *An Exploration of the Ramakrishna Vivekananda Tradition*. Shimla: Indian Institute of Advanced Study, 1993.

———. '"Kaliyuga", "Chakri" and "Bhakti": Ramakrishna and His Times'. *Economic and Political Weekly* 27, no. 29 (18 July 1992): 1543–1559, 1561–1566.

Sarkar, Tanika. *Hindu Wife, Hindu Nation*. Delhi: Permanent Black, 2001.

Sartori, Andrew. *Bengal in Global Concept History: Culturalism in the Age of Capital*. Chicago: University of Chicago Press, 2008.

Scheer, Monique. 'Are Emotions a Kind of Practice (And Is That What Makes Them Have a History)? A Bourdieuian Approach to Understanding Emotion'. *History and Theory* 51, no. 2 (2012): 193–220.

Schoonover, Karl, and Rosalind Galt. *Queer Cinema in the World*. Durham: Duke University Press, 2016.

Schwartz, Laura. *Infidel Feminism: Secularism, Religion and Women's Emancipation in England, 1830–1914.* Manchester: Manchester University Press, 2013.

Scriver, Peter, and Amit Srivastava. *India: Modern Architectures in History.* Glasgow: Reaktion, 2015.

Sen, Amiya P. *Hindu Revivalism in Bengal 1872–1905: Some Essays in Interpretation.* Delhi: Oxford University Press, 2006.

———. *Swami Vivekananda.* Oxford: Oxford University Press, 2000.

———. *Three Essays on Sri Ramakrishna and His Times.* Shimla: IIAS, 2001.

Sengupta, Debanjan, ed. *Nivedita o Jagadish Chandra: Ek Achena Samparker Sandhan.* Kolkata: Gangchil, 2010.

Sharma, Arvind. *The Concept of Universal Religion in Modern Hindu Thought.* Basingstoke: Palgrave Macmillan, 1998.

Sharma, Pandey Bechan ('Ugra'). *Chocolate and Other Writings on Male Homoeroticism.* Translated by Ruth Vanita. London: Duke University Press, 2009.

Sil, Narasingha P. 'Vivekānanda's Rāmakrsna: An Untold Story of Mythmaking and Propaganda'. *Numen* 40, no. 1 (January 1993): 38–62.

Singha, Radhika. 'The Great War and a "Proper" Passport for the Colony: Border-Crossing in British India, c.1882–1922'. *Indian Economic and Social History Review* 50, no. 3 (2013): 289–315.

Sinha, Mrinalini. 'Premonitions of the Past'. *Journal of Asian Studies* 74, no. 4 (November 2015): 821–841.

———. *Specters of Mother India: The Global Restructuring of an Empire.* Durham: Duke University Press, 2006.

Skaria, Ajay. 'Gandhi's Politics: Liberalism and the Question of the Ashram'. In *Enchantments of Modernity,* edited by Saurabh Dube, 199–233. New Delhi: Routledge, 2009.

Slate, Nico. *Coloured Cosmopolitanism: The Shared Struggle for Freedom in the United States and India.* Cambridge, MA: Harvard University Press, 2012.

Sohi, Seema. *Echoes of Mutiny: Race, Surveillance, and Indian Anticolonialism in North America.* New York: Oxford University Press, 2014.

Soja, Edward. *Postmodern Geographies: The Reassertion of Space in Critical Social Theory.* London: Verso, 1989.

Sprinker, Micheal, ed. *Edward Said: A Critical Reader.* Oxford: Blackwell, 1992.

Stanley, Liz. 'The Epistolarium: On Theorizing Letters and Correspondences'. *Auto/Biography* 12, no. 3 (2004): 201–235.

Steedman, Carolyn. *Dust.* Manchester: Manchester University Press, 2002.

Stoler, Ann. *Carnal Knowledge and Imperial Power Race and the Intimate in Colonial Rule.* Berkeley: University of California Press, 2002.

———, ed. *Haunted by Empire: Geographies of Intimacy in North American History.* Durham: Duke University Press, 2006.

Stoler, Ann. 'Tense and Tender Ties: The Politics of Comparison in North American History and (Post) Colonial Studies'. *Journal of American History* 88, no. 3 (2001): 829–865.

Suhrud, Tridip, ed. 'Gandhi and Aesthetics'. Special issue, *Marg* 71, no. 2 (December 2019).

Syman, Stefanie. *The Subtle Body: The Story of Yoga in America*. New York: Farrar, Straus & Giroux Inc., 2010.

Takaki, Ronald. *Strangers from a Different Shore: A History of Asian Americans*. Berkeley: University of California Press, 1998.

Thompson, Edward P. *Alien Homage*. Delhi: Oxford University Press, 1993.

Thomson, Mark. *Gandhi and His Ashrams*. Mumbai: Indiana University Press, 1993.

Tidrick, Kathryn. *Gandhi: A Political and Spiritual Life*. London: I. B. Tauris, 2008.

Tinker, Hugh. *A New System of Slavery: The Export of Indian Labour Overseas, 1830–1920*. London: Oxford University Press, 1974.

———. *The Banyan Tree: Overseas Emigrants from India, Pakistan, and Bangladesh*. Oxford: Oxford University Press, 1977.

———. *The Ordeal of Love: C. F. Andrews and India*. Oxford: Oxford University Press, 1998.

Trivellato, Francesca. 'Is There a Future for Italian Microhistory in the Age of Global History?' *California Italian Studies* 2, no. 1 (2011).

Twells, Alison. '"Eros the Great Leveller": Edward Carpenter, Sexual Cosmotopianism and the Northern Working Man'. *Journal of Colonialism and Colonial History* 22, no. 3 (Winter 2021).

Veer, Peter Van Der, ed. *Nation and Migration: The Politics of Space in the South Asian Diaspora*. Philadelphia: University of Pennsylvania Press, 1995.

Visvanathan, Susan. 'S. K. Rudra, C. F. Andrews and M. K. Gandhi; Friendship, Dialogue and Interiority in the Question of Indian Nationalism'. *Economic and Political Weekly* 37, no. 34 (2002): 3532–3541.

Viswanathan, Gauri. *Masks of Conquest: Literary Study and British Rule in India*. New York: Columbia University Press, 2015.

Vrajaprana, Pravrajika. *My Faithful Goodwin*. Calcutta: Advaita Ashrama, 1994.

Ware, Vron. *Beyond the Pale: White Women, Racism, and History*. London: Verso Books, 1992.

Weber, Thomas. *Gandhi as Disciple and Mentor*. Cambridge: Cambridge University Press, 2006.

Webster, Travis D. 'Secularization and Cosmopolitan Gurus'. *Asian Ethnology* 75, no. 2 (2016).

Young, Michael. *The Elmhirsts of Dartington: The Creation of an Utopian Community*. New York: Routledge, 1982.

Web Resources

Bayly, C. A. 'South Asian Liberalism under Strain c. 1900–1914'. Lecture Notes. https://www.qub.ac.uk/schools/happ/Discover/WilesLectureSeries/Secure-access/Filetoupload,695534,en.pdf. Accessed on 22 October 2019.

Chunder, Rajarshi. 'Tagore and Caste: From Brahmacharyasram to Swadeshi Movement (1901–07)'. https://www.sahapedia.org/tagore-and-caste-brahmacharyasram-swadeshi-movement-1901%E2%80%9307. Accessed on 16 January 2019.

Prabuddha Bharata, 1896–1912. https://archive.org/details/PrabuddhaBharata-July1896-Dec2001/page/n16. Accessed on 25 July 2019.

Rietzier, Katharina. 'Merze Tate and Women's International Thought'. https://blogs.sussex.ac.uk/whit/2018/12/05/toward-a-history-of-womens-international-thought/. Accessed on 30 August 2019.

Tagoreweb. 'The Complete Works of Rabindranath Tagore'. http://www.tagoreweb.in/. Accessed on 19 June 2021.

University of Massachusetts Amherst Libraries, Special Collections and University Archives. 'Letter from W. E. B. Du Bois to Rabindranath Tagore, February 19, 1929'. W. E. B. Du Bois, 1868–1963, W. E. B. Du Bois Papers (MS 312). http://credo.library.umass.edu/view/pageturn/mums312-b183-i406/#page/1/mode/1up. Accessed on 16 August 2020.

Unpublished Theses

Bower, Charles. 'The Gandhian Ashram and Its Contemporaries'. Unpublished Undergraduate Honors Theses 784, 2015. https://scholar.colorado.edu/honr_theses/784. Accessed on 12 September 2021.

Ebright, Donald Fossett. 'The National Missionary Society of India, 1905–1942: An Expression of the Movement toward Indigenization within the Indian Christian Community'. PhD thesis, Chicago, Fraser–Tagore Collection, University of Edinburgh, 1944.

Index